The
AXIS
of
EVIL

The
AXIS
of
EVIL

Iran,
Hizballah,
and the
Palestinian Terror

Shaul Shay

The Interdisciplinary Center, Herzliya

The International Policy Institute for Counter-Terrorism

Transaction Publishers
New Brunswick (U.S.A.) and London (U.K.)

This book is printed on acid-free paper that meets the American National Standard for Permanence of Paper for Printed Library Materials.

Library of Congress Catalog Number: 2004058039
ISBN: 0-7658-0255-4
Printed in the United States of America

Library of Congress Cataloging-in-Publication Data

Shai, Shaul.
    [Tsir ha-resha'. English]
    The axis of evil : Iran, Hizballah, and Palestinian terror / Shaul Shay.
      p. : ill. ; cm.
  Includes bibliographical references and index.
  ISBN 0-7658-0255-4 (cloth : alk. paper)
    1. Terrorism—Government policy—Iran. 2. State-sponsored terrorism—Iran. 3. Arab-Israeli conflict. 4. Hizballah (Lebanon) 5. Shiites—Iran. 6. Iran—Foreign relations. I. Title.

HV6433.I7S5313   2005
327.1'17'0955—dc22

                                          2004058039

Contents

Tables and Figures

Introduction

In the course of twenty-five years of Islamic rule (1979-2004), Iran has appeared to be a state that supports a radical foreign policy with no holds barred, including terror, in order to export the Islamic revolution and facilitate its political objectives. The use of terror as a tool to further political interests is not exclusive or unique to Iran, but there is no doubt that during the reviewed period Iran was among the most prominent countries to encourage terror and use it to realize its goals on the international level.

In a speech delivered in February 2002, U.S. President George Bush defined Iran as a member of the "Axis of Evil" that supports terror and is involved in an attempt to create weapons for mass destruction. Since the beginning of the 1980s, Iran has appeared on the U.S. State Department's list of states that support terror. Indeed, since the Islamic revolution in 1979, Iran was one of the leading countries to use terror to promote its objectives in the international arena.

This volume aspires to comprehend the motives behind Iran's methodical use of terror as a tool to achieve its international goals, and strives to elaborate the way that terror is actively integrated into achieving of these goals. It discusses the issue of Iranian state-supported terror from as wide an angle as possible, and does not limit itself to the Israeli aspect and the connection to the Arab-Israeli conflict. The study emphasizes that Iran views terror as an effective tool to further its objectives, as a substitute for or supplementary measure to diplomatic processes, and that terror constitutes a "legitimate" means in the Iranian regime's battle against its external and internal rivals and enemies. From an in-depth analysis of terror attacks perpetrated during the reviewed period (1980-2003), based on data provided by research institutes and publications in the media, it is possible to point to hundreds of international attacks perpetrated by Iranian entities or Shiite/Palestinian-sponsored organizations (on an average, slightly more than one attack per month over a period that exceeds twenty years). This study analyzes the phenomenon of Iranian and Shiite terror according to these characteristics:

- The ideological and religious background vis-à-vis the use of terror, and the Iranian intelligence and terror agencies;

1

- The various categories of Iranian state terror (terror perpetrated against foreign targets on Iranian soil, Iranian terror worldwide, and particularly Iranian terror "via proxy");
- The modi operandi of the Iranian and Shiite terror (suicide attacks, attacks against aviation targets, attacks via explosive devices, assassinations, and the kidnapping of hostages;
- The targets of Iranian terror.

The following restrictions and reservations apply to the current study: First, it is very difficult to provide a full description of Iranian and Shiite terror due to the lack of official and recorded data and because of attempts made by the perpetrators of terror attacks to cover their tracks. Moreover, a police investigation of a terror incident sometimes takes an extremely long time, and as a result, the identity of the suspected perpetrators changes. In addition, during the Iran-Iraq war, Iran and its proxies perpetrated hundreds of terror attacks against Iraqi targets, but this activity was often incorporated within the ongoing development of the war. Thus, the statistics in this study do not include these activities, with the exception of terror activities perpetrated against Iraq outside of its boundaries as well as terror activity perpetrated in Iraq after the war. We will also refrain from analyzing terror attacks perpetrated by the Hizballah organization against the Israel Defense Forces during the period that it was stationed in Lebanon.

Nevertheless, the issue of Iranian and Shiite terror against Israel is discussed at length on four main levels:

- Iran's approach to Israel and the Israel-Arab conflict;
- Attacks against Israeli and Jewish targets abroad;
- Attacks against Israel after its withdrawal from Lebanon (May 2000);
- Iranian and Hizballah involvement in the Al Aksa Intifada (starting from September 2000).

As stated earlier, Iranian terror activity is perpetrated judiciously. Iran endeavors to leave no "fingerprints" that might identify it as the force behind the terror activities. Moreover, in public declarations the Iranian leadership expresses its reservations regarding terror and condemns it; this is also true of sponsored organizations such as the Hizballah. Iran's attempt to conceal the terror activities that it perpetrates enables it to extract the maximum benefit from this activity. On the one hand, this prevents the terror victim from retaliating, while on the other, Iran sometimes presents itself as a mediator attempting to achieve a compromise between the victim and the terror organization. Using this method, Iran attains its goals from both directions.

Most of the information that has exposed Iran's involvement in terror activities has come to light after perpetrators of acts of terror were apprehended and brought to trial, as the result of comprehensive intelligence investigations of terror attacks worldwide, and following the perpetration of acts of terror where the claiming of responsibility by the responsible organizations included declarations and/or demands that clearly reflected an Iranian link between terror activity and Iranian foreign policy. Particularly evident is the consistent and methodical usage of terror in order to force other countries to accept Iranian demands after regular diplomatic channels failed to achieve these goals. Nevertheless, although Iranian terror policy may be portrayed as a rational and sober method to achieve Iranian goals, it is important to point out several other phenomena that have significant impact on the formulation of Iranian policy:

- The use of terror in the international arena constitutes a focal point for controversy in the higher echelons of the Iranian regime, between the circles often termed "moderate" and those considered "radical," and which support the uncompromising struggle against the enemies of the revolution. Thus, to a significant degree the scope of the use of terror and its objectives reflects the internal power struggles inside Iran.
- Iran has often conducted an ambivalent foreign policy, with the "moderates," aspiring to negotiate and reach compromise, while at the same time "radical" entities continue to be involved in acts of terror (sometimes with the aim of "torpedoing" the steps initiated by the "moderates"). Iran's ambivalent policy has provided it with flexibility in its political course and has made it difficult for its adversaries to formulate a forceful policy that will provide an adequate response to Iranian terror, due to the assumption that the moderate elements in the Iranian regime must be encouraged vis-à-vis the extremists, as they are "the lesser of two evils."

Khomeini's theory, which calls for "Shiite activism" and "revolutionary violence," paved the way and provided ideological and religious legitimization for the use of terror. Thus, Iranian terror is motivated by a combination of religious and ideological motives and political needs.

The dilemma regarding the issue of Iranian leadership (moderates versus extremists) stems primarily from an observation angle and judgment formulated according to Western norms and values. A close examination of the deeds and declarations of the Iranian leaders, both moderate and extremists, leads us to the conclusion that in reality the more accurate differentiation would be between radical and more radical leadership. As long as Khomeini's theories serve as a source for legitimization and as a guide for Iranian leadership, the differences between the radical elements and the moderate ones will be expressed in varying approaches to achieving goals, but not in their fundamental essence.

In general, Iranian involvement in terror can be divided into three main eras;

1. The "revolutionary" period, during Khomeini's regime—1979-1989, and the period of "Khomieni's successsors," which can be divided into two sections:

2.   The period of Rafsanjani's rule—1989-1997
3.   The period of Khatami's rule—1997-2003.

This study indicates a significant difference between the eras vis-à-vis Iranian terror activity, which was at its most intensive level during the Khomeini era but decreased significantly during the reign of his successors. During Khatami's term as Iranian president there has been a significant drop in Iran's involvement in terror, with the exception of the Arab-Israeli conflict in the Lebanese and Palestinian arenas. Iran was the first to introduce suicide terror into the combat arsenal of the Mid-Eastern arena (see further elaboration in chapter 3). In this regard, its approach has not changed since the 1980s, and even today it encourages the Palestinians to use terror and suicide attacks as a strategic means in their struggle against the State of Israel.

The war against global terror declared by the United States, which has been implemented in practical terms in Afghanistan and Iraq, constitutes a real threat to the Iranian regime as well. There is no doubt that the consequences of the American campaign in Iraq will seriously affect U.S. policy vis-à-vis Iran, but it appears that only a significant transformation in Iran's approach to two central issues will yield a real transformation in its relationship with the United States:

- Iran's expressed willingness to cease its attempts to acquire non-conventional weapons and launching means.
- Practical steps to end its involvement in terror and cessation of its support and aid to its sponsored organizations, led by the Hizballah, to Palestinian terror organizations, and more.

This type of rethinking in Iranian policy would trigger internal political power struggles between the moderate and radical factions, and at this time it is not clear which of these will ultimately prevail in this matter.

This study is partially based on the author's previous book, *Terror in the Service of the Imam: Twenty Years of Shiite Terror—1979-1999*, which depicted Iranian and Shiite terror up to the year 2000. The current study reviews and analyzes global and regional developments that have affected Iran's utilization of terror in the international arena since the year 2000: The "war against global terror" declared by the United States in the aftermath of the terror campaign of September 11, 2001, the IDF's withdrawal from Lebanon, the Palestinian Intifada, and the war against Iraq in 2003, which toppled Saddam Hussein's regime.

State-Supported Terror—Theoretical Background

Since the 1970s, following the increased intensity of international terror and the necessity to understand and contend with this phenomenon, a sort of research discipline has developed, mainly among Western democracies, which examines terror from various angles, such as the legal, psychological, sociological, and historical, and of course, the various political science aspects. The attention currently focused on terror is accompanied by a basic frustration on the part of the researchers due to the difficulty in formulating a universal definition of the phenomenon. The difficulty does not stem from an inability to define the phenomenon, but rather from the fact that each entity has its own definition and it is impossible to arrive at a definition that is universally acceptable to everyone.

There are various approaches to differentiate between the various groups of definitions. One of the differentiations is between normative and analytical definitions.[1] A representative of the normative stream is Connor Cruise O'Brien. His definitions are based on political values from which he derives standards for judging political actions. O'Brien characterizes terrorism in terms of the political context in which it is created, and defines it as "unjustified violence against a democratic country that permits effective forms of non-violent opposition."[2] According to this definition, a black man who detonates a police station in South Africa during the period of the apartheid is not to be considered a terrorist, while a member of the Irish Underground (the IRA) who attacks a British base is included in this category. This is an example of one of the major limitations related to normative definitions that examine the phenomenon from a subjective point of view, according to which an ally or friend is defined in positive terms (a freedom fighter) while an opponent is defined negatively (a terrorist). Thus, on the basis of a normative definition it is difficult to define the term "terror" in an unequivocal and universal manner.

On the one hand, the importance and benefit of the normative definition lie in the very proposition of the issue of the legitimacy of utilizing political violence as a standard of judgment. Left-wing terrorists may negate the state's legitimacy and claim that the use of violence against it is legitimate, while right-wing terrorists may negate the legitimacy of the opposition and argue that the use of violence to serve "law and order" is justified in order to protect the "status-quo."

Anthony Quinton points out a pivotal point vis-à-vis the issue of legitimization, stating: "A key aspect related to the state's method of handling terrorism is the defense of its legitimization to use violence and nullify the legitimization of the terrorist challenge."[3] To a great extent, the objective of terror is to win legitimacy from the point of view of the population (or part of it) and to negate the legitimacy of the ruling government. O'Brien defined it well when he stated, "Terrorism poses a challenge regarding the government's right to monopolize power in society and physically undermines its ability to maintain law and order."[4]

Other issues that stem from the normative approach address the moral aspects of terror. Martha Crenshaw argues that terrorism can be judged from two aspects; a moral examination of the consequences alongside a moral examination of the means. Regarding the consequences of terror activity, the criterion is whether the goal of the activity is to establish a just, liberated, and democratic government or if it serves the narrow and deplorable goals of establishing an authoritarian regime that will grant special privileges to a defined group and cause the discrimination of freedom vis-à-vis others.

The discussion regarding the issue of the morality of means leads us to an examination of the methods and means that terror uses, and particularly to an examination of the identity of the terror victims. Crenshaw defines two main groups of victims: The first group includes individuals that are vulnerable to terror acts due to the roles that they fulfill, and as a result of the fact that they are identified to a certain extent with the "unjust" policy that the terrorists are fighting; the second group includes citizens of the state who do not play an official role, or the citizens of other countries who have no connection to or direct influence upon the government's policy. The "transgression" of these people (according to the terrorists) is that they obey the laws of an "unjust" government, thus becoming accomplices to its deeds.

The issue of terror victims represents another example regarding the problematic aspect deriving from normative definitions. The observer's starting point is the factor that determines his moral approach to the case. For example, the way Israeli Jews view the attacks carried out by the Israeli underground National Military Organization against British soldiers may be different than their outlook vis-à-vis the hijacking of an Israeli passenger plane by a Palestinian terror organization. Therefore, it would appear to be impossible to develop objective moral judgment vis-à-vis the use of terror in various political circumstances; at the very most one might state that the definition of a deed as an "act of terror" does not in itself constitute a moral or ethical determination regarding its substance. While the normative school of thought strives to address the term of "terror" by examining it via normative and ethical aspects, the analytical school of thought attempts to find the formula for defining the phenomenon by constructing a neutral, theoretical definition that will be sufficiently general to cover the range of terror variations.

One of the most comprehensive studies in this area was conducted by Alex Schmidt.[5] His study is based on the assumption that despite the disagreement regarding the definition of terror, there exists a common denominator as to the customary images related to the terror issue, and this consent is clear enough to enable the construction of a model that will provide a common language for terror researchers. Schmidt compiled 109 different definitions of terror and conducted a "content analysis" of these definitions while striving to indicate the identical components among the definitions. His findings indicate twenty-five similar components, the most prominent being: the use of violence/force (appearing in 83.5 percent of the definitions), a political goal (in 95 percent), spreading fear (51 percent), threat and exerting psychological pressure (47 percent), addressing the difference between the terror victims (37.5 percent), methodical and / or planned activity (32 percent).

The list of parameters or components that Schmidt compiled cannot suffice to provide an exact definition of the phenomenon, but his study enables the indication of the main components connected to terrorism, on the basis of which Schmidt attempted to construct his definition of terror.[6] According to Schmidt, terrorism is a method of assault in which coincidental or symbolic victims serve as instrumental targets for violence. The victims are divided according to group characteristics that constitute the basis of their choice as victims. Previous usage of violence or a proven threat to use it also turns other individuals from the target group into victims due to the state of "chronic fear" in which they subsist. This indirect method of attack is meant to motivate the victims to act according to the wishes of the terrorists or to induce secondary targets to change their approach or behavior according to the terrorists' goals.[7] Schmidt's comprehensive study contributed to an understanding of the phenomenon and to the mapping of the joint components in the different definitions, but he, too, was unable to produce a universal definition of the phenomenon. The failure to provide a universal definition of the terror phenomenon also accompanies the study of the "by-products" of terror, such as international terror and "state-supported" terror, which are the focus of this study.

During the 1970s, two American research centers made an attempt to define international terror. The first study was conducted at the Rand Corporation, and in its framework the researchers defined international terror as follows:

> A single incident or a series of incidents that are contradictory to accepted law, accepted diplomatic arrangements and accepted laws of war. International terror is meant to draw international attention to the issue for which the terrorists are fighting and to spread fear. The objective of terror is to cause impact or change according to the wishes of the perpetrators, and the direct victim of terror is not necessarily identical to the entity that the terror is aspiring to influence.[8]

Researchers at Interate Project arrived at a different definition. They defined international terror as follows:

The use or threat to use violence for political aims by an individual or group acting on behalf of or against an existing government. The aim of the activity is to influence a target audience which is broader than the action's direct victims; and the victims, perpetrators or their links cross boundaries."[9]

The various forms of state involvement in terror have been united under the terms "terrorist states" or "state-sponsored terror." However, these terms create too coarse a generalization vis-à-vis the various levels of involvement of countries in terror. Thus, a more precise differentiation is required to classify the involvement of countries in terror according to the following categories:

- *States supporting terrorism*—This category includes countries that support terror organizations via financial, ideological, military, and operational aid;
- *States operating terrorism*—States that initiate, direct, and implement terror activity via sponsored organizations, while avoiding direct involvement of governmental agencies in the terror;
- *States perpetrating terrorism*—States that perpetrate terror worldwide through the state's security agencies (security and intelligence mechanisms).

Paul Wilkinson points out three conditions in which political terror becomes international terror:

1. When terror is directed against foreign citizens or targets;
2. When terror is directed by governments or organizations from more than one country;
3. When the terror is aimed at influencing the policy of a (different) foreign country.

By examining the definitions and the conditions related to international terror one may observe that state-sponsored terror, when activated against one of the targets specified above, constitutes a specific case deriving from the definitions of international terror. Indeed, Wilkinson defines state-sponsored terror as "direct or indirect involvement of a government, via a formal or informal group, in the creation of psychological and physical violence against political targets or another state in order to achieve tactical and strategic goals that it is striving to attain."[10]

State-sponsored terror characteristically takes an ambivalent approach to international law and order.[11] On the one hand, states that make use of terror are willing to deviate from the norms and international "game rules" in order to strike out at an opponent and achieve their objectives (a prominent example of this can be seen in the "student" takeover of the U.S. Embassy in Iran and the taking of diplomats as hostages in 1979), while on the other hand, they endeavor to conceal their involvement in this activity in order to prevent reprisal from the terror victim.

Cooperation between a state and a terror organization generally exists on the basis of religious, ideological, or political identification—or on the basis of joint interests. The "patron's" level of control over the terror organization will vary according to the basis for cooperation and the extent to which the sponsored organization is dependent on its patron. The involvement of the state in terror may be direct or indirect and express itself in various levels of aid and cooperation (moral, political, economic, operational). In the majority of cases the ties between the "patron" state and the terror organization are of a covert nature, often carried out by citizens of other countries, because this factor helps the country to deny responsibility when the activity is exposed, thus avoiding criticism and the imposition of sanctions by the international community.[12]

Terror can serve as an additional or alternative tool vis-à-vis the use of military force for the attainment of the country's objectives (when the state supports terror against a country with which it is in a state of war), but there may also be the use of terror between countries that are not officially involved in a state of hostility. Terror can be effective in obtaining goals that may be unattainable through direct military confrontation, such as undermining the political stability in the target country or harming its diplomatic and economic ties with other countries.[13] Some researchers, such as Ariel Merari and Robert Cooperman, identify state-supported terror as part of Low Intensity Conflicts (LIC). This relates to a relatively limited conflict that is reflected in standard local wars but where the risk of deterioration to a full-blown flare-up is low.

The concept behind this definition is based on the assumption that various countries have come to the conclusion that modern weapons are so expensive and deadly that it is preferable not to take action on the level of direct military conflict while unleashing the full extent of the country's power. The alternative is to attempt to attain political and military achievements through the use of means that will keep the conflict simmering on a relatively low level of violence, while being adequately effective to achieve the user's goals. The advantage inherent to this type of conflict lies in a positive cost/benefit ratio from the point of view of the party using it. This method may be cost effective, that is, there is a good chance of achieving military/political benefits at a reduced risk strategy, based on the assumption that the attacked party will not want to broaden the conflict or cause an all-out confrontation.

Among the various countries worldwide in general, and in the Middle East in particular, that make use of terror and which are defined as "states that support terror," Iran stands out for two main aspects:

1. Iran is characterized by a combination of radical ideology and religion alongside political considerations, which turn the use of terror within the Iranian political framework into a rational and inevitable component.

2.   During the reviewed period, the intensive use of terror by Iran in order to promote its objectives on the international level was particularly prominent.

During the period of over two decades since the Islamic revolution (1979), Iran stands out as a state that utilizes terror in order to facilitate and achieve its goals in the international arena. Several events have served as milestones in Iranian involvement in terror. Primarily, in the first years of the revolutionary regime in Iran (1979-1980), the regime's main thrust of power was focused on stabilizing the regime and on internal terror against the opposition, and most of the terror attacks against foreign targets (American, British) were conducted on Iranian soil. From the year 1980, when the war broke out against Iraq, the use of terror became an auxiliary/supplementary tool to support its conventional struggle against that country on two levels: First, the perpetration of terror attacks against Iraqi targets in Iraq and worldwide; and the other, attacking countries identified as supporters of the Iraqi war effort. A third milestone in Iranian involvement in terror was the dispatch of forces of the Revolutionary Guards to Lebanon and the incorporation of local Shiite organizations in the terror activity against Western entities in Lebanon, particularly against Israel, as well as terror activity worldwide as emissaries of Iran.

As noted earlier, Iran embodies the incorporation of two basic elements in its policy that turn the use of terror in its international relations into a "legitimate and effective" tool:[14]

1.   The first principle is the ideological and religious basis, at the center of which lies the aspiration to establish Islamic rule worldwide. The attainment of this objective necessitates "export of the revolution" and contending with the revolution's internal enemies (within the Muslim world) and the outside (mainly Western capitalism and Zionism), and any means used to achieve this goal is acceptable, including terror.

2.   The second principle stems from the political and military needs vis-à-vis Iran's enemies and their supporters (for example, Iraq and the countries that supported it in the Iran-Iraq War such as Kuwait or France).

The use of terror in cases such as these constitutes a complementary or alternative means to the activation of conventional military power and political steps in order to attain Iran's goals on various levels (tactical, operative, and strategic).

Iran is known for its sophisticated terror activity, generally by "proxy," meaning via sponsored organizations like the Hizballah that enable Iran to place itself in the position of "intermediary" between the terror victim and the perpetrating organization, and to enjoy the political/military benefit that this position yields.

Iranian foreign policy is characterized by a combination of revolutionary ideology and radical modi operandi, on the one hand, and pragmatic policy, on the other. To a large extent, this policy reflects the power struggles and the opposing political approaches within the Iranian leadership. This ambivalent policy, particularly in its attitude towards the West, has provided Iran with flexibility in its political maneuvering and has made it difficult for its adversaries to formulate a forceful policy that will provide an adequate response to Iranian terror, mainly due to ongoing and cautious optimism according to which moderate elements in the Iranian regime should be encouraged and "the burning of bridges" which might fortify radical elements should be avoided.

Notes

1. Martha Crenshaw, *Terrorism, Legitimacy and Power*, Wesleyan University, Middletown, CT, 1983, pp. 1-4.
2. Ibid., p. 3.
3. Ibid., p. 1.
4. Ibid., p. 2.
5. Alex P. Schmidt and Albert I. Jongman, *Political Terrorism*, Transaction Publishers, New Brunswick, NJ, 1983.
6. Ibid., p. 110.
7. Ibid., p. 111.
8. Rand Corporation, Chronology of International Terrorism.
9. Interate Project—International Terrorism: Attributes of Terrorist Events.
10. Paul Wilkinson, *Terrorism and the Liberal State*, Macmillan Education Ltd., 1977, p. 182.
11. Ray S. Kline and Yona Alexander, *Terrorism as State Sponsored Covert Warfare*, Fairfax, VA, 1986.
12. Walter Laquer, *Terrorism*, Little Brown, Boston, 1997.
13. Shaul Kantzler, *International Terror—Ideology, Organization and Implementation*, Am Oved, Tel Aviv, 1999.
14. Martin Kramer (ed.), *Shi'ism, Resistance and Revolution*, Westview Press, Boulder, CO, 1987, pp. 47-51.

1

The Ideological and Religious Background and the Organizational Infrastructure of Terror in Iran

The Ideological and Religious Background for the Use of Terror by Iran Shiite Entities

Comprehension of the ideological and religious motives for the use of terror by Iran and Shiite entities necessitates a discussion of three main areas and the reciprocal ties among them: First, the general phenomenon of Islamic fundamentalism must be examined; subsequently, the basic principles of the Shiite faith must be studied; and, finally, an analysis must be conducted vis-à-vis Khomeini's philosophy, which combines Islamic radicalism and fundamentalism with the unique principles of the Shia, and translates them into a policy that counts terror as one of the tools for its fruition.

Fundamentalism is a foreign term of Christian-Protestant origins, which was adopted by Western people (researchers, politicians, journalists) to define the phenomenon of radical Islamic believers. Muslim religious extremists regard the use of this term in connection to Islam as a form of Western intellectual imperialism, and the term that they commonly use to define themselves is Islamayun—Islams or Islamic loyalists (as opposed to the Muslimun, which means one whose religion is Islam, but whose lifestyle may be secular).[1] The semantic meaning of the term "fundamentalism" refers to a fervor for the principles of religious beliefs, a way of life that stems from the latter and includes adherence to all of its manifestations; adopting religious symbols in daily life, behaving according to the normative codes of Islam, or organization and activity to preserve all of these principles and their dissemination in society.[2] By their very existence, the fundamentalist organizations, associations, and movements embody the full scope of this phenomenon's manifestations, signifying an ideology that facilitates its goals through the use of political means. The fundamentalist movements are essentially ideological, and their worldview is based on the holy writings of the Islam.[3] This type of ideology, which is rooted in "divine revelation," is driven by a rejection of any other ideology, as the latter is the creation of human conception, which is inherently perceived as flawed. An expression of this type of rejection can be observed in various slogans, such as "Islam is the solution" or "Not East, not West," which are widespread in the fundamentalist propaganda. Those faithful to Islam believe that "the realization of Allah's will on this earth," meaning the establishment of an Islamic society and state, is the only solution to the maladies plaguing human society.[4]

Islamic fundamentalism is not made up of one single approach. It contains major differences in the interpretation of Islamic history (Sunni, Shiite), as well as in the interpretation of commandments deriving from the principles of belief and the operative approach that best serves the ideology.[5] The fundamentalist movement may use different methods, from violent activity patterns (Jihad), severance of any connection with the infidels (Hijra), or service in the form of an organization that regards an investment in education and indoctrination (Dawa) as its ultimate goal—each group adheres to its own approach. The basic common denominator, shared by all of the movements, is the perception of Islam in its current state as a culture that is becoming extinct. This assessment feeds the sensation of urgency and pessimism, and constitutes one of the basic cultural-psychological motivations vis-à-vis their actions. Islamic fundamentalism is not a new phenomenon. Its roots lie in the previous century, and among its heralds were Jamal al Din Afghani, Muhammad Abdu, and Rashid Rida. Movements like the Salfiya had already appeared at the end of the nineteenth century within the Sunni population, and in the mid-twentieth century they became movements of mass appeal bearing a political message that spread throughout the Arab states in the form of the Muslim Brotherhood.[6]

At the end of the 1950s, the Shia also began to awaken, and Shiite fundamentalism as an ideological-political movement started developing in the religious center of Najef, radiating its influence upon the Shiite population of Iran and Lebanon. Najef of the 1960s and 1970s became an intellectual, revolutionary melting pot, in which the radical worldview of Lebanese Shiite religious leaders was fused, the same individuals who later became the leaders of the Hizballah in Lebanon.[7]

It is possible to identify several events and processes in the history and development of Islamic fundamentalism that constituted "defining events" vis-à-vis its approach and concepts:

The Encounter with the West—The expansion of fundamentalism is thought to be rooted in this encounter, which also serves as momentum for its present escalated strength. The encounter with the West involves many facets: The military, technological, scientific, and economic superiority of the West, cultural estrangement, the Imperialist "scheming," a modernism which alongside its blessings instigates major changes in traditional lifestyles. The problematic issues triggered by this encounter, which rapidly evolved into confrontation, make it possible to define fundamentalism as one of the forms of addressing this issue, or as the Islamic response to Western culture.[8]

Physical confrontation with the infidels—This stems from the overall experience of the encounter with the West, but it contains significant inherent influences both because of the emotionally charged aspect of these confrontations, but also due to the pointed emphasis placed on the inferiority of the Islamic East vis-à-vis the West.[9]

Thus, fundamentalism represents a radical ideology, which negates the existing order and expresses an aspiration for a more just society. This constitutes a struggle for social and economic change as part of an overall battle to bring Islamic peoples back to their authentic roots. Fundamentalism combats a failing socioeconomic reality as well as modernism, which cannot meet the materialistic and social expectations that it arouses, and seeks a cure for the social maladies at the root of Islamic societies, according to traditional, authentic standards rather than foreign, Western, and modern standards.

The awakening of Shiite fundamentalism is a part of the general phenomenon of Islamic fundamentalism, whose origins we have already discussed, but the Shia is unique in its sensation of historical discrimination which is not only the result of its backwardness and discrimination vis-à-vis the West, but is also due to the fact that the Shiites have been an oppressed minority in the Muslim world for hundreds of years.[10] The sensation of discrimination is rooted in the Shiite "Foundation Myth," which is based on the issue of the historical injustice perpetrated against the House of Ali after the death of the Prophet, when the former was deprived of his right to assume power in the Islamic world. The controversy with the Sunna and the feeling of ongoing political, social, and economic discrimination fuelled and empowered Shiite fundamentalism, which awakened and surfaced under Khomeini's leadership.

Basic Principles of the Shia

The basis of the Shia (or its literal translation, "the Ali Faction"), and at the focus of the controversy with Sunni Islam, is the belief that the lawful heir of the Prophet Muhammad is his son-in-law and cousin Ali Ibn-Talb, and that the reign over the Muslim community must be placed in the hands of his descendants. The basic principles of the Shia are closely linked to the events surrounding the Prophet Muhammad's death (in the year 632). According to descriptions in Sunni historical sources, Muhammad died without appointing an heir or establishing procedures for the election of a ruler. After a brief power struggle Muhammad's father-in-law, Abu-Backer (who ruled 632-634) was appointed the role; he was subsequently declared the first caliph (*calipha* actually means a substitute—i.e., the Prophet's substitute). With his demise, the reign passed on to Omar Ibn-al Qattab (634-644) and after him to Othman Ibn-Afhan (644-656)—both were Muhammad's sons-in-law and members of his tribe (Koriesh). The characteristics and method of appointing the first three caliphs became a Sunni tradition that served as a model for establishing the laws related to handing down the rule in the following centuries.

This concept of the nature of government is poised at the roots of the controversy between the Shiites and the Sunnis; the latter claim that Muhammad appointed a certain person as his successor (none other than Ali Ibn-Talb), an appointment rooted in divine command. According to the Shiite point of view, the reign of the first three caliphs was merely arbitrary theft of the Prophet's birthright from its legal owners; this is the source of the Shiites' feelings that they were the victims of injustice from the very start.

Ali did rule for a short time (656-661), but he was assassinated and his eldest son Hassan lost control to the first Umai ruler Muaviya (661-680). About twenty years later, Ali's second son Hussein tried to claim the throne, but he was brutally murdered with his family by the army of the Umai ruler Yazid Bin Muaviya at the Battle of Carbala (October 680). The murder of Hussein made a deep impression on the consciousness of the Shiites and became the root of the martyrdom that is so characteristic of their worldview. According to their outlook, Hussein intentionally chose death as an expression of his love for Allah and out of his desire to defend his faith.[11]

The participation of the faithful believers in the pain of Hussein and his family is considered a religious command, and for hundreds of years the Shiites commemorate the events at Carbala with ceremonies that culminate with the Ashura (the tenth of the month of Mukharam, which according to Shiite tradition is the anniversary of Hussein's death). The ceremonies include a reconstruction of the battle, the recitation of lamentations, and processions in which the participants afflict themselves until they shed their own blood. According to the traditional Shiite concept, this battle symbolized the end of the era of active opposition, as from that time most of the community leaders sided with passive behavior (*Kaud*), leaving the time for the realization of their goals in the hands of Allah. With the practical relinquishment of the achievement of their political goals, those leaders began to develop the religious dimension of their claims with great fervor; this is the basis for the development of the Shia as a religious movement rather than just a political party.

One of the prominent Shiite philosophers was Jaafar al Zadek, one of Ali's descendants, who recorded the principles of the Shiite religious rulings in a composition called "The Four Hundred Basic Elements," a document that served as a basis for literature related to Shiite religious rulings that subsequently developed. At the heart of the Shiite religious theory that took shape in the days of al Zadek and his disciples was the principle related to devotion and loyalty to the Imam (the leader), from the descendants of Ali and his wife Fatma (the Prophet's daughter). According to this belief, starting with Hussein (Ali's son), the reign is to be passed down from father to son. As the identity of the Imams was predetermined by divine command, the Shia obviously dismisses the principle of appointing a ruler, which was the ruling of the Sunni religious scholars. The Imams are privileged to rule not only due to the fact that they are descendants of the Prophet's family, but also because of their inherent qualities—perfect knowledge, part of which was inherited from their forefathers, and the other part, which was acquired through reading secret writings in their possession. The Imams serve as models for the faithful and they are immune to error and sin. Due to their status as those who provide guidance to the community, they continue in Muhammad's footsteps, and the only difference between them and him is that they are not prophets because they were not privileged to behold a direct divine revelation.

While both the Sunnis and the Shiites regard the sayings and deeds of Muhammad as the second source of religious law after the Koran (which contains the words of Allah), the Shiites also add the sayings and deeds of the Imams to this source. The Shiite belief in the Imams, alongside the Prophet Muhammad, plays an important role on the Day of Judgment because they will intercede before Allah on behalf of the faithful, and thanks to them even a believer who sinned will reach the Garden of Eden. This leads to the conclusion that affiliation with the Shia promises salvation.

Thus, the Shiite is different than the others not only because of his devotion to "the true religion" but also due to the material from which he is made. This elitist approach is also expressed in terminology: The Shiites are the chosen ones (*al Khatsha*), while other mortals (led by the Sunnis) are the masses (*al Amma*).

Another byproduct of the loyalty to the Imams is the complete repudiation (*Bra'a*) of their opponents; this has far-reaching implications because from a religious point of view the first three caliphs (which in the eyes of the Sunnis constitute the "golden generation" of the Islam), are viewed by the Shiites as sinners and infidels.[12] The concept of the Bara'a is one of the most difficult dilemmas in the Shiites' approach to the Sunnis. On the one hand, it is problematic to regard the Sunnis as infidels on the level of Jews and Christians, but, on the other hand, the Sunnis reject the faith in the Imams so they cannot be regarded as believers. The solution to this issue is based on the classification of people into three categories: believers, Muslims, and Infidels. According to the Shiite school of thought, the believers are Shiites, while the Muslims are those who recognize the uniqueness of Allah and Muhammad as His emissary, but do not adhere to the principle of devotion and loyalty to the Imam (Vilaya).

The difference between the Sunna and the Shia in this regard is substantial. The Sunnites also distinguish between believers and Muslims but regard them as one bloc facing the world of infidels. The world is therefore divided into two sections: The area of Islam (Dar al Islam), where the Islam is in control; and the area of the infidels (Dar al Kufer), which Islam must conquer. The Shiites, on the other hand, divide the world into three types of territory: The area of faith (Dar al Iman), under Shiite rule; the area of Islam; and the area of the infidels.

The interesting fact is that according to the Shiite theory of Jihad, the initial battle must be waged against the "Islam area," in order to convert it into "the area of belief," and only subsequently should the struggle against the infidels be launched. But theories aside—for almost nine hundred years there were actually no areas that could be called "the areas of belief," and the Shiites, who, in the past (and in the present), constitute a minority in Islam, lived mostly in "Islam area."

This reality eventually brought about the existence of another significant principle in the Shiite faith—the principle of caution (*Takiya*). As throughout history, the Shiites were a persecuted minority, this principle established that in times of danger the Shiite is permitted (and sometimes even obligated) to conceal his true faith. The Shiites justify this by the fact that even the faithful were forced to rely on this principle during times of distress.

Another central principle connected to the Takiya deals with the disappearance of the twelfth Imam. The Shiites believe that Allah predetermined that there would be twelve Imams, the last of which would be the messiah (*mahadi*). According to Shiite sources, after the assassination of the eleventh Imam, his son, who was a small child at that time, entered a cave in the basement of their house in Samra, and was never seen again. If he had not hidden, the life of this Imam would also be in danger just like his predecessors, but in contrast to them there would have been no one to take his place if he had been killed, and thus there was no choice but to disappear. "The great disappearance" continues to this very day and will end with the return of the "vanished Imam" as the mahadi.

The period of disappearance is considered a trial period during which the Shiite's allegiance to the Imam is tested. This allegiance includes the continuance of the adaptable line adopted by the Imams; the factor that alleviates the Shiite's suffering is the belief that the mahadi, who will deliver the message of salvation, will also redeem the Shiites from their enemies and restore justice to the world.

In the absence of the Imam the community of believers is to be led by the *mujtahidun* (religious scholars) that act according to his philosophy. These religious scholars defined their role as the preservation of religious principles and to serve as substitutes for the "vanished Imam." One of the important ramifications of this principle is the invalidation of the legitimacy of any existing secular regime, and the demand that the religious scholars must rule until the foundation of the utopian regime with the return of the "vanished Imam."

The Main Principles of Khomeinism

Khomeini's theory is based on his interpretations of several key issues in Shiite Islam and the adaptation of the solutions to the new reality of the twentieth century. A central principle is his stance that calls for taking an active approach in order to facilitate the goals of Islam and achieve salvation. Khomeini's philosophy grew and spread against the background of the Shiites' historical feelings of frustration, a harsh socioeconomic reality and the intensification of fundamentalist leanings in the Muslim world.

In their study, Marvin Zonis and Daniel Brumberg[13] indicate eight principles in Khomeini's theory that lead to the basic outlook that calls for Shiite activism and realization of goals via "revolutionary violence." *The first principle* deals with the granting of legitimacy to Shiite activism. Most of the Shiite philosophers espoused a passive approach which opines that the return of the "vanished Imam" must be awaited and that the principle of the Takiya must be applied; the ongoing repression and injustice are signs that herald the imminent return of the mahadi. Admittedly, even before Khomeini there were interpreters that called for a struggle against the corrupt rulers in an attempt to restore justice and shorten the waiting time till the mahadi's return, but these constituted a minority in the Shiite community. The activist worldview was conceived by Khomeini in the 1970s. Khomeini provided legitimization for the idea that it was permitted for man to act to facilitate his fate, and that this principle applied to all of society, and therefore the Muslims must act to achieve their goals instead of waiting for a change that will come at its own pace. This resolution opened the door for the definition of the goals for the necessary social changes and the steps that the Muslims must take in order to achieve their objectives.

The second principle discusses the legitimacy of regimes until the return of the "vanished Imam." As long as the utopian "just society," which is to rise upon the return of the "vanished Imam," has not yet been established, there is no regime that is worthy of complete legitimacy in the eyes of the Shiites. Nevertheless, during the "transition period," the ulma (the Muslim scholars who deliver religious rulings in matters related to faith and customs) granted different degrees of legitimacy to various regimes according to their treatment of the Shiite community and their attitude to the laws of Islam. This also applies to Sunni regimes that adopted the laws of Islam but were granted only partial legitimacy. Khomeini claimed that the only country that came close to the proper and correct implementation of the Islamic laws was revolutionary Iran. According to Khomeini, the degree of legitimacy to be awarded to the Sunni regimes was dependent on their willingness to change and improve their ways. If these countries do not adopt reforms (according to his philosophy), it is Iran's right to oblige them to do so, even through the use of force. A precondition for achieving legitimacy is the eradication and rejection of any foreign influences (social, economic, and cultural) by the international powers as this leads to corruption, weakness, and rifts in the Muslim world.

The third principle deals with the way the Shiite minority handles the coercion of the majority positions. Khomeini approaches this issue in two "state cycles" and indicates the reciprocal influences between them. In light of the basic assumption (stated above) that the Sunni regime has not been granted legitimacy, thus the Western regimes standing behind them are not deemed legitimate either; therefore Khomeini believed that it was permissible to use violence not only in the "Muslim circle" but also against the international powers (this concept does not even need to rely on the concept of Jihad, which grants legitimacy for war against the infidels in any case). Moreover, Khomeini claimed that as the correct understanding of the Koran was bestowed upon the Shia (a claim that reverts to the elitist approach), it is the fate of the Shiites to exist in a world in which the majority is heretic or mistaken in its understanding of Islam. This led to Khomeini's derivation of two concepts that justified violence for the achievement of Islamic goals.

- First, the world is divided into two parts—the oppressors and the oppressed. Therefore, the strongest powers (the superpowers) are also the less-legitimate and the less-just. According to Khomeini, these powers are responsible for all of the evil and corruption in the world, and the Muslims must encourage the oppressed nations to rise up and throw off the control of the domineering nations. This process is to be achieved through the use of violence and in a way that will teach these powers a lesson.
- Secondly, Khomeini did not recognize the superpowers' values and norms (particularly the Western ones, but also communism). Values such as liberalism, democracy, human rights, socialism, and others are merely empty slogans. Moreover, Khomeini did not accept international norms and laws, and the UN is simply a tool whose reason for existence is to bestow legitimacy upon interests and concepts that serve the superpowers. Among the various countries, the United States was considered the "Great Satan," due to its presence and involvement in Iran and in the Middle East, and its attempts to instill the influences of its corruptive culture in Muslim states.

In light of this concept, Khomeini believed that action should be taken against the "forces of evil;" the level of deserved punishment varies according to circumstances (France's aid to Iraq, for example, caused the former to be promoted to the status of "a Great Satan.")

The fourth principle deals with the philosophical issue of the essence of human nature and its implications. Khomeini believed that the average human being, as opposed to the Prophet and the Imams, is basically weak and vulnerable, and he can be tempted by evil. These weaknesses are inherent to mankind. Society is also afflicted by a "natural wickedness," and it contains a "satanical self" that demands to slake its urges, lusts, and selfish physical needs, instead of striving to fulfill spiritual needs and those of the entire community. Society must cleanse itself of the evil that it contains by establishing "a just society" based on Islamic values. The road to achieving this goal is strewn with stumbling blocks, and therefore the latter must first be overcome.

An example of a serious hurdle is the Muslim regimes that enable the infiltration and dissemination of foreign cultures and values. According to Khomeini, these regimes must be ousted and replaced by a single Islamic state (the concept of Islamic unity) through peaceful methods or by taking forceful and violent action.

Based on the definition of the conflict's objectives as well as the definition of human substance, Khomeini reaches one of the central and innovative issues in his theory, which permits the sacrifice of an individual's life for Muslim society. The individual lives in a corrupt society, whose main goal is to satisfy physical needs; therefore, when an individual sacrifices himself, he sacrifices something physical for a spiritual objective that will benefit all of society, and thus it is permissible to sacrifice the "physical I" in favor of the "spiritual I." The encouragement of self-sacrifice among young people, the "martyrs," constitutes an extreme expression of this concept regarding the cleansing of society and the individual.

Khomeini was not the first or the only Islamic philosopher to point out the link between the use of violence and the promotion of the goals of Muslim society. He was preceded by the philosopher Sayyid Jamal al Din Afghani, who claimed that Muslims must resist corruptive foreign influences with any available means, including murder. But Khomeini's uniqueness lies in the fact that he was the first Shiite philosopher to permit self-sacrifice (suicide) for Islamic goals.

The fifth principle also deals with the justification of self-sacrifice from another aspect. The death of Hussein and the demise of other Imams represent a central theme in the Shiite faith. The Shiites believe that when Hussein embarked on his long journey from Higaz to Carbala, he knew he would not return and that he would die a cruel death, but this death was important for the Shiite community in order to claim the crown of Islamic leadership, and therefore Hussein continued on his journey. Hussein's death is relived each year at the Ashura ceremonies, but according to Khomeini this is not enough to propel people into action, and certainly not to self-sacrifice. Khomeini encouraged the faithful to relive Hussein's sacrifice not only on the Ashura holiday, but also through daily self-sacrifice in the service of Islam. In the matter of self-sacrifice, the issue of Jihad is also worthy of mention, as Khomeini also contributed an innovative concept to the principles of Shiite faith in this regard.[14] In the past, the Shiites were very doubtful regarding their obligation to initiate Jihad as long as the "vanished Imam" had not yet returned, because Jihad can be declared only on the basis of a command from a legitimate political authority, and from the point of view of Shiite legal theory, this type of legal authority has not existed since the disappearance of the twelfth Imam. In its emphasis on the need for Jihad, Khomeini's philosophy deviates sharply from this line of thought. I will subsequently address the source for the legitimization of this conceptual change.

The *sixth principle* deals with the universality of the Shiites' struggle (this topic is also linked with the issue of self-sacrifice). Traditionally, the Shiites regard themselves as the victims of oppression at the hands of evil regimes in the present, and as the victims of historical injustice when attempting to claim the Islamic leadership. Khomeini universalized this concept. In his view, the Shiites actually represent all of the oppressed peoples on this earth. The Islamic revolution is the spearhead of this struggle, and it calls on all subjugated nations to struggle in order to oust their oppressors.[15] This is a universal worldview, but ultimately, its main target audience is the Shiite community of believers. Nevertheless, this appeal also fell on a receptive audience in Islamic fundamentalist Sunni circles.

According to Khomeini, one of the main tools at the disposal of the oppressed in their battle against their oppressors, whose strength is obviously superior, is the willingness of the Shiites to sacrifice themselves in order to achieve their goals. Khomeini understood that in order to win the trust and support of the faithful for his philosophy, the sources for legitimization and authority would have to be shown to the elite, which would then hoist the ideological banner and also provide justification for the status and philosophy of the leader himself, who sets the path for the community of believers.

The next two principles (the *seventh* and the *eighth*) deal with the issue of the source of Khomeini's governmental authority. The privilege to lead the community of the believers was given to the Prophet Muhammad, and after him to the twelve Imams. Since the disappearance of the twelfth Imam, due to their attributes and knowledge of the Islam, the mujtahidun were given the responsibility to guide the masses of believers. Khomeini believed that the senior and most educated mujtahid must lead and serve as the main guide, while the actual government should be placed in the hands of an elite group of religious leaders. Thus, the authority for his government stems mainly from the fact that he perpetuates the sequence of leadership from the Prophet via the Imams. Among Khomeini's supporters an attempt was even made to confer a mystical dimension upon his return to Iran, according to which even if Khomeini's return was not comparable to that of the "vanished Imam," it might reduce the waiting time until the latter's return. Therefore, it would seem that one of the main sources of Khomeini's reign was the charisma and the mystical faith in his power and spiritualism.

An additional issue related to the source of authority for Khomeini's regime is connected to an esoteric perception of the knowledge of the Koran. According to Khomeini's theory, the understanding of the Koran and the truth is beyond the capabilities of the average person. This ability was awarded only to a select few from among the religious scholars, who due to their characteristics and studies are the successors of the Imams. These scholars, with Khomeini at their head, have been given the right to pass religious rulings and their interpretations are entirely valid and are impervious to objections. This makes it easier to understand Khomeini's ability to introduce innovative religious rulings that sometimes contradicted hundreds of years of interpretation provided by Shiite philosophers.[16]

To summarize, Khomeini's philosophy is characterized primarily by a belief in messianic salvation, which is achievable via the adoption of an active line that includes political activity or the use of violent force as required. This messianic inclination was reflected in the bestowment of the appellation of Imam on Khomeini and other charismatic religious leaders. This usage gave the title of "Imam" a modern-day meaning of a leader who combines secular and spiritual authority in his character.

Khomeini regarded "revolutionary violence" as a central tool for the solution of the problems within Islamic society as well as a solution for the individual's problems. The struggle is primarily focused upon the purification of Islamic society from within, initially inside the Shiite community, and subsequently in the wider Islamic circle. The struggle does not end in the Islamic arena but it is also designated to obliterate the "source of evil"—the superpowers that cause the corruption of the world. Thus, Khomeini's revolutionary message is universal, with the Shiites representing all of the oppressed on this earth.

Khomieni provides the ideological/religious and rational justifications for the use of violence in order to promote the objectives of Islam, and places the Jihad and "self-sacrifice" at the ideological front of his philosophy. This fact gave the Shia the worldwide reputation of being a violent faith that demands self-sacrifice of its followers to promote its goals.

Exporting the Iranian Revolution

The aspiration to export the Iranian revolution to all of Muslim society (as well as all of humanity) is an inseparable part of the philosophy of the Islamic revolution, and at its basis is the aim to promote the Islamization of the Muslim society, forge Muslim unity, and return Islamic society to its proper status in human society.[17]

Khomeini and his disciples strove to ignore the religious differences between the Sunnis and the Shiites, as well as national divisions, and aspired to create a unified revolutionary Islamic power that "would include a billion Muslims."[18] In Khomeini's view, this concept constituted justification for interference in the "internal" business of other Muslim countries and societies, in the form of rhetoric calling for Muslim populations to rebel against their governments (which he regarded as lacking religious legitimization and as lackeys of imperialism). Even during his exile in Iraq Khomeini had stated that the leaders of Muslim countries "live as infidels and animals...and they do not pay heed to the poor populace that suffers from poverty and need."[19] Khomeini ignored the political boundaries separating Muslim populations in various states, and declared that Iran "views all of the Muslim countries as part of us and ourselves as part of the Muslim countries."[20]

Although the revolutionary message was meant for all of human society, the Muslim states were the first target, and the Shiite community in these countries was naturally designated to serve as the standard bearers of the revolutionary concept. An examination of the movements in the Muslim world that adopted Khomeini's outlook indicates that most of them were Shiite organizations, some of which had been established prior to Khomeini's ascension to power (such as the al Dawa movement and the Islamic action organization in Iraq) and had undergone radicalization,[21] and others arose after the revolution and were inspired by it, such as the Jundullah and the Hizballah in Lebanon. In the eyes of the leaders of these movements, such as the Sheikh Fadallah in Lebanon or al Khakim in Iraq, the Iranian revolution constituted the epitome of "Husseinism," the concept of self-sacrifice for Islam as Hussein had demonstrated in the battle of Carbala. They lauded the achievements of the Iranian revolution, and its lessons were studied in the publications of radical Lebanese and Iraqi circles.[22]

The Iranian model grants legitimacy to an armed struggle, and, and bases its political policy on Shiite Khadits that explain when and why it is permissible to use violence, and what regime should be established after ousting a heathen and sinful government (see elaboration in the previous section, which discusses the principles of Khomeini's philosophy). These movements recognize Khomeini as the representative of the "vanished Imam" and also as the leader of the Islamic nation, whose authority is valid throughout the Muslim world.[23]

Among the religious scholars in Iran there were those who viewed the revolution as a gateway towards the modification of all of human society and as an opportunity to turn Muslim society into a leading power in human civilization. Ayatollah Mashkini, one of the extreme advocates in favor of "exporting the revolution," went so far as to state that "the objective of the revolution is to force the Koran on the entire world."[24] However, for the most part even the more radical religious leaders viewed the revolution as no more than the presentation of a message and a model for emulation for oppressed nations. Ali Khamenei expressed the stance of the regime by stating that "the revolution knows no boundaries and cannot be imprisoned by walls, but rather it must be exported."[25] Khamenei compared the affect of the revolution in the Muslim world to that of "whispering coals that will naturally ignite the black reality that encompasses them."[26] Thus, according to his view, the Islamic revolution was only the first stage in the "world revolution." The Iranian Foreign Minister in 1981, Mussawi, declared that the goal of his ministry was to "convey the messages of the revolution to the world." He added that if Iran persuades the world that it possesses a "message, solution, a model for emulation, then there will be a chance to create a large revolutionary movement throughout the world."[27]

During the years of Khomeini's regime, Iran continued to espouse the principle of exporting the revolution and aiding the "freedom movements" in the

Muslim world. However, gradually and over time realism and moderation crept into the Iranian declarations, due to pragmatic considerations related to Iranian foreign policy needs; these declarations mainly carried a message regarding the dissemination of the principles of the Iranian revolution for simulation "in peaceful ways." In 1983, Khomeini passed a ruling according to which although the course of history turns the export of the revolution into an unstoppable process, Iran is not interested in "crawling like a worm [into the other countries], but rather prefers to enter through the front door like an invited guest." Until then, it must act to disseminate the revolutionary values and create an awareness of Iran's achievements as a means "to encourage these invitations."[28]

Iran took myriad steps to export the revolution: Starting from its presentation as a model for emulation; through its use of terror, encouragement of radical movements and its assistance in establishing revolutionary Islamic movements (Hizballah in Lebanon and Islamic movements in the Gulf and Magreb); and finally dispatching forces of the Revolutionary Guards to Lebanon. The means and methods changed in accordance to the character of the society of destination ("third world" countries, Muslim countries or Shiite societies) and its internal situation.

A central means for the export of the revolution was propaganda activity aimed at disseminating its values, which was carried out by Iranian embassies, special information delegations, and "culture houses" established in various countries, including Western Europe. Students who underwent ideological training and religious clerics were sent to various countries throughout the world in order to convert people and promote the concept of the Iranian revolution. Another method for the dissemination of the Iranian revolution was based on Iran's presence in international organizations, which it used as a stage to present its worldview. At the same time an effort was made to draw religious clerics from other Muslim countries to the revolution, mainly by inviting them to attend conferences or visit to Iran as well as by hosting various Islamic conventions. For example, in May 1983, some five hundred clerics convened at the "world conference for Imams" and ruled that they regarded Khomeini as a man "who has the required qualifications for Muslim Imams," and they undertook "to call on Muslims to follow the path of their appeal."[29]

In the framework of its attempts to export the revolution and to make its ideas attractive for Sunni Islamic circles, the Khomeini regime made use of two separate layers of propaganda: Shiite propaganda for internal consumption, and an ecumenical approach (an approach that strove to play down and lessen the controversy between the two schools) for external consumption. In order to address the challenge of exporting the revolution, Iranian propaganda in Arabic[30] emphasized the messages shared by all of the Islamic movements, underscored the activities of the Iranian revolution to realize the message in the economic sphere (redistribution of income and property) and the moral area (woman's status, imbibing wine, etc.), and played down the conflict between the Shiites and the Sunnis. An example of this ecumenical effort can be viewed in the approach to the Shiites' fundamental myth—the myth of Hussein and the battle of Carbala. The ecumenical approach grants this myth an all-Islamic and universal significance in the form of the struggle against injustice and suppression, a struggle that is not to be postponed to the "end of days," but rather it is the duty of every Muslim to participate in it even today.[31]

The dispatch of the Revolutionary Guard to Lebanon in 1982 constitutes an example of an aggressive operational method—the export of the revolution also via military power, and not only through influence and persuasion. Although the Revolutionary Guards were not directly involved in the combat against Israel, they established the Hizballah organization that spearheaded the armed struggle against the Western and Israeli presence in Lebanon.

Iran regards the solidification of the Hizballah in Lebanon as its greatest success (and only one to date) in exporting the Islamic revolution. Even after the IDF withdrawal from Lebanon (in 2000), Iran continues to view Lebanon as its forefront against Israel, and the Hizballah as a key factor in leading the struggle.[32]

Over time, Khomeini's movement became the Muslim world's symbol for the power of Islam in its struggle against the oppressor, whether from within or via external imperialism, but its practical influence did not usually exceed organizations formed by minority militant groups. Several factors combined to limit its influence and prevent it from becoming a leading trend in Islam:[33]

- The Iranian revolutionary regime failed to provide satisfactory solutions for Iran's social and economic problems; therefore, in practical terms it was not perceived as a suitable model for emulation.
- The regimes in Muslim countries were aware of the danger posed by radical religious groups, and therefore took ruthless action against them.
- The promotion of Khomeini's ideas came up against an objective obstacle because they were accepted by a Shiite minority in a Muslim world which was mostly Sunni and was hostile to the Shiites.

In this connection, it is to be noted that the Iranian revolutionary regime made significant efforts to expand its influence and connections to radical Sunni Islamic circles. In this framework, close cooperation was established with the various Islamic Jihad groups (Palestinian, Egyptian), and with radical Islamic movements in the Magreb.

Due to the obstacles that made it difficult to export the Islamic revolution (as specified above), subversive activity to disseminate Khomeinism and the use of terror gradually turned into the main tools to achieve the objectives of the Iranian regime. Subversive pro-Iranian factors instigated riots and agitation in many Muslim countries, and translations of Khomeini's philosophy to local languages became an integral part of the arsenal of fundamentalist propaganda in these countries.

The assassins of Anwar Sadat in Egypt brought up Khomeini's name during their trial as a source of inspiration for their acts. During a television interview, King Hassan of Morocco accused Khomeini of being behind the wave of riots that struck Morocco in 1983. A series of suicide attacks in Lebanon against French, American, and Israeli targets was perpetrated under Iranian inspiration and direction, with the aim of banishing the foreign presence in Lebanon as the first step towards an "Islamic Republic" in that country according to the Iranian model.[34]

The period of the regime of Khomeini's successors in Iran is characterized by the fortification and stabilization of the Islamic rule, the implementation of the revolutionary theory, the resolution of the Iranian people's problems and distress, the setting of the revolutionary path, and the continued export of the revolution.[35]

External observers distinguish between radical and moderate entities in the Iranian leadership. Power struggles between radical and moderate elements had already taken place during the presidency of Rafsanjani, but the struggles became more intensive during the term of his successor to the presidency—Khatami. Khatami appears to be a reformer who aspires to carry out internal

Figure 1.1
The Governmental Structure in Iran

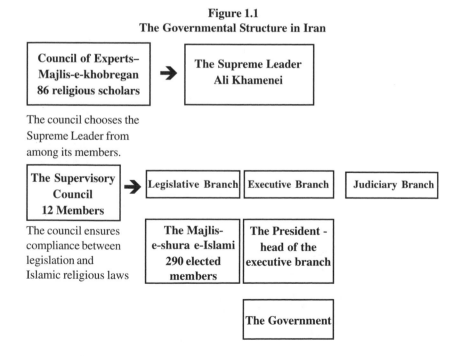

reforms in Iran and improve its ties with countries worldwide, but his ability to realize his vision is restricted due to the power wielded by the traditional circles headed by the spiritual leader Ali Khamenei.

The pragmatism of the Iranian governmental system stems from social and economical problems, and from the knowledge that in order to survive, it is necessary to increase cooperation with the laws of the international systems, and Iran's foreign relations have improved accordingly. The main events that took place in the international arena during the 1990s, which had an impact upon Iran were: the collapse of the Soviet Union, the U.S.-led coalition's war against Iraq in the Gulf War, the Middle East peace process, and the Islamic fundamentalist awakening. The influence of these events was reflected in the intensification of Iranian aspirations to cement its status as a regional leader, while viewing the situation as an opportunity to fortify Iranian hegemony in the Gulf, as a chance to hoist the banner of the Islamic struggle against Israel, and as a means to disseminate Islam through linkage with movements that were not trained or supported by Iran when they were first founded (the Hamas, for example).

It is clear to the Iranian leaders that the degree of Iran's stability and success will ultimately stem not from the extent that Islam is implemented, but rather from its success in solving the social and economic problems. This is why they incorporate pragmatism and realism, and, as a rule, when the revolutionary interests conflict with the country's interests, preference will be given to the latter.

The examples to be brought below do indeed reflect the duality of Iran's approach. On the one hand, in regions and at focal points where Iran believes it can act intensively and uncompromisingly to promote the concepts of the Islamic revolution, it aids radical Islamic organizations in terror acts and subversion aimed at ousting secular regimes and striking out at Western interests. This category includes Iranian involvement and cooperation with Sudan in disseminating radical Islam in North Africa (mainly Egypt and Algeria) and in the Horn of Africa (Somalia, Eritrea, etc.), as well as Iranian support of the Hizballah in Lebanon and Palestinian terrorist organizations in their battle against Israel.

On the other hand, at spots where there is a fear that Iranian subversion may be exposed, thus resulting in damage to Iranian interests, Iran adopts a more pragmatic policy. A prominent example in this category is the moderate stand adopted by Iran towards the neighboring Islamic republics, with the aim of maintaining sound relations with Russia and Turkey, and for the time being able to prevent the creation of a threatening reality that will cause conflicts with these countries.

To summarize, it is reasonable to postulate that Iranian policy is currently motivated by radical revolutionary ideology, but its implementation is examined vis-à-vis pragmatic considerations that ultimately dictate Iran's steps.

The American campaign against terror following the attacks of September 11, 2001—including the U.S. war in Afghanistan and subsequently in Iraq—has created a new strategic reality along Iran's borders, which necessitates Iran to reexamine its goals vis-à-vis the export of the revolution and terror.

Intelligence and Terror Functions in Iran

Khomeini's revolutionary regime was forced to provide a response to several central challenges that threatened its very existence:

- Coping with opposition to the revolutionary regime from among the followers of the previous regime (that of the Shah), as well as with some of its revolutionary partners which later turned into its enemies, such as the (communist) Tudeh party, the Mujahidin Khalq, and the Fedayeen Khalq;
- Coping with the Iraqi invasion of Iran (in 1980);
- Coping with the threat posed by foreign powers that supported the Shah's reign and were unwilling to recognize the revolutionary regime in Iran (the United States, Britain, and others).

Aside from coping with these weighty challenges, the revolutionary regime was committed to its revolutionary ideology and to the principle of "exporting the Khomeini Revolution" to the entire Muslim nation. Thus, the regime had to set up intelligence, operational, and propaganda agencies within a short period of time in order to meet the demands (see figure 1.2).

The Islamic regime initially used the apparatus that served it during the period of the struggle against the Shah's reign and in the course of the revolution, like the Hizballah militias and the Revolutionary Guard, which had carried the burden of the struggle against the Shah's government. Their most important mission, after the success of the revolution, was to wipe out the military and security power points that supported the Shah's reign.[36] After these entities were eradicated, jailed or fled the country, the regime's main effort was directed against the opposition organizations (Khomeini's allies during the period of the revolution), while at the same time the regime was forced to deal with the Iraqi invasion in a head-on military confrontation, as well as with Iraqi and Western aid offered to the opposition circles that were active against the revolutionary regime.[37]

As the army and the Iranian intelligence agencies in Iran had identified with the Shah's regime, the Khomeini regime was forced to establish new intelligence forces and agencies that would be based on loyalists to the revolutionary regime. The Khomeini revolution in 1979 brought about the eradication of the Iranian intelligence service dating from the Shah's reign—the SAVAK—which served as a central tool for securing the Shah's government, as well as pursuing and eliminating his opponents. During the revolution and in its aftermath, the leaders of the SAVAK became central targets of the revolutionary regime, and many of them were imprisoned and executed.[38]

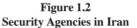

Figure 1.2
Security Agencies in Iran

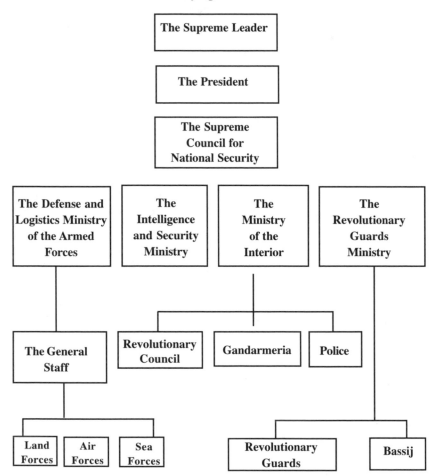

According to the Iranian constitution, the spiritual leader is the chief commander of the Iranian armed forces. In practice, there are several "armies" and semi-military forces acting under the command of the various political powerbrokers in the Iranian establishment, as will be detailed subsequently. Already in 1979 Khomeini's regime had founded its own intelligence service called the SAVAMA; its main role was in the area of internal security (persecuting and eliminating the regime's opponents), and gathering intelligence about Iraq.[39] The first director of the SAVAMA was General Faradost (who was arrested in 1985 and was charged with espionage for the USSR). The SAVAMA acted simultaneously with the Hizballah's branches and the Revolutionary

Guards, which handle missions that were identical to those of the intelligence service. In 1984, the SAVAMA underwent reorganization: Muhammad Kishari was appointed its director and its name was changed to VEVAK (the Ministry of Intelligence and Security).

The Ministry of Intelligence and Security (VEVAK)[40]

The VEVAK inherited the SAVAMA's roles while expanding its intelligence activities vis-à-vis Iraq and other foreign targets, and incorporating them in "revolutionary export" missions. In order to boost its operational capabilities, military intelligence service intelligence experts (from the Shah's time) and junior SAVAK agents who specialized in Iranian leftists and in the Iraqi and Arab arena were called back to service.

It appears that during these years VEVAK renewed the intelligence infrastructure established in Iraq and in Arab countries during the reign of the Shah, and utilized the intelligence capabilities for the promotion of Iran's goals despite the difference in ideological approaches between the revolutionary intelligence service and its predecessor.

Due to the allocation of generous funding and extensive personnel, within a short period of time the Ministry of Intelligence and Security became one of the most powerful and influential agencies in the Iranian regime. In 1988, Ali Falahian was appointed the Minister of Intelligence. Thanks to his qualifications, connections, and status in the regime, he succeeded in establishing work procedures and coordination mechanisms between the various security and intelligence entities, as well as founding and heading the supreme council for intelligence matters, which supervised and coordinated all of Iran's intelligence and subversive activities.

The Ministry of Intelligence and Security is officially subordinate to the president, but in practice the heads of the Ministry are appointed from among the close associates of the supreme leader and act according to his instructions. The Ministry is composed of twelve departments that activate over 20,000 agents inside and outside of Iran. The first department is responsible for internal security, and enjoys a substantial part of the budget allocated for covert activity within Iran to secure the regime. The second department—the popular intelligence—is responsible for the bazaars, markets and mosques, and in practice strives to supervise public places and focuses on group associations. The third department—external security—is responsible for gathering intelligence information, underground activity, and terror activities abroad. The department operates the Al Quds organization, spread out at various points worldwide, including Turkey, Pakistan, Germany, Switzerland, and more. The technical service provides communication equipment to agents and supported terrorist organizations; the finance department and administrative center deal with the budget and payroll, while the training bureau deals with the agents' training and instruction. The department for external security and the bureau of revolutionary movements are involved in links and operational activity vis-à-vis Islamic and other organizations that cooperate with Iran and are recipients of Iranian funding.

The Ministry of the Revolutionary Guards (Pasdaran)[41]

The aim of the activities of the Revolutionary Guards was mainly to defend the Iranian revolutionary regime against internal opposition. After the Iraqi invasion of Iran (in 1980) the Revolutionary Guards became a central nucleus of the Popular Military Forces, which bore the brunt of the combat against Iraq, due to the weakness of the Iranian army, which underwent purges as a result of the revolution. The Revolutionary Guards number about 120,000 members, including independent land, sea, and air forces. The land forces are divided into thirteen regional commands and twenty divisions (a division of the Revolutionary Guards is parallel to a military division). The Revolutionary Guards are deployed along the borders of Iraq and Afghanistan with the aim of defending the country, and in Iran's large cities for internal security missions. In addition, they are responsible for Iran's non-conventional combat means. Parallel to their missions related to safeguarding the regime and protecting the Iranian homeland, the Revolutionary Guards also undertook tasks related to the "export of the revolution," mainly through the use of terror and aid to Islamic terror organizations worldwide.

The Revolutionary Guards Ministry, which was established in 1983, handles all areas of activity inside and outside of Iran. In all matters relating to activities outside of Iran, the Revolutionary Guards are based on two central entities: (a) the committee for intelligence abroad; (b) the committee for operations abroad. The activity of Revolutionary Guard members abroad is generally conducted under a diplomatic, cultural or commercial guise. The Revolutionary Guards support the training, instruction, and indoctrination of activists in Islamic terror organizations worldwide. These activists undergo training in Iran, Sudan, Lebanon, or Afghanistan (during the period of the war that took place in this country). Revolutionary Guard members also assist in the establishment of Islamic terror organizations, such as the Hizballah in Lebanon, and support Islamic entities in conflict arenas worldwide such as Bosnia or Chechnya.

The "Al Quds Force" ("Jerusalem Force") of the Revolutionary Guards, which has been deployed in Lebanon since 1983, is an Iranian entity that leads Iranian activity in the region and its support of the Hizballah. This force deals with the direction and provision of military aid in terror activity against Israel, particularly that of the Hizballah, and Islamic and secular Palestinian organizations. The entity includes several militia forces that operate under the auspices of or in connection with the Revolutionary Guards:

- The Bassij—This militia constitutes a national guard and is charged with the supervision of law and order in the country, and handling disorderly conduct and threats against the regime. The militia is based on civilians who can be recruited as needed. The Bassij is subordinate to the Revolutionary Guards.
- Law enforcement forces—These forces are subordinate to the Ministry of Interior, but in practical terms are operated by the leaders of the religious establishment and serve as a kind of "religious police."

The Ministry of Direction and Propaganda[42]

The ministry is responsible for religious and cultural activity, and for the dissemination of the Islamic revolution abroad. In this framework it is responsible for the establishment of mosques, cultural centers, associations, student unions, and religious services worldwide. The ministry is allocated considerable resources, which serve for the financing of propaganda activities, communication, and education. The ministry's activity centers abroad often serve as a guise for Intelligence Ministry members, and enable the identification and recruitment of Islamic activists abroad among Muslim communities where ministry members are active.

The Foreign Ministry[43]

The Foreign Ministry is in charge of Iran's foreign policy and its diplomatic ties with states and organizations all over the world. It also assists in the dissemination of the Islamic revolution, and the diplomatic representations abroad serve as central focal points for entities affiliated with the Revolutionary Guards and the Ministry of Intelligence.[44] The Foreign Ministry provides diplomatic camouflage for the activity of intelligence members and terror activists, and aids in the provision of documentation (passports, visas, etc.) and in the transfer of combat means and equipment via diplomatic pouch (which according to international law is not supervised by the host country).[45] Iranian diplomats also deal in the gathering of intelligence and surveillance of potential targets against which Iran intends to perpetrate attacks.

The Supreme National Security Council

The council was established in order to supervise the implementation of the Islamic revolution and protect the national interests of the Islamic republic as well as the sovereignty and territorial integrity of the state. In accordance to clause 177 in the Iranian constitution, the council is responsible for the following issues.

- To establish policy regarding national security issues according to the general policy framework formulated by the spiritual leader;

- To coordinate the political, intelligence, social, cultural, and economic activities in keeping with the general security policy;
- To develop the country's strategic, economic, and security infrastructures in order to provide an adequate response to internal and external threats.

Various committees function within the Council, such as the defense committee and the national security committee. The president or a member of the council appointed by the president heads the committees. Here follows a list of the council members:

- The leaders of the legislative, judiciary, and executive branches;
- The chief commander of the armed forces' supreme council;
- The head of the planning and budgetary institution (PBO);
- The council's secretariat appointed by the supreme leader;
- An additional representative appointed by the supreme leader;
- The Foreign Minister;
- The Minister of the Interior;
- The Intelligence and Security Minister
- A representative of the Revolutionary Guards

The Supreme National Security Council discusses Iran's security issues but in essence this body mainly plays a consulting role rather than a decision-making one. The council's executive responsibilities are limited due to its composition and because it is headed by the president, which means that its recommendations are only executed by the implementers after the spiritual leader grants his approval.

The Iranian Terror System[46]

Terror activity, subversion, and the elimination of the regime's opponents abroad are subject to the approval of the top decision-makers in the Iranian regime, including the spiritual leader (*Valiat Fakia*). Ideas and initiatives in these areas are first raised for discussion and approval in principle within a small forum composed of the president and four ministers. Following their authorization, these proposals are transferred to the Supreme National Security Council, which processes the recommendations and prepares them for the approval of the spiritual leader. After gaining the approval of the spiritual leader, they are then transferred to the Supreme Council for Intelligence, which ensures implementation via the relevant ministries and the executive branches.

The trial of Iranian agents in Germany, who were tried and convicted of murdering four Kurd émigrés in the Mikonos restaurant in Berlin, constitutes a prominent example of the Iranian decision-making chain, and the German court unequivocally indicated the responsibility of the Iranian government's top leaders for the terror activity. In his verdict, the German judge pointed to the personal and direct involvement of the Iranian Intelligence Minister

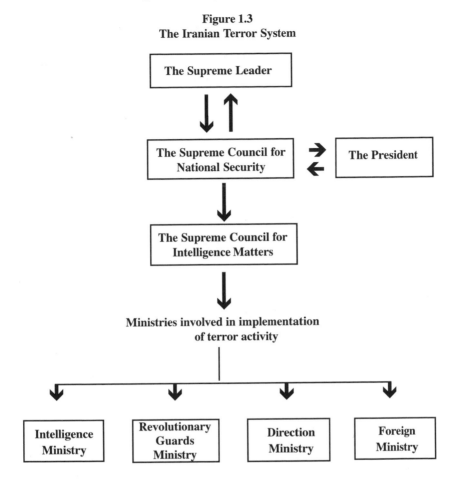

Figure 1.3
The Iranian Terror System

Falahian in the planning and implementation of the terror activity and issued an arrest warrant against him (in absentia).[47]

Since the early 1990s, the Supreme Council for Intelligence and the Ministry of Intelligence and Security have played a central role in initiating, planning, and conducting terror activity abroad. The Supreme Council for Intelligence and its head are responsible for coordination between the relevant ministries in all matters related to the planning and perpetration of an operational activity.[48]

As stated earlier, the various agencies that deal in the export of the revolution and international terror recruit and activate terrorists all over the world, who undergo underground training in Iran or Lebanon.[49] For example, terror activity against foreign targets was perpetrated by the Hizballah's Special Security Agency in Lebanon[50] and by various cells of Hizballah members abroad, based on Iranian diplomatic infrastructure.

Imad Muraniya heads the Special Security Agency and receives his instructions directly from Iran.[5151] The Special Security Agency was responsible for the hijacking of airplanes, the kidnapping of Western hostages in Lebanon, and terror attacks worldwide (see elaboration in following chapters).

Notes

1. Bernard Lewis, "Islam and Liberal Democracy," *The Atlantic Monthly* (February 1994), pp. 10-14.
2. Emanuel Sivan, *Islamic Extremists*, Sifriat Ofakim, Am Oved, Tel Aviv, 1986, pp. 192-195.
3. Lawrence Kaplan (ed.), *Fundamentalism in Comparative Perspective*, University of Massachusetts Press, 1992, pp. 6-7. David Menshari, *Iran in a Revolution*, Hakibbutz Hameuad, Tel Aviv, 1988, pp. 203-205.
4. Martin Kramer (ed.), *Protest and Revolution in the Shiite Islam*, Hakibbutz Hameuhad, Tel Aviv, 1985, pp. 11-15.
5. A.B. Lughud, *Arab Rediscovery of Europe*, Princeton U.P. 1963, pp. 69-158. A. Hoorani, *Arab Thought in the Liberal Ages 1939-1978* ,Oxford U.P. 1962, pp. 34-102.
6. Ibid.
7. Anat Kurtz, Maskit Burgin, and David Tal, *Islamic Terror and Israel*, Papyrus Publishing, Tel Aviv University, 1993, pp. 24-25.
8. A. Hoorani, *Arabic Thought in the Liberal Ages 1939-1978*, Oxford University Press, 1962, pp. 32-34.
9. J. Waardenburg, "World Religions as Seen in the Light of Islam," in A. Walch and P. Cachia (eds.), *Islam Past Influence and Present Challenge*, Edinburgh University Press, 1979, pp. 255-265.
10. Joseph Olmert, "The Shi'is and the Lebanese State," in Martin Kramer (ed.), *Shi'ism, Resistance and Revolution,* Westview Press, Boulder CO, 1987, pp. 189-198.
11. Eitan Colberg, "The Renewed Shia," in Martin Kramer (ed.), *Resistance and Revolution in Shiite Islam*, Hakibbutz Hameuhad, Tel Aviv, 1985, pp 11-15.
12. Emanuel Sivan, *Islamic Extremists*, pp. 196-197.
13. Marvin Zonis and Daniel Brumberg, "Shi'ism as Interpreted by Khomeini: An Ideology of Revolutionary Violence," in Martin Kramer (ed.), *Shi'ism, Resistance and Revolution*, pp. 47-54.
14. Emanuel Sivan, *Islamic Extremists*, p. 122.
15. David Menashri, *Iran in a Revolution*, pp. 51-57.
16. Chava Lazarus-Jaffe, "The Shia in Khomeini's Political Philosophy," *The New East* 30 (1991), pp. 99-106.
17. Alan Taylor, *The Islamic Question in the Middle East Politics*, Westview Press, Boulder, CO, 1988.
18. David Menashri, *Iran in a Revolution*, p 217. An interview with the Ayatollah Ali Montzari, *Jamhuri Islami*, December 8, 1984.
19. Shaul Bakash, *The Reign of the Ayatollahs in Iran and the Islamic Revolution*, Unwin Paperbacks, London, 1986, p. 21.
20. David Menashri, *Iran in a Revolution*, p. 217.
21. Magnus Ranstorp, *Hizballah in Lebanon—The Politics of the Western Hostage Crisis*, St. Martin's Press, New York, 1997, pp. 25-30.
22. Amir Taheri, *The Holy Terror—The Inside Story of Islamic Terrorism*, Sphere Books, London, 1987, p. 287. Examples of these types of publications: *Alliue Altsadar*, bulletin of the "Islamic Revolution of Iraq"; *Alhakima*—a Shiite quarterly edited by Muhammad Hussein Fadallah, published in Beirut.

23. David Menashri, *Iran in a Revolution*, p. 217.
24. *Kihan*, December 14, 1982.
25. *Atla'at*, November 2, 1981.
26. *Jamhuri Islami*, January 26, 1984.
27. *Atala'at*, August 23, 1981.
28. Ayatollah Khomeini, *Al-Khakoma al-Islamiya*, pp. 18-22, pp. 133-139.
29. David Menshari, *Iran in a Revolution*, p. 57.
30. Ibid., pp. 51-57.
31. Ibid. Graham E. Fuller, *The Center of the Universe*, Westview Press, Boulder, CO, 1991, pp. 12-14.
32. *Hizballah*, Special Collection of Information, the Center for Intelligence Heritage, the Information Center for Intelligence and Terror, March 2003, p. 45.
33. Graham E. Fuller, *The Center of the Universe*, pp. 271-273.
34. Ibid., pp. 119-122.
35. Edgar O'Balance, *Islamic Fundamentalist Terrorism*, 1979-1995, New York University Press, 1997, pp. 137-139.
36. Ibid., pp. 40-48.
37. Ibid.
38. Ibid.
39. Iran—*A Country Study*, U.S. Library of Congress Federal Research Division, 1996.
40. Ibid.
41. *Ma'ariv*, Tel Aviv, June 28, 1996; Iran—*A Country Study*, U.S. Library of Congress Federal Research Division; Amir Taheri, *The Spirit of Allah*, Hutchinson Press, London, 1985.
42. *Ma'ariv*, Tel Aviv, June 28, 1996; Amir Taheri, *The Spirit of Allah*.
43. *Ma'ariv*, Tel Aviv, June 28, 1996.
44. *U.S. News and World Report*, March 6, 1989.
45. *Independent*, July 1, 1987.
46. *Ma'ariv*, Tel Aviv, June 28, 1996.
47. *Der Spiegel*, April 9, 1997.
48. *Ma'ariv*, Tel Aviv, June 28, 1996.
49. Marvin Zonis, Daniel Brumberg, "Khomeini, The Islamic Republic of Iran and the Arab World," *Harvard Middle East Papers* 5 (1987), p. 34.
50. A. Fishman, *Hadashot*, February 18, 1992.
51. *Ma'ariv*, Tel Aviv, February 2, 1987.

2

Categories of Iranian State Terror

Iranian Terror against Foreign Targets on Iranian Soil

The use of terror in Iran against foreign targets situated on its soil constitutes an integral and even central component of the Iranian view of terror as an essential tool for promoting its political goals. Naturally, it is clear that foreign targets located in Iran are the easiest to attack, but on the other hand, in the event of this sort of attack the direct responsibility falls on Iran as the host country, thus exposing it to retaliation. The targets included in this category are primarily diplomatic ones (embassies and consulates), as well as economic or cultural institutions owned by foreign states or that represent foreign states or citizens.

When a state activates terror against targets belonging to a foreign country located on its soil, it has at its disposal the optimal means and resources required for this purpose. Terror activities can be perpetrated via non-official entities (for example the students who took over the American Embassy) that supposedly "take justice into their own hands"—then the country can claim the status of a neutral entity striving to resolve the problematic issue between the victim and terrorists. Alternatively, the state can operate official security entities, which through the use of a legal pretense may arrest or take action against foreign citizens under the pretext that the latter are foreign agents or that they have violated local laws. Another method is to initiate covert terror activity against foreign targets and citizens, based on the assumption that the perpetrators will never be exposed because the victim is unable to launch any genuine investigation in Iran with the aim of capturing them.

Yet another method applied in Iran is the perpetration of an act of terror that commences outside of the state's boundaries but ends inside of it, for example, the hijacking of an aircraft and its landing in Iran, followed by a continuation of the bargaining vis-à-vis the victim with Iranian "arbitration." This method precludes almost any possibility of attempting to use military force to liberate the hijacked plane, and enables Iran to pose as "mediator." In the majority of cases, these types of events end in the capitulation of the hijacking victim.

The most prominent example of terror against a foreign target on Iranian soil is the invasion of the U.S. Embassy in Teheran.[1] The revolutionary regime in Iran demonstrated a basic ideological hostility towards the United States—"the Great Satan." The desire to strike out at the latter took on even greater momentum due to the fear that the United States would act to oust the regime. The Shah's hospitalization in the United States for treatment only reinforced the Iranian regime's conviction that the United States constituted an immediate existential threat.

In a speech delivered on November 1, 1979, Khomeini appealed to the public to increase its attacks against the United States and stated that November 4—the memorial day for students killed a year earlier—was the most appropriate day to take action. On that date, "the students that follow the line of the Imam" obeyed Khomeini's instructions and seized the U.S. diplomats (who were defined as spies) in their embassy.[2] The affair of the Teheran hostages went on for 444 days, revealing the weakness of the Americans and the "triumph" of the Islamic revolution. This incident served as a central milestone for the Iranian regime and encouraged it to make use of terror in the future as well. Here follow several central points in this connection:

- The takeover was supposedly perpetrated by students (in reality, members of the Revolutionary Guards), but there is no doubt that the act was planned and executed under official guidance.
- The definition of the attackers of the embassy as students motivated by ideological reasons, purportedly exempted the Iranian regime of any responsibility for the events, and enabled Iran (at least at the initial stages of the affair) to claim the neutral stance of a "mediator" which "could understand the students' feelings" but aspired to find a solution to the problem.
- In the course of the affair, mainly due to the U.S. response, which demanded that the Iranian government put an end to the invasion and subsequently enacted retaliatory measures against the latter, the (allegedly neutral) Iranian stance underwent gradual erosion until it became clear that the perpetrators and the Iranian regime were one and the same.
- The affair itself constituted a substantial infringement of the most basic international "game rules," due to its invalidation of the immunity granted by international law to foreign representations and foreign diplomats.

During the negotiation process and towards the end of the affair, the following official Iranian conditions for it to come to an end were stipulated:[3]

- The Shah's extradition;
- The return of Iranian funds frozen in the United States;
- The cancellation of American monetary demands vis-à-vis Iran;
- A U.S. promise not to interfere in internal Iranian matters in the future.

The U.S. capitulation to several of the Iranian conditions (return of some of the funds and a promise not to interfere in its internal affairs) was perceived by the Iranian regime as a victory and as proof of the ability of a small but determined country to bring the United States "to its knees." It would appear that this precedent encouraged the Iranians to turn the use of terror into a central tool for the achievement of their political goals.[4]

The activation of the threat to take over embassies became a tool that the Iranians used several times during crises with Western countries (although in practical terms no incidents similar to the events at the U.S. Embassy ever recurred). A noticeably similar incident, which did not deteriorate to "invasion of the embassy," took place in 1987, when the French Embassy was placed under siege in Teheran (against the background of the "Gorgi" incident in Paris). The siege was withdrawn only after France caved in to Iranian dictates.

Attacks against foreign embassies in Iran also serve as an additional means to deliver messages regarding alleged dissatisfaction of radical elements in Iran with the policy of one foreign government or another. Examples can be seen in the following attacks:

- On November 8, 1993, two hand grenades were lobbed into the yard of the French Embassy in Teheran. On the same day a French citizen was injured from the explosion of a hand grenade flung at the offices of Air France in Teheran. An organization calling itself "the Hizballah Committee" claimed responsibility for the attacks and announced that they were perpetrated in retaliation for the French government's support of the Iranian opposition organization Mujahidin Khalq.
- On January 4, 1994, gunshots were fired at the British Embassy in Teheran. No one was hurt and no group claimed responsibility for the attack, but it would appear that the attack was perpetrated in order to protest the alleged anti-Iranian British policy.

In these types of attacks, the perpetrators generally avoid causing serious damage or injuries, and their main aim is to provide deterrence and pose a threat against countries whose embassies were hit.

A different modus operandi of Iranian state-terror is reflected in the terror campaign that Iran conducted against the British presence and interests in Iran.[5] The terror campaign began in 1979 with the murder of the head of the Anglican community in Shiraz, and between June and October 1980 the Iranian authorities took over the Christian hospitals and missions in Shiraz and Isfhahan. The main victim of the Iranian terror was the Anglican bishop; in September 1980, members of the Revolutionary Guards took over his home and office, and confiscated documents. In October 1980 an assassination attempt was made against the bishop during which his wife was injured. In May 1981, his son was murdered. During the years 1980-1981, several British missionaries in Iran were attacked, injured, and arrested. The Iranian terror campaign culminated at the end of 1981, when all activities of the Anglican Church were stopped and its members left the country.

In the framework of the purges initiated by the Iranian revolutionary regime against its internal enemies, hundreds of Iranians who had foreign citizenships and carried foreign passports were arrested and executed. Most of them were eliminated due to the Iranian claim that they were secret agents serving imperialism.[6] For example, Roger Cooper (a British citizen) was arrested in 1986 in Teheran on the pretext that he had been spying for Britain. This arrest is essentially similar to the taking of hostages (much like the kidnapping of Western citizens in Lebanon), but in this case it was done through official (supposedly legal) channels, and his detention was accomplished openly according to Iranian law.

In 1984, two incidents of aircraft hijackings occurred, that of an Air France plane departing from Frankfurt, and of a Kuwaiti airplane flying from Dubai. Both airplanes were diverted to Iran by the hijackers. In both cases, Iran served as the "mediator." The refusal of both France and Kuwait to cave in to the kidnappers' demands led to the detonation of the Air France plane in Teheran, and in contrast—to the release of the Kuwaiti aircraft, although two of the hostages were murdered. It is important to stress that in both cases the hijackers were not brought to trial, a fact that points to a link between the kidnappers and the Iranian authorities.[7]

Iranian Terror Worldwide

Iranian/Shiite terror activity worldwide is based on an organizational and operational infrastructure that includes five levels:[8]

- Iranian embassies and consulates (which enjoy diplomatic immunity);
- Iranian institutions, organizations, and companies (the Iranian national carrier, shipping companies, banks, etc.)
- Institutions, organizations, and companies belonging to Iranian or Muslim residents living all over the world, which are prepared to assist Iran or its emissaries;
- Cooperation with radical Islamic states and organizations (such as Sudan);
- Terror "by proxy" through sponsored organizations such as the Hizballah.

The Iranian/Shiite terror system regularly makes use of these components in order to spread a broad, worldwide infrastructure designated to serve terror activity. This infrastructure includes a large network of collaborators and intelligence sources, secret hideaways, stockpiles of weapons, and transportation and escape means enabling the perpetrators of terror to reach their destination and flee as soon as their mission is completed. Some of the collaborators, residents of various countries, are sent to Iran or Lebanon for religious, ideological, and military training and, subsequently, return to their countries of residence where they aid the Iranian terror mechanism in perpetrating missions.[9]

The involvement of official Iranian representatives and of Iranian embassies in Europe in terror activities has been exposed several times during the last decade, and this fact strained the relationship between Iran and the host country, sometimes to the point of severing relations.[10] Prominent examples of these types of incidents are reflected in the "embassy wars" between Iran and France in 1987, due to the exposure of the Iranian terrorist Wahid Gorgi who found asylum in the Iranian embassy in Paris; the "siege" on the Iranian Embassy in Vienna in 1989 against the background of suspicions that the assassins of Kasmelo, head of the Kurd underground, had sought refuge there; and the expulsion of Iranian diplomats from London following the "Rushdie affair."

The key component in the perpetration of Iranian/Shiite terror attacks is the attack team, which generally arrives in the countries of destination from Iran or Lebanon, avails itself of the infrastructure prepared for it by Iranian representatives and activists, and flees back to Iran or Lebanon after completing the mission. Most of the Iranian/Shiite attacks have been perpetrated by terror cells including several (4-5) terrorists, and sometimes by larger terror networks, but there are also examples of terror attacks conducted by a single terrorist, such as the hijacking of the Air Africa flight in July 1987.

Iranian/Shiite terror entities use a range of methods to transfer the weaponry required for the perpetration of terror attacks to the countries of destination. One of the methods is the smuggling of weaponry via designated cells or couriers,[11] and there have been several incidents in which terrorists attempting to smuggle weaponry into various European countries were caught:

- In November 1984, Shiite activist Hanni al Atat was arrested in Switzerland while carrying weaponry designated for terror activity in Italy.
- In January 1987, Hizballah member Hudar Beshir was arrested while carrying ten kilograms of explosives (camouflaged as candy), detonators, and activation devices for explosive charges.
- In January 1987, Hizballah member Abas Hamadi was arrested in the possession of explosives intended for the organization's terror network in Europe.

Another method, utilized mainly when smuggling large amounts of weaponry, is dispatch in the guise of merchandise.[12] An example of this method of smuggling was reflected in the exposure of a large consignment of explosives and weaponry on a ship that set out in November 1989 from Lebanon for the port of Valencia in Spain in the guise of a food shipment. The consignment had been sent by a Lebanese company in Shtura (in the Lebanon Valley) and contained seventeen tons of preserves and jams packed in jars. A police inspection revealed that some 220 kilograms of C-4 plastic explosives had been concealed in jars of humus and fig jam, as well as 258 electronic detonators and four hand grenades.

Subsequently, the Spanish police arrested eight men suspected of membership in the Hizballah, who were to have received the weaponry for use in terror attacks.[13] The cell was headed by Imad Ali Muhammad Sabiti, a thirty-one-year-old Shiite with Lebanese citizenship. The other detainees carried passports from other countries (four Iraqis, one Kuwaiti, one Brazilian, and one Sudanese). Sabiti had founded a company in Spain called al Yaster, which was to have served as a cover for the network's activities and was the designated recipient of the explosives concealed in the shipment.

It appears that the Hizballah had planned to establish an activity base in Valencia and exploit the relatively unproblematic border control between Spain and France in order to perpetrate a wave of attacks against Israeli, American, French, and other West-European aviation targets, as well as against the "reactionary Arabs" in the Gulf States, including attacks against Arab vacationers who visited the Costa del Sol.

On May 2, 1990, a senior leader of the Hizballah warned Spain to treat the eight Hizballah detainees "cautiously" in order to avoid incurring the movement's wrath:

> We are not Spain's enemies but the current arrests may arouse hostile feelings and various responses that will turn the feelings of friendship that radical Muslims feel for Spain into hatred.... Spain is a base because we have good relations with Spain, since it did not participate in the suppression of the Shiites or the Lebanese. There are countries that share a border with Spain (referring to France—SS) which acted against us and planned terror attacks against us.[14]

The Mortar Affair[15]

On March 14, 1996, customs authorities in Antwerp, Belgium, discovered a consignment of weapons. The equipment was discovered in a container that was unloaded from the Iranian ship *Kolahdoos*, which was to have contained food products. An inspection of the weapons uncovered a special mortar with a particularly wide diameter (some 300 mm.), along with shells that contained about 125 kgs. each of TNT, and a timing device that causes a bomb to explode in the air before hitting the ground. Additionally, the mortar's range was about 700 meters.

At the time of the discovery, the Iranian ship had already continued on its way from Antwerp to Hamburg. In Hamburg, the German security authorities arrested the ship's crew, and the following findings were revealed during their interrogation:

- At least two of the crewmembers were identified as members of the Intelligence Ministry and Iranian Security (VEVAK).

- The shipment was sent by a Teheran food supplier (Jifort Food Inc.) whose president was known to be an active member of the Republican Guards.
- In order to conceal the identity of the dispatcher, the name was changed on the bill of lading, and the container was sealed by the Iranian customs authorities.
- On February 20, 1996, Jifort made a request to add additional items to the shipment (about a quarter of a container). It was resealed according to the procedures of the customs authorities, and the ship sailed from the port at Bandar Abbas in Iran on February 23, 1996.

The assessment of the German security officials was that the weapons were introduced into the container between February 20 and February 23, 1996. The investigators believed that the mortar was intended for use in a terror attack against a protected target in Europe; its purpose was to overcome security measures surrounding the target (a wall, fence electronic means, and guards).

A similar weapon was confiscated in Iraq in May 1995, and interrogation of the members of the attack cell who had smuggled the mortar into Iraq as piping parts revealed that their aim was to attack the home of Massud Rajavi, leader of the Mujahidin Khalq (an organization that opposed the Islamic regime in Iran). The mortars intercepted in Antwerp and Iraq attest to Iran's direct involvement in the planning of terror attacks. Iran dedicates technological means for the development of unique weapons to provide an operational response for the neutralization of security measures surrounding targets designated for attack.

In the majority of cases, the Iranians aspire to export the weapons in various ways, and the cell that is charged with the mission of perpetrating the attack receives the weapons in the country of destination. However, there have been other cases in which the cells brought the equipment required for the attack along with them. The most prominent example of the latter is the hijacking of the TWA airplane in June 1985, when the hijackers brought the weapons from Lebanon to Greece and used them to perpetrate the hijacking.[16]

In most of the attacks carried out worldwide it is difficult to indicate unequivocally the perpetrating organization and Iran as the country behind the planning and the execution. Therefore, most of the information on this matter is based on cases in which the perpetrators were caught. The perpetrators usually publish their responsibility for the attack under cover names such as the "Islamic Jihad," "the Depressed on earth," "the revolutionary justice organization," "the committee for solidarity with Arab and Middle Eastern political prisoners in Europe," among others. The use of cover names prevents attributing the responsibility for the attack to any organization or country, thus making it hard for the terror victim to take forceful action against the perpetrators.

The Infrastructure of Shiite Terror in Africa

The African continent constitutes an important and influential activity arena for Iranian and Shiite terror organizations. The Iranian and Shiite terror infrastructure in Africa developed at two focal points:

- East Africa—on the basis of the links between Iran and the radical Islamic regime in Sudan (since 1989);
- West Africa—on the basis of emigrant Shiite populations that settled in West African countries following the civil war in Lebanon (1975).

The Iranian and Shiite terror activity developed mainly in East Africa, an area that constituted the focus of the confrontation between the United States and radical Islam (the main center was in Somalia in 1993). West Africa constituted a focal point for Shiite activity mainly at the end of the 1980s, but beginning in the 1990s Shiite activity has been concentrated in East Africa. However, West Africa continues to serve as a base for the consolidation of terror infrastructures on the African continent.

West Africa

The infrastructure of Iranian and Shiite terror that developed in West Africa in the mid-1980s is based on a large Shiite population originating from Lebanon, which is estimated at several hundred thousand Shiites spread out over the Ivory Coast, Senegal, and Guinea. The Lebanese presence in Africa experienced accelerated growth after 1975 as a result of the civil war in Lebanon, and the majority of the emigrants have Shiite origins.[17] It is important to note that Islam in "black Africa" is mostly Sunni, and the African lifestyle is incompatible with the rigid rules dictated by Shiite Islam of the Iranian school.

The Shiite population is generally organized around community activity and maintains close ties with their families in Lebanon. The majority of the Shiite population in Africa is not fundamentalist, but the Lebanese dispersion in Africa contributes to the financing of the Shiite groups and organizations in Lebanon, and there are fundamentalist circles that aspire to cast their authority on the Shiite community in Africa. These circles are radically oriented and constitute a convenient infrastructure for the Iranian and Shiite terror activity in Africa.[18]

African countries serve as a fundraising source for the Iranian-sponsored Hizballah organization.[19] Here we must point out again that Africa constitutes a base, infrastructure, transit station, and even an actual arena for the perpetration of terror activity against Western targets. Several examples of this activity as it was exposed during the 1980s are as follow:[20]

- On July 24, 1987, an Air Africa flight en route from Italy to France (the airplane had originally departed from Africa) was hijacked. Shiite terror activists from the African community were involved in the hijacking.

- On August 18, 1988, a stash of weapons was found in the apartment of a Lebanese Shiite in Abidjan. During his interrogation, the man revealed that some of the weapons had been concealed in holy books and smuggled from Lebanon to the Ivory Coast, and that they were to be used for perpetrating terror attacks in the Ivory Coast and France.
- In August 1989, a Lebanese Shiite named Mustafa Maza, who had arrived from Africa, was killed in a "mysterious explosion" in a London hotel room. It would appear that a bomb went off as he was trying to assemble it.
- On September 1989, a UTA passenger plane exploded in African airspace. The Islamic Jihad claimed responsibility for the incident. One of the widespread suppositions regarding the perpetrators (who have yet to be apprehended) is that they were acting in the name of a Iranian/Shiite terror organization, and that the attack was executed as a threat or to avenge renewed French involvement in the Lebanese arena. (This conjecture has never bee proven, and there are also well-based suspicions that Libyan entities may have been responsible for the attack.)

East Africa

Sudanese-Iranian ties. The radical Islamic regime in Sudan headed by Omar al Beshir and Hassan al Turabi operated a policy of exporting the Islamic revolution, while turning Sudan into a center for fundamentalist Islamic organizations. Against this background, Sudan acted to strengthen its ties and formulate a strategic alliance with Iran. The foundation of the ties between Iran and Sudan was based upon the following principles:

- Sudanese willingness (despite the fact that it was a Sunni state) to regard the Iranian revolution as a model for inspiration and adopt "the Iranian revolutionary message";[21]
- The Sudanese regime's vital need for economic and military aid due to the ongoing war in the south and the regime's political isolation (particularly due to its support for Iraq during the Gulf War);
- Sudan's geopolitical location (it borders on eight countries, some of which are Muslim), which in the view of the Iranians turns the country into an important base for disseminating the Iranian revolution;
- Sudan's huge area, which enables the concealment of training bases and infrastructures for Islamic terror organizations;
- Sudan may serve as a substitute for the activity bases of the Revolutionary Guards and the Hizballah in Lebanon, in the event that they are forced to cease their activity due to Israeli or Syrian pressure;[22]
- Sudan's economic and military problems enable Iran to acquire an important base of influence at a relatively low economic price.

The consolidation of the special relations between Sudan and Iran began in 1990, after al Beshir's regime stabilized and the National Islamic Front, led by

Hassan al Turabi, reinforced its status as a dominant entity in the new regime. In October 1990, the level of diplomatic relations between Sudan and Iran was raised to that of ambassadors. Ali Akbar Mohtashami, who had played a key role in the invasion of the U.S. Embassy in Teheran by the Revolutionary Guards in 1979, was appointed the Iranian ambassador to Sudan. He was also one of the founders of the Hizballah in Lebanon during his term as ambassador there in 1982. At the same time, intensive efforts were initiated to tighten the economic, political, and military ties between the two countries. In this framework, the Iranian Cultural Minister visited Khartoum (in May 1991) and laid the foundations for an Iranian cultural center in Sudan. Since 1991, Iran has been operating widespread propaganda-religious activities in Sudan, through a network of religious and cultural centers founded with Iranian funding or operating under Iranian patronage. Iran grants students from Sudan and throughout Africa scholarships for studies at Islamic centers in Sudan, Qum, and Teheran, and encourages the exchange of religious delegations between the two countries.[23]

On April 25-28, 1991, al Turabi convened the Islamic Arab People's Conference—a roof organization for all of the fundamentalist Islamic movements, which he himself headed. Representatives of radical Islam from fifty-five countries attended the conference, and this was the first attempt to organize a radical Islamic Sunni front in response to the challenge posed by the West when it defeated Saddam Hussein in the Gulf war. The organization's main resolutions were not formulated in the expanded forum, but rather in a smaller framework in al Turabi's home in Manshia. During the conference, it was decided to establish the Popular Islamic Conference (PIC) whose proclaimed aim according to al Turabi was to plan the struggle against the West. In addition, a permanent committee was established in Khartoum with the participation of representatives from those fifty-five countries in which the battle of radical Islam was being fought.

Shiite Iran was impressed with al Turabi's determination and with the success of the conference in Khartoum, and promised him assistance in promoting his concepts despite the Sunni leanings of the organization and its leader. Iran helped to establish a control headquarters for the PIC, and several days after the end of the conference in Khartoum, the head of Sudanese Intelligence, Colonel el Fatah Urva left for Teheran for consultations and to promote cooperation. Upon his return he brought Teheran's contribution with him—advanced and encrypted communications equipment for use between the PIC headquarters and its entities active in various countries.

Within a short period of time, Iranian experts and advisers arrived and, together with Afghan alumni, began establishing an effective terror infrastructure in Sudan. The two main campsthat were established and trained Islamic terrorists at the beginning of the 1990s were the al Shambat and al Mazra'ah bases. Training at these camps included the use of light weapons and explosives, the preparation of improvised explosives, the use of night vision and setting ambushes.

On October 18, 1991, Iran convened the International Conference of the Islamic revolution in Teheran in support of the struggle of the Palestinian people, with over 400 delegates from sixty countries. Among those invited to the conference was Hassan al Turabi, who enjoyed the special esteem lavished on him by his Iranian hosts. Upon his return to Sudan, al Turabi acted determinedly to improve the operational capabilities of the Islamic movements affiliated with the PIC. Al Turabi believed that these organizations lacked the tools and experience to act outside of their native countries, and thus welcomed the Iranian support in promoting the intentional operational capabilities of the Islamic terrorists.

In September 1991, a senior Iranian military delegation visited Sudan and apparently prepared the groundwork for the anticipated visit of the Iranian President Hashemi Rafsanjani in Sudan. Rafsanjani arrived in Khartoum on December 13, 1991, for a six-day visit, at the head of a delegation counting 157 members, including the Foreign Minister, the Defense Minister, the head of Intelligence, the Commander of the Revolutionary Guards and the Minister of Commerce. Rafsanjani's visit to Sudan represented the culmination of the rapprochement process between the two countries, as this was the first visit by an Iranian president since the Khomeini Revolution, a fact that attested to the close relations between the two countries and the importance that Iran attributed to its ties with Sudan.[24] During Rafsanjani's visit it was decided to launch strategic cooperation between Iran and Sudan, and a series of economic and military agreements was signed between the two countries. In the military field, Iran promised to provide support in the form of training and weapons (at a scope of $20 million), aid that was essential to Sudan for the war against the south,[25] and in the economic area Iran agreed to supply Sudan with oil, food products, and various goods.[26]

At the same time, it became apparent that Iranian advisers were present in Sudan,[27] and possibly members of the Revolutionary Guards as well, who administered military consulting and training in addition to disseminating the Iranian Revolutionary message.[28]

The cooperation between Iran and Sudan, which was firmly established and officially recognized via the strategic alliance signed between the states, turned Sudan into a front base for the export of the Islamic revolution.

In 1992, a militia of the National Islamic Front—the Popular Defense Units—was established in Sudan. The role of the militia, which was founded with Iranian aid and based on the model of the Iranian Revolutionary Guards, was to ensure the control of the Islamic movement in Sudan, constitute a counterbalance to the Sudanese army in the event of an internal crisis, and serve as a spearhead for the Sudanese government's forces in the war against the south. From the time of its establishment, the militia was granted preference over the army in matters related to the allocation of manpower, resources, and weapons. Its officers underwent training in Iran,[29] and the size of its forces grew steadily and was estimated at 90,000 fighters and volunteers.[30] The militia served as the mainstay of the Sudanese regime, to the dissatisfaction of the commanders of the Sudanese army, who were demoted to a secondary role in the country's political system for the first time since Sudan had been granted independence.

Alongside the establishment and consolidation of al Turabi's militia, additional ties were developed and strengthened on the military level between Iran and Sudan, in the framework of which Iran helped to train Sudanese air force personnel,[31] provided spare parts and weapons, and dispatched Iranian consultants who aided the government forces in the war in south Sudan.[32]

Due to the reinforcement of al Turabi's status as a significant Islamic leader, and Iran's support of the Sudanese regime, Sudan gradually became a "magnet" for fundamentalists from the Arab states, North Africa, Black Africa, and other areas.[33] This process was consistent with al Turabi's aspiration to turn Sudan into an Islamic fundamentalist center—initially in relationship to North Africa and the Horn of Africa, and, subsequently, regarding the entire Muslim world. As stated earlier, al Turabi believed (much like Khomeini) that Islam knows no boundaries, and that it bears a universal message regarding the establishment of a just Islamic state that will serve as a model for emulation for all of human society.[34]

The Sudanese aid provided to Islamic movements was reflected in the following areas:[35]

- Convening Islamic conferences, propaganda activities, maintaining offices and Islamic fundamentalist study centers;
- Maintaining fundamentalist training camps for the entire Muslim world, under the training of Iranian or Sudanese instructors (usually from the ranks of the Popular Defense Units), or members of fundamentalist movements from various locations;
- Providing weapons and sabotage materials to fundamentalist terrorists;
- Providing assistance in the form of documentation, financing, and the transfer of fundamentalist activists from Sudan to their native countries.

The fundamentalist activity in Sudan posed a threat to a series of Arab regimes (Egypt, Algeria, Tunisia, and Saudi Arabia), and positioned Sudan at a confrontational front with these countries (particularly Egypt), a fact that increased the isolation of the Sudanese regime. In August 1993, the American administration placed Sudan on the list of states that support terror.[36] Consequently, economic steps were taken to prevent aid from reaching the regime, its political isolation grew, and sanctions were imposed by the Security Council.

Hassan al Turabi, who was aware of the fears in the Arab and Western world vis-à-vis Islamic fundamentalism and Iranian activity on Sudanese soil, attempted to play down the importance and scope of the ties between Sudan and Iran, and denied accusations that his country supported Islamic terror.[37] Nevertheless, there seemed to be a large gap between the placating messages transmitted by al Turabi in interviews with the Western media, and his statements in internal forums in Sudan and his writings in the Arabic language. For example, in his book, *The Islamic Movement in Sudan*, he addressed the need for mutual aid among Islamic movements in order to achieve their goals, and he openly mentioned the aid presented by his movement to the Palestinian Islamic Jihad, the Egyptian Islamic Jihad, the Alnahda movement in Tunisia, and the Islamic Front in Algeria.[38]

Sudan's role as a magnet for Islamic fundamentalism attracted many of the Afghan alumni, with Osama Bin Laden in the lead. The preparations for Bin Laden's move had already begun in 1991, due to the strained relations between Bin Laden and the Saudi Arabian government following his harsh criticism of the Saudi monarchy in the matter of the Gulf War. Jamal al Fadel, Bin Laden's aide, traveled to Sudan and purchased several properties designated to serve Bin Laden and his organization if they were to relocate to Sudan.[39] In April 1991, Bin Laden left Saudi Arabia and moved to Pakistan. From there he moved on to Afghanistan and finally arrived in Sudan at al Turabi's invitation.

Bin Laden and al Turabi developed a symbiotic relationship—Bin Laden enjoyed complete freedom in Sudan and in exchange invested millions of dollars in that country. He purchased communication equipment and weapons for the National Islamic Front (NIF) headed by al Turabi, and in exchange Sudan provided Al Qaida with 200 Sudanese passports, which enabled organization members to move from one place to another with new and fictitious identities.[40]

The years 1991 to 1993, during which Bin Laden lived in Sudan, were also decisive years in all matters related to the character and nature of the Islamic state in Sudan. At that time, the Arab world was beginning to recover from the Gulf War, which was perceived as a traumatic event where secular regimes in Muslim countries had joined forces with the infidels from the West in order to crush another Muslim state (Iraq). The period was termed by radical Islamic circles as *al Atzma* (the crisis), a term that comes second in severity only to *al Nakba* (the disaster), which relates to the establishment of the State of Israel. It was again proven to radical Islamic circles that secular regimes in the Muslim world, such as the regimes in Kuwait or Saudi Arabia, survive only thanks to their dependence upon the power of the United States. This led to the conclusion that the way to establish "real" Islamic regimes in the Muslim world was by launching a relentless struggle against the United States, patron of the corrupt secular regimes.

The feeling of emergency and the perception that the struggle of each of the Islamic movements against the secular regime in its particular country is in fact waged against two strong enemies simultaneously—the secular regime from within and the West from without—led to the need for consolidation of all of the Islamic forces in a struggle against the more powerful forces. In the beginning of the 1990s, this newly developed perception led to the consolidation of the Global Jihad Front, which served as a sort of umbrella association for Islamic terror organizations worldwide. The leading entities in most of these movements were Afghan alumni, who had accumulated extensive operational experience during the Jihad in Afghanistan.

From the early 1990s, the Islamic movements began to dispatch fighters of the armed Islamic branch to confrontation points between Islam and its foes worldwide. Osama Bin Laden, who at the time was living in Sudan, played a crucial role in establishing the training of the Islamic entities, dispatching them worldwide and founding terror infrastructures to perpetrate attacks against Islam's enemies.

The Iranian and Sudanese Involvement in Somalia

As noted earlier, the escalation and deterioration of the Somali situation took place concurrently, and perhaps as part of an Iranian-Sudanese attempt to export the Islamic revolution to East Africa. In 1990-1991, an infrastructure of training camps was established in Sudan that was run by the National Islamic Front (NIF). Islamic volunteers arrived from Ethiopia, Eritrea, Kenya, Uganda, and Somalia. One of al Turabi's henchmen, Dr. Ali Alhaj, was responsible for managing the training camps and training foreign terrorists.

In autumn 1992, al Turabi issued instructions to escalate the campaign to undermine the stability of the regimes in East Africa, and terrorists who had completed their training were sent back to their native countries in order to promote and to lead the subversive Islamic activity. Al Turabi initiated this step at approximately the same time that the United States decided to send a humanitarian task force to Somalia.

The civil war and anarchy that prevailed in Somalia constituted an expedient opportunity for Iran and its ally Sudan to obtain influence and a foothold in a neighboring Muslim state, situated at an important strategic location on the shores of the Red Sea. The American involvement in Somalia was perceived by Iran and Sudan as a threat to the interests and steps that they aspired to facilitate in that country and as renewed American imperialism under the guise of humanitarian aid. Thus, Iran and Sudan regarded the U.S. forces as a prime target to be dislodged from Somalia through the operation of a terror and guerrilla network, based on local Somali powerbrokers that were hostile to the Americans and the UN. Sudan aided Islamic terrorists trained in its camps to infiltrate Somalia in various ways (via the sea, Ethiopia, and Kenya), and provided them with weapons.

Bin Laden and Al Qaida were partners in the formation of the Iranian-Sudanese strategy for the dissemination of the Islamic revolution in the Horn of Africa. Although most of the tasks assigned to Bin Laden were logistic and organizational, they enabled him to acquire considerable experience in the organization of the infrastructure that supported the complex campaign against the United States in East Africa, and to fit in as a major player in the decision-making process and its realization in the framework of the Iranian-Sudanese coalition.

The organization of an effective front of Islamic terror organizations in the Somali arena necessitated the foundation of a logistic and financial infrastructure that would enable the flow of fighters, weapons, and money. As stated above, the task of establishing and managing this infrastructure was assigned to Bin Laden, who made use of his economic and organizational experience as well as his worldwide connections, and within a short period of time was able to place an effective financial and logistic infrastructure at the disposal of Iran and Sudan. Bin Laden set up several international companies in neighboring Ethiopia, which dealt in agricultural development. These "companies" established agricultural farms in the Ogaden Desert along the Somali border that served as camouflage for Somali terrorist training facilities, provided storage for weapons, and the flow of money to fund the activities.

In the framework of the preparations for the escalation of the struggle against the U.S. forces in Somalia towards mid-1993, Bin Laden orchestrated a complex campaign involving the transfer of Afghan alumni from Pakistan, Afghanistan, and Yemen to Somalia. Some of the fighters were transferred via a fleet of fishing boats, which dropped them off on desolate beaches along the Somali coast—from there they were transferred to the combat zone in Mogadishu by the local infrastructure; others were flown in on light aircraft which landed under the cover of darkness on improvised landing strips in Somalia; still others infiltrated Somalia through its joint borders with Ethiopia and Kenya.[41]

General Aidid—one of the two main powerbrokers struggling for control in Somalia—was Sudan's key ally in Somalia, but the extent of the Sudanese or Iranian influence on his steps was relatively limited. Sudan granted Aidid funding and military aid in order to expand and deepen its influence in Somalia, and al Turabi even sent volunteers trained in Sudan to fight alongside Aidid against the forces of Ali Mahdi Muhammad—Aidid's rival in the struggle to gain control of Somalia.

As stated earlier, through Bin Laden al Turabi established a covert financial and logistic infrastructure enabling the flow of financial aid to al Turabi's allies. In 1992, al Turabi established the Somali Islamic Union Party—the SIUP—in Somalia. This umbrella organization united several radical Islamic bodies with a common denominator of tribal loyalties. The SIUP became the main platform for infiltrating Sudanese influence into the Somali arena under the guidance of al Turabi.

The formal leader of the SIUP was Muhammad Othman who resided in London and dealt mainly in propaganda and information activity; the subversive activity and fighting were orchestrated by local commanders in Somalia that were directly activated by Sudan and Somalia. The SIUP initiated its military activity in June 1992 in an offensive in the area of Bossaso, north Somalia, but failed. Due to the military failure, a delegation of experts arrived in Marka, Somalia, in August 1992. The delegation was headed by Rahim Safawi, deputy-commander of the Iranian Revolutionary Guards, and Ali Othman Taha from Sudan, who inspected the military, assessed other needs of the SIUP, and outlined plans to improve its operational capabilities. From autumn 1992, weapons were transferred and training camps were established for the organization in Somaliland and in Ogaden inside Ethiopian territory. (Bin Laden played a major role in the establishment of the camps in the territory of Ethiopia.)

After the landing of the marines in Somalia, a joint decision was reached by Sudan and Iran to fight the American presence there, based on Sudan's allies in the Somali arena and on the terror infrastructure established in the country prior to the arrival of U.S. troops.

At the beginning of summer 1993, Iran and Sudan's preparations were completed in anticipation of the campaign in Somalia, and the Islamic terror cells started acting against the UN forces from the neighborhoods of the capital Mogadishu, which were under Aidid's control. These actions included ambushes and the planting of explosive devices.[42] These actions culminated on June 5, 1993, in an ambush that the terrorists laid for the Pakistani UN force in which twenty-six Pakistani soldiers were killed. In the aftermath of the brutal attack against the Pakistani force, the UN outlawed the SNA (the Somali National Alliance headed by General Aidid). Aidid was officially expelled from the discussions regarding Somalia's economic and political rehabilitation, and the commander of the UN forces in Somalia declared a twenty-five thousand dollar prize for anyone who could bring about Aidid's capture.

The attack, which was attributed to Aidid, reinforced his status with the Somali public, and tribes and many powerbrokers joined the SNA coalition, which he led. Aidid's radio station countered the UN action by offering a $1 million prize to anyone who terminated or captured Admiral Howey, the commander of the UN forces in Somalia. Following the heavy losses sustained by the UN forces, the latter began to respond with heavy fire against the terrorists, and Somali residents were often injured in the crossfire.

On June 11, 1993, Aidid set out for Khartoum with some of his senior aides in order to coordinate the coming moves with Sudan. The Sudanese propaganda machine accused the United States and the UN of causing the deterioration in Somalia, and claimed that the United States was plotting to take over all of the Horn of Africa, and that Somalia was merely the first target in an overall American plan. The Sudanese Foreign Minister even issued a warning to the United States according to which if the latter attacked Sudan it would encounter serious resistance and a declaration of Jihad.

Following Aidid's visit to Khartoum, and based on Sudanese instructions, Bin Laden sent weapons and additional fighters to reinforce the combat capabilities of the Islamic entities. In June 1993, the Islamic forces in Somalia included the following:[43]

- Aidid's forces under the umbrella of the SNA (whose commanders were located in Mogadishu and Galacio);
- The SIUP forces (whose commanders were located in Marka);
- The forces of the Somali Revolutionary Guards (SRG), along with Iranian advisers (whose main base was in Bossaso).

The forces were armed and prepared for a prolonged guerrilla and terror campaign against the U.S. and UN forces, according to the policy and guidelines set by Iran and Sudan.

In the course of the campaign that developed in Somalia, the United States suffered heavy casualties, and as a result decided to pull its forces out of that country as of March 1, 1994. The withdrawal of the U.S. forces from Somalia was perceived by Sudan, Iran, Bin Laden and the radical Islamic organizations as an important victory over the United States and as testimony to its weakness due to its sensitivity to casualties. This perception is reflected in Osama Bin Laden's remarks in an interview that he granted in 1999 to the Al-Jazeera television network, in which he stated:

> Based on the reports that we received from our brothers, who participated in the Jihad in Somalia, we learned that they saw weakness, frailty and cowardice of U.S. troops. Only eighteen U.S. troops were killed. Nonetheless, they fled in the heart of darkness, frustrated after they had caused great commotion about a New World Order.[44]

In 1995, Al Qaida initiated cooperation with the Hizballah. Despite the religious and ideological dispute between the Shiite Hizballah and the radical Sunni Al Qaida, the two cooperated against the common enemy—the United States. Al Qaida members traveled to Lebanon, where the organization purchased a guesthouse, and organization members were trained by the Hizballah in how to detonate large structures. The explosions perpetrated by the Hizballah at the Marine headquarters and the U.S. Embassy in Beirut in 1983 constituted a model that Bin Laden aspired to emulate. Bin Laden believed that using this method he could force the Americans to withdraw from Saudi Arabia, just as the Hizballah had done in Beirut in 1983.[45] According to the testimony of Muhammad Ali (an Al Qaida member who turned state witness in the United States against members of the organization), Bin Laden even met with Imad Muraniya, head of the Hizballah's security agency.

In 1996, due to American, Egyptian, and Saudi pressure, Bin Laden was forced to leave Sudan and returned to Afghanistan. According to official sources in Sudan, Bin Laden's extradition to the United States or Saudi Arabia was under consideration, but the fear of rioting on the part of the strong Islamic circles in Sudan convinced the Sudanese regime to be satisfied with his expulsion from the country. As to Bin Laden's exile, the Sudanese claimed that the United States had raised the matter for discussion with Sudan and had demanded that he not be allowed to go to Somalia, but the CIA had no objection to his move to Afghanistan. According to economic sources in Sudan, as a result of Bin Laden's expulsion and the closing of his businesses in that country, the latter lost about $30 million.

The attacks of September 11, 2001, the war against terror declared by the United States, and the American offensive in Afghanistan all motivated Sudan to revise its policy, for fear of becoming the target of a future U.S. military campaign, and to support the counter-terror coalition. Sudan is currently careful about involvement in terror and its support of radical Islamic organizations has decreased (at least for the time being). This is also true of its ties with Iran in connection to the support of terror.

South America—Islamic Terror Activity at the Tri-Border Area

South America, like the African continent, constitutes a focus for the development and fortification of terror infrastructures for Iran and the Hizballah on the basis of a Muslim community residing in that area. The continent serves both for fund-raising and as an arena for perpetrating attacks (see subsequent elaboration in the discussion of the attacks in Argentina). The tri-border area between Argentina, Brazil, and Paraguay constitutes a central focus for Shiite terror. This area traditionally serves as a focal point for crime, particularly smuggling, and a haven for terror organizations. This fact stems mainly from the limited supervisory capabilities of the countries in the area and the difficulty in coordinating activities between them.

A large Muslim community exists in the tri-border area, which mainly consists of Palestinian and Shiite expatriates from Lebanon. This community serves as a refuge and activity base for Islamic terror organizations.[46] Indeed, according to intelligence sources, various Islamic terror organizations are active in this area including the Hizballah, Hamas, the Egyptian Jama'a al-Islamiya and the Islamic Jihad, which have strong links with Al Qaida.[47]

The activities of the Islamic terror organizations in the area focus mainly on logistic and economic aspects, but in the attacks against Israeli and Jewish targets in Buenos Aires, Argentina—in 1992 against the Israeli Embassy and in 1994 against the Jewish Community Building (Amia)—the perpetrators' tracks led to the tri-border area.

According to intelligence sources, Ciudad Del Este, the district capital of Paraguay, serves as a central focus for terror activity, and according to Argentina that is where the attacks against the Jewish and Israeli targets in Argentina were prepared.[48] On September 12, 2001, following the terror attacks in the United States, the Argentina News Agency reported that security measures had been tightened around all airports and roads leading to the tri-border area.[49] At that time, urgent meetings were held between FBI agents and intelligence entities from all three states in order to coordinate security measures to prevent activities by terrorists and collaborators of Islamic terror organizations from this region.[50] The working premise was that dormant terror cells were located in the tri-border area that might go into action. In consequence, the Paraguayan authorities arrested twenty-three individuals suspected of belonging to and affiliated with Islamic terror organizations, mainly the local Hizballah and Hamas, but in actual fact some were released and others were charged with membership in a criminal organization, tax violations, and the use of counterfeit papers.[51]

Authorities were unsuccessful in their attempts to arrest Assad Ahmed Barkat, against whom an international (Interpol) arrest warrant had been issued; the latter was suspected of heading the Hizballah organization in the region. According to the Argentinean prosecution, Barkat played a central role in the attacks in Argentina between the years 1992 and 1994. Barkat is one of the owners of Galeria Page—one of the largest shopping centers in Ciudad Del Esta, and according to investigators, the commercial activity serves as camouflage for his covert activity involving fundraising and the transfer of funds for Hizballah. A raid on his apartment revealed large amounts of subversive material belonging to the Hizballah and information attesting to the fact that he dealt in "money laundering" for the organization. Among other things, a letter written by Hassan Nasrallah thanking Barkat for his fund-raising activities was found on the premises. According to the investigators, Barkat also had links with Al Qaida. In this connection, the Paraguayan authorities are investigating forty-six bank accounts that served for the transfer of some $50 million to charity funds in Iran and Lebanon.[52]

Legal proceedings are now underway in Uruguay for the extradition of Jama'a al-Islamiya activist Sayyid Hassan Mukhlis, at Egypt's request. The activist was arrested in Uruguay on the suspicion that he was using counterfeit documents. As noted earlier, the Jama'a al-Islamiya has close ties with Al Qaida.[53]

However, it would appear that despite the activities of the security entities in the tri-border area, that area will continue to serve as an important focal point for the activities of Islamic terror organizations, and due to the dislodging of Al Qaida activists in other areas in the world, it is reasonable to assume that this region may serve as a haven and activity center for the organization's members. This assumption has been reinforced by several recent arrests of individuals connected to Al Qaida in the tri-border area.

Iranian Terror by Proxy

In 1981, the Khomeini regime established the "Islamic Revolutionary Council," whose goal was to disseminate the Islamic revolution to Muslim countries through a combination of information and propaganda means, on the one hand, and terror activity on the other.[54] Primarily, target states with a Shiite population that might hoist the banner of the Iranian revolution were chosen (Lebanon, Iraq, Kuwait). The agents of the Islamic Revolutionary Council were activists in the al Dawa Party (the Call), the Islamic Amal Movement (the Hope), and, subsequently, in the Hizballah (God's Party), mainly in Lebanon.[55]

The Iranian activity did not limit itself to these countries, but expanded to other Muslim countries in Asia and Africa such as Tunisia, Morocco, Afghanistan, Turkey, India, and Malaysia. Fired by Iranian inspiration, pro-Khomeini parties were established in these countries, which acted to disseminate Khomeinism.

In the framework of Iran's efforts "to export the revolution" thousands of activists from the Islamic target countries underwent military and ideological training in the holy city of Qum (Khomeini's city of residence) and returned to their countries as "emissaries of the true Islam." Special emphasis was placed on training Lebanese and Iraqi Shiites for the perpetration of terror attacks against Saddam Hussein's regime in Iraq and against Israel and Western targets in Lebanon.[56] Iran's most prominent success in establishing pro-Iranian strongholds outside of its boundaries was in the Lebanese arena, where the existing conditions made it possible for the Iranian influence to penetrate.

The Shiite System in Lebanon

The origins of the Shiites in Lebanon are apparently in the Amla tribe, which joined the Shiite community during the Ummite period. They were mainly concentrated in southern Lebanon; the area between the Awali River and the Israeli border was named Jabal Amal after them. Other concentrations of Shiites were to be found in the northern Bakaa, in the Ba'al Beq and Harmel areas.[57] The Shiite society constituted an often-persecuted minority, which sought areas of habitation as far removed as possible from the arm of the Muslim rule (Sunni or Ottoman); this is what led to Shiite isolationism in marginal areas in the Bakaa and southern Lebanon.

The establishment of the French mandate in Lebanon caused a significant change in the Shiites' status. In January 1926, the French authorities recognized the Maktab el-Ja'afri (the Shiite religious ruling system) and founded courts that would rule according to this system. This was the first time in the history of the community in Lebanon that it was recognized as a religious group separate from the Sunnis and entitled to its own judicial system.[58] The objective of the French was to appease the Shiites at a time when the Druze and

Sunnis in Syria and Lebanon were in a rebellious frame of mind, as well as to introduce a step that would drive a wedge between the Shiites and Sunnis and prevent the formation of a homogenous Muslim front in Lebanon against the French rule and its allies, the Maronite Christians.

The French policy opened a new era in the annals of Shiite history in Lebanon. For the first time, there was a real political interest on the part of the Shiite leadership in the existence of an independent Lebanese state, because only in that state was recognition granted to the Shiites as a community separate from the Sunnis, along with an independent status and real political weight, factors that were the stuff of dreams in an Ottoman state or in an enlarged Syrian state (that would include Lebanon) with its large Sunni majority.

In 1932, the first and last population census in the history of Lebanon took place (to date), according to which the Shiites constituted some 18 percent of the overall population and were the third largest group after the Maronites and the Sunnis.[59] In practical terms, in matters related to representation in the government, control of economic resources and the level of education and health services, the status of the Shiites was far from what should logically have followed from their relative demographic weight.

With the establishment of an independent Lebanon, after World War II, the distribution of internal political power was agreed upon (which endured until the civil war in 1975), according to which the president would be a Maronite, the prime minister a Sunni, and the Shiites would be granted only the secondary role of the Speaker of the Parliament. This role quickly turned into a pivotal conflict point within the Shiite community, with each of the central Shiite families aspiring to have its candidate elected to the post, thus becoming the leading entity in the entire community.

During the crisis in 1958, the Shiite community was faced with a dilemma: Ostensibly, this was a confrontation between Christians and Muslims, and one would have expected the Shiites to take the anti-Christian side, but in actual fact it was a struggle between the preservers of the pro-Western independent Lebanon and those who preferred a more "Arab" Lebanon. The Shiites as an ethnic group did not take a stand, but there was no doubt that they preferred to maintain the status quo rather than boost the Sunni control and strengthen the pro-Syrian, pan-Arab link.

The late 1950s and early 1960s, under the government of Fuad Shaab, were characterized by his attempt to establish a stable Lebanon with an effective central government that would extend its authority over all areas of the state. The new administration strove to introduce national priorities while considering the welfare of the populations that had been propelled into the margins of the political-economic activity in Lebanon, including the Shiite population.

At about this time the Palestinian problem began to emerge, the pan-Arab radical Ba'ath regime took power in Syria and emanated its influences, and in Lebanon a political-social awakening took place in the form of the growth of various "left-wing" movements such as the Communists and the Nasserists. The processes of change and development did not skip over the Shiite community, but the Shiites did not control this process taking place from within, nor did they initiate or analyze it, but rather played only a passive role for three main reasons:[60]

1. This period was characterized by massive migration of Shiites from the periphery to the urban centers, particularly Beirut. These Shiites cut themselves off from the community's traditional leadership, which remained in south Lebanon and the Baq'a, and became "easy prey" to the new political leftist movements developing at the time. The Shiites that joined these organizations became assimilated and did not function as Shiites representing their community's interests.

2. The awakening of the left was accompanied by close cooperation with entities from outside of Lebanon (Syria, Iraq, Libya, Egypt). This link exposed one of the traditional weaknesses of the Shiite community—the lack of an outside supporter. The only Shiite state in the region was Iran, which during the Shah's era advocated Lebanon in its current status, and was not inclined to cooperate with Shiite minorities outside of Iran.

3. The Palestinian influence upon the rise of the Lebanese left was significant. Here, too, the Shiites had a problem due to the fact that the Palestinian organizations were Sunni. This made it hard for the Shiites to establish a basis of trust with them along the lines of the link between those Palestinian organizations and other Lebanese groups that received financial aid and military supplies from Palestinian sources.

Thus, in the mid-1960s the Shiites again found themselves in a situation of significant backwardness, just as their country was in the midst of a process involving essential change. However, at that time the Imam Mousa al Sader appeared in the arena, ushering in a highly significant new stage in the annals of the Shiite community in Lebanon.

The origins of the Sader family were in southern Lebanon but some of them moved to Iraq. Mousa's father, a senior religious leader, moved to the city of Qum in Iran, where Mousa was born. Mousa acquired his initial education in Teheran. He subsequently moved to the holy city of Najef in Iraq, where he studied Shiite law, reached the status of Mujtahid, and in 1959 returned to Lebanon and settled in the city of Tyre. From the mid-1960s until August 25, 1978, Mousa al Sader was the prominent leader of the Shiite community in Lebanon. In the framework of his efforts to boost the political status of the Shiites in Lebanon he established the Supreme Shiite Council, whose goal to this very day is to represent the Shiite demands vis-à-vis the Lebanese administration.[61]

Al Sader offered the Shiites in Lebanon an alternative path to that espoused by the traditional political leadership. He presented an active approach in the framework of which the Shiite community shifted from the status of a passive religious movement to a dynamic political movement. In 1959, he established the first political Shiite movement—"Harqat al Mukhramin"—whose basic objective was to conduct a peaceful struggle for the achievement of justice, and social and economic equality for the Shiite population of Lebanon. After it became obvious that in the Lebanese reality it was impossible to achieve the movement's goals in a peaceful manner, al Sader reached the conclusion that "there was no other alternative but to rebel and use force."[62] He founded the Amal militia, and from 1975 the militia began to play an important role as a Shiite military force that protected the Shiite population and its interests during the civil war.

The success of the Islamic revolution in Iran served as a source of pride and had a major influence on all of the Shiite populations worldwide. The basic principles of al Sader's theories contributed significantly to his links with the new Iranian regime, which for the first time granted the Shiite community in Lebanon state patronage similar to the status of most of the other communities in Lebanon.

In contrast to the Iranian approach, the Shiite population in Lebanon, which headed the Amal movement, preserved its identity and national character, and aspired to solve the problems of the Shiite community in the framework of the Lebanese state. Therefore, Amal's policy advocated the establishment of a central government universally accepted by all of the communities, accompanied by a just distribution of resources, and with relatively moderate and pragmatic policies.[63] Although Amal did not adopt the Iranian approach, which advocates the establishment of an Islamic regime in Lebanon based on the Iranian model, it generally maintained fairly close ties with Iran and with its representatives in Lebanon.

The disappearance of Mousa al Sader during a visit to Libya in August 1978 left a vacuum that Amal, under the leadership of Nebil Beri, found difficult to fill. Amal's relationship with Iran gradually deteriorated due to the secular leanings (national-Lebanese) that Amal advocated, and also because of Iran's support of the PLO in its struggle against Amal for control in south Lebanon and Beirut. The relations between Amal and Iran reached a crisis level with the outbreak of the war in Lebanon in 1982, when Nebil Beri joined the "National Rescue Front" headed by President Sarkhis, with the participation of all of the Lebanese leftwing parties. From the Iranian point of view, Amal symbolized the conquest of Lebanon by alien elements, and it ceased to regard Amal as a central factor to promote its goals in Lebanon.

As a result of the split with Amal, Iran started to invest efforts in establishing an alternative Shiite Lebanese organization that would accurately reflect Iran's positions and constitute a substitute for Amal's control of the Shiite population in Lebanon. This organization was established under the patronage of the Iranian Revolutionary Guards, which arrived in Lebanon in 1982, in the form of the Hizballah.[64] Nevertheless, despite the controversy and the declared support of Iran for the Hizballah, it did not sever its ties with Amal but rather made every effort to influence the organization to adopt Iran's positions. However, in the power struggles that erupted between Amal and the Hizballah over the control of the Shiite community in Lebanon, Iran actively aided the Hizballah despite its declared policy to try and reconcile the rival factions and achieve unity within the Shiite community. Iran's policy regarding the power struggles of the Shiite community in Lebanon and its support of the Hizballah gradually pushed Amal into increased cooperation with Syria, which even today serves as Amal's main patron.[65]

The reciprocal relationships between Iran and Syria on the strategic level and in the Lebanese arena, and the relationship between these two countries and their Shiite-sponsored organizations are extremely intricate and complicated, however, it is important to emphasize several basic components that are vital to the comprehension of the impact that these relationships have on the terror activity of the sponsored organizations.

First and foremost, on the strategic level Iran and Syria were allies in their struggle against Iraq during the Iran-Iraq war, and in the Lebanese arena there was also a consensus between the two states regarding two main goals: Banishment of the Israeli presence in Lebanon and removal of the Western (American and French) involvement in this country.[66] On the operative level, the agreement regarding these targets generated cooperation in the activation of these two Shiite-sponsored organizations, both Amal and Hizballah, to perpetrate terror activity in Lebanon against Israel and the West.

However, beyond the tangible objectives, the ultimate goals of the two states regarding the Lebanese issue were completely different. Via the Hizballah, Iran aspired to establish an Islamic state in Lebanon according to the Iranian model, while Syria sought to establish a pro-Syrian secular regime that would put an end to the interethnic struggles in that country. The conflict of interests between the two "patrons" also brought about the perpetuation of the internal controversy within the Shiite community between Amal and Hizballah.[67]

Theoretically, both organizations set the struggle against Israel as their main target, but in practical terms basic differences of opinion also surfaced in this matter. Amal believed that the struggle against Israel must focus on the security zone, and that even this struggle should be constrained in order to prevent harsh Israeli retaliation against the Shiite population in south Lebanon. Hizballah, on the other hand, regarded the struggle against Israel as an overall confrontation, one in which the banishment of Israel from the security zone was only the first step leading towards its annihilation, and therefore believed the scope and intensiveness of the struggle should not be limited or restricted.

Amal's terror activity focused on achieving specific goals that did not necessarily match Iran's objectives or the radical line represented by the Hizballah. However, there were several incidents in which the organizations cooperated under Iranian inspiration against Western and Israeli targets in Lebanon. A prominent example of this was the hijacking of the TWA passenger plane in 1985, in which both Amal and Hizballah activists were involved under Iranian sponsorship.

Amal's terrorist activity in the international arena was focused mainly against Libya (an Iranian ally during the Gulf War), based on their demand to release the Imam Mousa al Sader, who according to Amal had been kidnapped by the Libyans. Foreign (Western) citizens were kidnapped by Amal members with the sole aim of bringing about the release of organization members who had been arrested in various countries, and from 1985 the organization acted on the international level very rarely. In the struggle against Israel, Amal focused on attacks only in the security zone, and refrained from perpetrating attacks inside Israeli territory.

The Hizballah

The Hizballah organization was established in 1982 with Iranian help and inspiration as part of the Khomeini regime's efforts to export the "Islamic revolution" beyond Iran's boundaries. Lebanon constituted a preferred target due to the large Shiite population residing there and also because of the political reality that made penetration of the Iranian influence into this country fairly easy. The Hizballah is an umbrella organization that consolidates Shiite organizations, groups and religious clerics that adopted the Khomeinist worldview and recognized Khomeini as the supreme religious adjudicator (Valiat Fakia), and as their undisputed religious and political leader. The organization was founded by members of the Revolutionary Guards who arrived in Lebanon in the summer of 1982.[68] Its founders include Abas Musawi, Sheikh Tsubhi Tufeili, and Sheikh Muhammad Yazbak. During 1982, Hussein Musawi joined the organization. Musawi was the leader of the Islamic Amal movement (an organization that had split from Amal, advocated a radical line on the ideological level, and perpetrated scores of terror attacks against the IDF forces in Lebanon), as well as other religious Shiite organizations such as the Muslim Students' Union, the Lebanese Muslim Ulama Union, and the al Dawa Organization.

Most of the founders of the Hizballah were alumni of Shiite seminaries in the holy cities of Najef (Iraq) and Qum in Iran, who returned to Lebanon in the late 1970s and established religious Shiite colleges that disseminated a radical school of thought among the Shiite population of Lebanon.

The Hizballah ideology is based on the principles of Iran's "Islamic revolution," in the center of which was the demand for activism via a violent struggle (Jihad), with the aim of ousting the tyrannical ruler. In this connection the Jihad is perceived as a legitimate defensive war. At the head of the struggle stands the learned scholar who will also lead the Islamic state, based on religious law, when it is established. This is not a local message but rather a universal one, and its goal is the establishment of a global Islamic regime.[69]

The goals of the Hizballah organization are:[70]

1.   The establishment of a revolutionary Islamic republic in Lebanon based on the Iranian model (as a strategic goal and as a stage in the establishment of a global Islamic republic);
2.   Fighting "Western Imperialism" in Lebanon, reducing its influence, and forcing Western entities (mainly French and American) to leave the region;
3.   Fighting the Israeli presence in a way that will not be restricted to its banishment from Lebanon, but also concentrating efforts on its annihilation in order to impose Islam upon Jerusalem;
4.   Establishing and consolidating the organization's status as the "leading" Islamic organization in Lebanon."

Hizballah's radical Shiite religious ideology played a major role in its formation and in drawing young Shiites to its ranks, by offering an attractive and active alternative to the community's political and religious establishment. The Hizballah perceives the struggle against the West and Israel as part of an overall struggle between Islam and the forces of evil, which are described as dynamic forces: The United States is the "Great Satan," while France and Israel are the "Small Satan." The United States, along with France and Israel, are considered the root of evil and the focus of heresy in its world; therefore, it is the duty of the Hizballah to eradicate their control.[71] The focus of the struggle was in Lebanon, particularly after the invasion by Israel, which, according to the Hizballah's view, plans to enslave the Lebanese people and turn their land into an imperialist base in cooperation with France and the United States. Therefore, their expulsion and the eradication of their influence in Lebanon were among the supreme objectives of the Hizballah.

The struggle against Israel will not end with the banishment of its presence from Lebanon, but with the triumph of Islam over Judaism. The Hizballah views the current struggle in this area as the continuation of the historical struggle between the prophet Muhammad and the Jews.[72] Moreover, the State of Israel was allegedly based on the theft of Arab land, a fact that according to Islamic religious ruling obligates every Muslim to act for the return of the stolen land to its owners. In addition, every Muslim has the basic obligation to liberate all Islamic areas (Dar-al-Islam) from the presence of foreign occupiers. Thus, the Hizballah negates the very existence of the State of Israel, and the struggle against Israel in Lebanon constitutes only the first step in the overall battle.[73]

However, in the array of considerations that guides the leaders of the Hizballah it is possible to discern more pragmatic thinking along the radical line, particularly when addressing issues that were controversial among the religious scholars. There are several prominent examples:

- In the matter of founding an Islamic republic in Lebanon, the organization recognized its inability to impose this type of regime upon Lebanon in the near future, and therefore this principle remained in the framework of a long-term strategic objective which will be realized when the time is right.
- Regarding the question of the struggle against Israel, the organization "compromised" at the initial stage and was satisfied with limiting itself to a struggle against its presence in Lebanon (the security zone).
- After the withdrawal of the IDF from Lebanon (May 2000), the organization redefined its objectives and placed the liberation of the "Shab'a Farm" and support for the Palestinian struggle at the head of its priorities.

The various organizations that joined forces with the Hizballah to a certain extent maintained their separate status within the organization, although not in a manner that would impair the organization's unity and activities. This apparently stems from the undisputed personal authority of the organization's leaders—religious clerics—in the eyes of their followers at the Shiite centers, colleges, and villages, where they are active and where their powerbase lies. It is also important to note that in this traditional environment, particularly in south Lebanon, considerable importance is attributed to family connections.[74]

Hizballah is structured upon a hierarchy of councils (*Shura*) headed by the Shura (Majelis), which numbers anywhere between seven to seventeen members during different periods. In 2003, the council members included Sheikh Hassan Nasrallah, Sheikh Naim Kassem, Hashem Tzafi Aldin, Sheikh Ibrahim Amin Alsayed, Sheikh Muhammad Yazbak, Haj Imad Muraniya, and two Iranian representatives. The inherent integration of Iranian entities into the organization's leadership reflects unequivocally the organization's identification and link with Iran.[75]

The Shura is headed by the secretary-general—Sheikh Hassan Nasrallah. This council controls the secondary councils—including the political council, the military council, and the judiciary council—as well as other entities. Therefore, unified leadership controls the organization's various branches, including the military-terrorist activities. The activity of all of the secondary committees, particularly the political and military councils, is determined by the organization's secretary-general and the Shura, and is translated into an established policy stemming from the organization's ideology and strategy, alongside a series of considerations and constraints rooted in the interests of Iran and Syria, which support the organization.

Sheikh Muhammad Hussein Fadallah, a native of Najef and a pupil of Abu al Qassam al Hawi (the supreme Shiite religious authority during his time), was granted the status of the organization's spiritual leader. Fadallah returned to Lebanon in 1966, established many educational and charitable institutions, and founded a radical ideological school of thought that opposed Mousa al Sader's theory and negated his efforts to achieve legitimization within the existing regime. Even so, Fadallah's approach is currently considered pragmatic and moderate in comparison to the attitudes of the other Hizballah leaders. Fadallah espoused the implementation of the goals of an Islamic state in a peaceful manner and through educating the public, while reconciling themselves to a certain degree of pluralism in Lebanon, at least at the initial stage.[76] Fadallah also opposed suicide attacks at the time, and refused to provide them with the support of a religious ruling (fatwa), although he gave them his blessing after the fact. In the matter of taking hostages, he also regarded this issue as damaging to Islam's moral image and as detrimental to the belief pertaining to the more just character of the Islamic state when it was founded.[77]

In any case, it is important to keep in mind that these disputes had no effect on Hizballah's adherence to the extreme line that it had adopted against its enemies inside and outside of Lebanon, nor did it limit the use of terror to achieve its goals. The organization had a military branch that relied on the infrastructure of the Shiite population. The number of militia members was estimated at several thousand, although the majority was made up of activists who were only partially recruited. The organization possessed an infrastructure that included bases, commands, hideaways, and ammunition depots. The activities were conducted in small groups. Also, the familial ties between many of the members and the joint origins—ethnic or geographical (from the same village in south Lebanon)—made it easier to maintain organizational loyalty and confidentiality.

The senior military command was mostly in the hands of the religious leaders Abas Musawi (until his termination) and Hussein Musawi, who were known as the masterminds of the Hizballah's attack policy in south Lebanon. This policy was executed by religious clerics such as Sheikhs Abd al Karim Obeid and Afif a-Nabulsi. In addition to the military training provided by the Revolutionary Guards to the Hizballah members, the organization also enjoyed financial support and the provision of a wide range of combat means.[78]

In 1989, in the framework of the "Ta'af Agreement," Syria forced the Lebanese government to allow the Hizballah the status of the sole militia organization in Lebanon, while the other ethnic militias were disarmed. The special status of the Hizballah and the weakness of the Lebanese government enabled the organization, from then to this very day, to exploit its strength for military and civil conquest of south Lebanon (and several areas in the Lebanon Valley) while usurping the Lebanese administration's place. This process has continued since the withdrawal of the IDF from Lebanon.

The area of south Lebanon has basically turned into a "state within a state" ("Hizballahstan"), much as it was when the Palestinians controlled it up to 1982 ("Fatahland"). The Hizballah has become the decisive factor in this area, while the control of the Lebanese government is shaky and is expressed mainly in the development of economic projects (subject to the organization's approval). The Hizballah established an extensive operational military infrastructure in south Lebanon numbering hundreds of activists skilled in various types of combat (in addition to the thousands of fighters that the organization can mobilize in emergencies). The fighters have various types of weapons, including a large amount of sabotage means, light weapons, anti-aircraft missiles (including "Taw" and "Sager" anti-missiles) as well as artillery including mortars, cannons, and rockets.

Hizballah entities that dealt in "mega attacks"—suicide attacks against American and French targets in Lebanon, the kidnapping of foreign citizens in Lebanon, and terror attacks worldwide—acted under cover names like the Islamic Jihad, the Revolutionary Organization for Justice, and the Organization of the Depressed on Earth. On the other hand, the organization that claimed responsibility for terror activities against the IDF and the SLA in south Lebanon was the Islamic Resistance, which is another cover name for the Hizballah.[79] The use of various cover names spreads confusion regarding the identity of the party that perpetrated the terror attack and restricts the ability of the "terror victims" to retaliate or apply punitive measures.

The Hizballah acted as Iran's emissary in the power struggles in Lebanon and in terror directed against Israel, Western and Arab states in Lebanon, and in the international arena. Two main types of attacks were characteristic of this organization: Suicide attacks against Western targets in Lebanon and Kuwait and against Israeli targets in Lebanon, and the kidnapping of foreigners on Lebanese soil. The section in charge of these attacks was the Special Security Agency, which was headed, as noted earlier, by Imad Muraniya.

Imad Muraniya and the Attack Mechanism

Imad Muraniya was born on July 12, 1962, in the village of Tir Daba in south Lebanon, some fifteen kilometers from Tyre. He is the eldest of three sons and a daughter, and his father, who was a religious Shiite, died in 1979.

Imad Muraniya spent most of his childhood in Bir al-Abed—one of the disadvantaged sections of Beirut. His family was poor, but the Muraniya clan is considered to be of top lineage in Shiite society, and in the 1970s one of its leaders, Sheikh Muhammad Muraniya, was considered a *marja taklid*, a senior religious title in the Shiite community.

In the late 1970s, after dropping out of high school, Muraniya joined the Fatah and underwent training in guerrilla warfare. He subsequently joined Force 17—the Fatah's security unit—and was among Abu-Iyad's bodyguards.

In 1982, during the Lebanon War, when the Fatah was about to evacuate Beirut, Muraniya decided to stay in Lebanon and joined the Islamic al Dawa organization, and, consequently, became a member of its successor, the Hizballah.

In 1983, Muraniya married his cousin Sa'ada Bader a-Din, and the couple had two children—Fatma (August 1984) and Mustafa (January 1987). In contrast to other young leaders of the Hizballah such as Abas Musawi, Subhi Tafeili or Hassan Nasrallah, Muraniya had no religious or political authority, and his activity focused in the operational area. His first role in the Hizballah was to serve as the bodyguard of Sheikh Fadallah—the Hizballah's spiritual leader. Shortly afterwards he transferred to another job, but his brother Jihad inherited his place, so that Imad Muraniya continued to be responsible for Fadallah's security by "remote control."

Also in 1983, a decision was made by Iran and the Hizballah to perpetrate terrorist attacks in an effort to remove the American and French presence in Lebanon. Imad Muraniya volunteered to execute the attacks, while aspiring to boost his status within the Hizballah and in the eyes of his patrons in Teheran. Muraniya did indeed orchestrate the series of terror attacks against the U.S. Embassy in Beirut and against the Marines headquarters and French forces in Beirut. Due to his "successes" he was appointed head of the "Special Security Agency" of the Hizballah, or to use its other name—"the Islamic Jihad."

The Special Security Agency, under Muraniya's command, was responsible for a series of attacks in Kuwait against U.S. and Kuwaiti targets in 1983. On December 12, 1983, his men detonated the U.S. Embassy in Kuwait and attacked other targets, including a shopping center in Shueiba and the control tower at the Kuwaiti airport. Five people were killed in these attacks and eighty-six were injured. The Kuwaiti authorities arrested seventeen suspects and sentenced seven of them to death. One of the condemned men was Mustafa Bader a-Din, Muraniya's brother-in-law and friend; another was Hassan Musawi, cousin of the Hizballah's secretary-general, Abas Musawi, who was terminated in a targeted attack by Israeli helicopters in 1992.

Imad Muraniya regarded the liberation of the accused as a central goal and used every means at his disposal to achieve their release. After the Kuwaiti royal family refused to release them, Muraniya initiated an assassination attempt against Emir Jaber a-Sabah, via a Shiite suicide attacker who detonated his car near a convoy in which the Emir was traveling in Kuwait City on May 25, 1985. Both of the Emir's bodyguards were killed but he emerged unscathed. Subsequently, Muraniya's people hijacked a Kuwaiti passenger plane (flight 211 from Dubai to Karachi), forced it to land in Teheran, and killed two American government employees before turning themselves in to the Iranian authorities in exchange for political asylum.

Starting from the mid-1980s, Muraniya's agency was involved in the kidnapping of Western citizens in Beirut in order to apply pressure on Kuwait through these countries to release the condemned men, and for the purpose of achieving additional objectives vis-à-vis the Western countries according to the interests of the Hizballah and its patrons in Teheran.

In June 1985, Muraniya was responsible for the hijacking of TWA flight 847 from Athens to Rome. The airplane landed in Beirut, and in the course of the hijacking an American soldier on board was killed. On April 5 1987, Muraniya's henchmen hijacked a Kuwaiti airplane on flight from Bangkok to Kuwait and forced it to land in Mashad in north Iran. From Mashad the hijackers flew with their hostages to Larnaca, Cyprus, and the incident finally ended in Algeria where the hijackers reached an agreement with the authorities, released the aircraft and its passengers, and "disappeared."

As stated earlier, since the 1980s, Muraniya has been behind most of the Hizballah's terror attacks against Western targets inside and outside of Lebanon. To this very day there is no clear picture of the hierarchical structure and subordination relationship of Muraniya and the agency that he heads, in relationship to the parent organization of the Hizballah and Iran. Within the Hizballah there is an entity that coordinates the attacks called Shurat al Jihad, which is comprised of two agencies: One is responsible for gathering information, and the second, the "Islamic Jihad," perpetrates the attacks. The agency headed by Imad Muraniya is part of the attack mechanism of the Hizballah, but due to Muraniya's status and importance, there exists a direct link with Iran. Therefore, there is a certain vagueness regarding the hierarchical subordination of "Muraniya's agency."

Muraniya constitutes an important target for intelligence services worldwide, particularly in Israel and in the United States. The United States has placed him on the list of the twenty-two most wanted terrorists, alongside Osama Bin Laden. Although over the years several opportunities have arisen to arrest him during his travels around the world under false identities, he has not been caught, and he continues to direct the terror activities of the Hizballah and Iran. (In 1988 he was almost arrested at Charles de Gaulle Airport in Paris, and in April 1995 he was almost caught during a stopover of the airplane in which he was traveling in Riyadh, Saudi Arabia.)

The Hizballah's Infrastructure in Canada[81]

The Hizballah has infrastructures of supporters and collaborators in many places all over the world. In order to illustrate the organization's infrastructure and modi operandi we provide the example of the organization's infrastructure in Canada.

A large community of Lebanese expatriates resides in Canada, mainly in Toronto, Montreal, and Ottawa. These are closed groups that meet all the needs of their members: educational institutions, culture, social welfare, places of worship, newspapers and Internet sites. These communities naturally became fertile soil for activities of fundamentalist Islamic organizations, which recruit members locally and collect funds for financing their military activities. The Canadian angle of the arrest of Hizballah activist Fauzi Ayub in Israel (see elaboration below) honed the controversy regarding the issue of whether the Canadian government should toughen its policy against terror. In contrast to the United States, the Hizballah is not included on the Canadian list of terror organizations, and Canadian law differentiates between the organization's military branch, whose activity is banned by Canadian law, and its social and political arm, al Dawa, which includes the organization's social services system.

Canadian Foreign Minister Bill Graham claimed that outlawing the organization would hurt "innocent people"—individuals about whom there exists no proof that they deal in terrorism. The Canadians, who operate multinational diplomacy, fear that the ostracizing the organization would deprive Canada of the possibility of involvement in the Middle East peace process. Evidence of the Canadian approach can be discerned in the participation of Prime Minister Jean (Poutine) Chrétien in a conference of Francophone countries in Beirut, with Sheikh Hassan Nasrallah, leader of the Hizballah, in attendance.

The Canadian opposition, on the other hand, has repeatedly called for the Hizballah to be outlawed and accuses the government of irresponsibility. Stockwell Day, the opposition member in charge of Canadian foreign affairs, was quoted in the media as saying, "the government is mistaken if it believes that money collected for one branch of the organization is not transferred to its military branch." The Jewish lobby of North America (AIPAC) joined the campaign and established a lobby in the Canadian Parliament in order to change the legal status.

In the early 1990s, a Hizballah agent named Muhammad Hussni al Hussni was caught in Canada. He confessed to the intelligence agencies that various channels of the organization are involved in terror and that they are all controlled by the same man—Hassan Nasrallah. The Canadian Security and Intelligence Service (CSIS) has had Hizballah agents in this country under surveillance for over a decade. Recently a "special agent" of the Hizballah was expelled from the country after confessing to planning attacks against Israeli settlements. The agent had arrived in Toronto in September 1998 with a Belgian passport and requested refugee status. His fictitious marriage to a Canadian expatriate was annulled after it became clear that she was legally underage.

Secret documents in the hands of the Canadian intelligence services attest to the organization's widespread activities in Canada. The documents indicate that the organization has laundered hundreds of thousands of dollars in Canadian banks; these funds were designated for the purchase of military equipment for the organization. Organization agents used the money to purchase night vision equipment, computers, and photography equipment to document attacks that the organization perpetrates against the IDF. In their investigations, the Canadians also revealed that the Internet site of the Hizballah serves for communication between activists and the organization's senior leaders in Lebanon.

Another instance that illustrates the Hizballah's activities in Canada occurred several years ago. The Canadian police discovered a cell that was involved in the theft of luxury cars and their smuggling to Lebanon and Eastern Europe. The affair was exposed after the luxury cars had been observed in Lebanon, in the use of organization leaders. The cars smuggled into Eastern Europe, on the other hand, were aimed at raising a profit, 10 percent of which was handed over to support the organization. Another investigation exposed a cell of activists involved in financial violations, mainly theft and the forgery of credit cards, for the purpose of purchasing military equipment for the organization. In another case, the theft of Canadian passports and their transfer to Hizballah members, with the aim of enabling Hizballah activists to travel between countries under fictitious identities, was revealed.

In 2001, Canadian intelligence agents had two Hizballah agents, Hamad al-Adham and Muhammad Hassan Dabuk, under surveillance and succeeded in eavesdropping on their conversations. In one of their conversations the two discussed a "successful" Hizballah attack in Lebanon, which had gone off "well" thanks to the organization's improved capabilities. The two agents had purchased military equipment in Vancouver and at a weapons factory in Canada and were searching for equipment that "could smash boulders." In April 2002, Canadian intelligence entities reported that during the years 1999 and 2000, the Hizballah had sent its agents in Vancouver, Toronto, and Montreal a "shopping list" of military equipment. The equipment was purchased and shipped to Lebanon by sea.

The problem in Canada is that even when the intelligence services believe that they are dealing with terrorists, they cannot arrest them because the laws in this connection are too lax. Moreover, up to now the Canadians have been fairly indifferent to the terror issue because they assumed that it did not pose a threat against the interests and security of Canadian citizens. The September 11 attacks and American pressure have altered this approach, to a certain extent.

The Kidnapping of Foreign Citizens in Lebanon

Hizballah and entities identified with the organization or associated with it have made extensive use (sometimes with Iranian guidance and at other times at the organization's initiative) of kidnapping foreign citizens (as well as local Jews) and holding them hostage. In the years 1984-1989, ninety-six foreign citizens were kidnapped in Lebanon, most of whom were American and French. About fifty-five of them were kidnapped by the Hizballah and entities linked to the organization.[82]

At the heart of the attacks against the West, including the kidnapping of foreigners, stood the ideological hostility towards the United States and Israel, and towards any foreign presence in Lebanon, but there were also other motives, sometimes even stronger ones, such as:[83]

- Obtaining a bargaining card for the release of imprisoned Shiites worldwide. The most prominent targets of terror attacks for this purpose were the United States, Kuwait, France, Britain, and Germany. Among the leading activists in this type of terror attack were relatives of the imprisoned Shiites abroad.
- The implementation of the Iranian terror policy, which believes in activating terror to achieve political goals (including as a means of placing pressure on countries that supported Iraq during the Iranian-Iraqi war).

The kidnapping of foreigners in Lebanon ceased in 1989, apparently due to the end of the Iran-Iraq war and Iran's desire to improve its relations with the United States and Western countries. The last hostages were released in 1991 and 1992, via the mediation of a special UN envoy.[84]

The Popular Front for the Liberation of Palestine— The General Command (PFLP-GC) (Jibril's Front)

This organization was founded on April 24, 1968, by Ahmed Jibril and some of his supporters who had split away from the Popular Front for the Liberation of Palestinian due to personal differences with the organization's head, George Habash.

Ahmed Jibril, a Palestinian whose family had departed for Jordan prior to 1948, is an alumnus of the Military Academy in Damascus and served in the Syrian army, where he reached the rank of major. In 1958, when the union was formed between Egypt and Syria, Jibril was ousted from the Syrian army under suspicion of having communist leanings. Immediately after his expulsion, Jibril moved to Cairo where he founded, together with a group of Palestinian officers, an underground cell called the "National Palestinian Front."[85] At that time, he distributed proclamations at night, and in the mornings edited the underground flyers and attempted to recruit additional members from among the Palestinians students. He appointed his wife Samira as head of the women's cell, parallel to his organization.

Jibril's subversive history in the 1950s and 1960s expressed itself in the dismantling and establishment of factions and organizations. At the end of the 1960s, Jibril joined Yasser Arafat's Fatah organization. In 1967, he left the Fatah in order to establish the Popular Front for the Liberation of Palestine, together with George Habash. Habash needed him because Jibril had earned prestige and the reputation of a man of action with military knowledge.[86] A year later, Jibril had a falling out with Habash and split away with his supporters to establish the Popular Front for the Liberation of Palestine—The General Command (PFLP-GC).

During its years of activity, the organization proved to have considerable operational capacity to perpetrate attacks against Israel, and against Israeli and American targets worldwide. Among its most prominent attacks are the following:

Attacks inside Israel

* The attack against the children from the town of Avivim who were on a bus to Safed (May 1970);
* The murderous attack in the town of Kiryat Shmona (April 1974);
* The hostage-bargaining attack at Kibbutz Shamir (June 1974);
* An aerial attack using a glider at a military camp in the northern sector of the country (November 1987).

Attacks worldwide

* Detonation of a Swissair flight en route from Zurich to Israel (February 1970);
* Detonation of an explosive device on an Austrian passenger plane (February 1970);
* Detonation of an explosive device on an El Al plane on the Rome-Lod line (August 1972);
* The hijacking of a KLM passenger plane (September 1976);
* Attacks against American military trains in Germany (September 1987, April 1988);

Up to 1984, it was important to the Fatah leadership, particularly Yasser Arafat, to preserve the unity of the Palestinian camp within the Fatah; thus, the head of the PLO maintained a regular political dialogue with Jibril's Front, even at the price of ideological concessions. But the tension between the Front and Fatah sometimes caused violent friction to erupt, as in the years 1981-1982, when Arafat's men, who had undertaken to cease attacks against Israel on the northern border, forcibly prevented Jibril's men from attacking the northern Israeli border south of Lebanon. Due to the circumstances, the days of the IDF siege on Beirut in the summer of 1982 brought about a unification of the ranks of the Fatah and the other organizations (including Jibril's organization) in a combined battle, despite the sharp ideological differences. But this situation did not endure for any length of time and did not prevent the yawning breach that gaped immediately after the evacuation of Beirut. At that time, as a Syrian satellite organization, Jibril's group came out publicly against the Fatah's central stream, while supporting the rebels in the Fatah's ranks.[87]

At the end of 1983, Jibril's fighters took an active part in the siege laid by pro-Syrian Palestinian organizations and the Syrian army on Arafat's fighters who had entrenched themselves in the refugee camps in northern Lebanon—the Albard River and Badawi—until the latter's evacuation by sea from Lebanon in December 1983.

As a result of the unstinted support that Jibril's men gave to Syria against the mainstream of the PLO, and in light of their participation in the siege on Arafat's loyalists in northern Lebanon at the end of 1983, on November 26, 1984, the organization was ousted from the National Palestinian Council and from other Fatah institutions, and since that time the organization has not been represented in the Fatah's executive committee.

When three Israeli soldiers—Hezi Shay, Nissim Salem, and Yosef Grof—were taken captive by the organization's members in Lebanon in the summer of 1982, this boosted the organization' status and granted Jibril considerable inter-Arab prestige, after his success in blackmailing Israel during prolonged negotiations into releasing 1,150 Palestinian prisoners on May 20, 1985, in exchange for the three Israeli soldiers ("the Jibril deal"). Another feather in the organization's cap vis-à-vis Israel occurred on November 25, 1987, in what is called "the night of the gliders" (or the Kibia action, in the organization's lexicon), when a terrorist affiliated with the organization succeeded in infiltrating Israeli territory on an air glider under the cover of darkness and after breaking into a military camp, killed six IDF soldiers and injured seven others. There are those who expressed the assessment at the time, that this attack, which garnered praise throughout the Arab world, contributed to the outbreak of the uprising in Gaza and the areas of Judea and Samaria (the Intifada) about a month later.

The organization currently has several hundred members stationed at the organization's bases in Lebanon, but its offices are located in Syria, and it has a radio station which broadcasts from Damascus.

The ties between Jibril's Front and Iran started developing in December 1987, following a meeting between Ahmed Jibril and the Iranian Foreign Minister Valyatiin in Tripoli, Libya. The improved relations between Jibril's organization and Iran stemmed from the organization's aspiration to reduce its financial and operational dependence on Libya and Syria.[88] In exchange for Iran's economic, political, and military aid, the organization offered considerable operational skills and the willingness to perpetrate terror attacks for Iran.

The discussions between Iran and the organization continued throughout 1988, when Jibril was a partner to an unsuccessful Iranian attempt to establish the "Islamic Front for the Liberation of Palestine," which was to have replaced the PLO (discussions between Jibril's representatives and members of the Palestinian Islamic Jihad in this matter were held in April 1988 in Teheran).[89]

On July 3, 1988, an American destroyer in the Persian Gulf shot down an Iranian airliner by mistake, and all of the passengers were killed. Jibril offered to perpetrate an attack in retaliation for the downing of the plane. During the month of October 1988, a terror network belonging to Jibril was exposed in

Germany, an incident known as the "Delckamony Affair." Various combat means were found in the cell's possession, which were to have served for the execution of a series of terror attacks in Europe (including the detonation of five European passenger airplanes in Germany).

Following the exposure of the terror network in Germany and the attack on a Pan-Am flight (on December 21, 1988), which was initially attributed to Jibril's Front, the United States and other Western countries (such as Britain and Germany) put heavy pressure on Syria, Jibril's patron, to expel him from Syria and clip his organization's wings. These efforts were fruitless, but this activity pressed the organization into tightening its ties with Iran to serve as an alternative in the event of a crisis in its relationship with Syria. Another expression of Jibril's loyalty to the Iranian line is reflected in the issue of the author Salman Rushdie. In February 1989, Khomeini issued a religious ruling in which he sentenced Rushdie to death for offending Islam and the prophet Muhammad in his book *The Satanic Verses*. After the issuing of the religious ruling, Ahmed Jibril announced that he regarded himself obligated to carry out Rushdie's sentence.[90]

Another terror attack in which Jibril's organization was suspected of involvement at Iran's command occurred on September 19, 1989, when a UTA French passenger plane exploded over Niger in Africa. Investigation of the attack revealed that the aircraft apparently had been detonated by a barometrically activated explosive device similar to the devices found during the "Delckamony Affair." The explosion took place at a time when tension between France and the Hizballah and Iran was soaring, due to France's support of the anti-Syrian and anti-Iranian administration of General Michel Unn, and the dispatch of French navy ships towards the Lebanese coast. The Hizballah threatened that it would attack French interests if the gunboats were not removed and if France did not stop supporting General Unn's administration. At the time of these events, discussions were held between Jibril's Front, the Hizballah, and Iran, and it is possible that these talks led to the terror attack. Nevertheless, no one has been able to prove that Jibril's organization was involved, and most of the evidence pointed to Libya as the guilty party.

In any event, the ties between Jibril's Front, Iran, and the Hizballah are still going strong and the organization constitutes a central ally for Iran in the Palestinian camp. In the past, this fact was reflected in Jibril's call to establish officially an Iranian-Palestinian alliance to promote the struggle against Israel and the West (particularly the French and the Americans).[91]

The alignment of the resistance organizations under Iranian leadership was reflected immediately prior to the opening of the Madrid Conference (on October 31, 1991), when a counter-conference was convened in Teheran of entities opposing the peace process, including representatives of the Palestinian and Shiite terror organizations. Iran's President Hashemi Rafsanjani declared his willingness before the participants of the conference to advance forces for a war against Israel. Khomeini's son, Ahmed Khomeini, promised that Iran would provide financial and military aid to the Palestinians, while Ahmed Jibril defined the ties between Iran and Syria as a key to the future.[92]

Following the signing of the Oslo Agreements, Jibril's Front took a rigid stand against the Palestinian Authority and strengthened its ties with entities within the Palestinian camp that opposed the peace process. Since the beginning of the Al Aksa Intifada (September 2000), Jibril's Front has aided Palestinian organizations in the areas of Judea, Samaria, and the Gaza Strip through the transfer of combat weapons and via attack attempts initiated from Lebanon as the organization's expression of solidarity with the Intifada. An obvious expression of the organization's involvement can be seen in the *Santorini* affair (see elaboration in chapter 4).

The Palestinian Islamic Jihad (the Fathi Shkaki Faction)

The Palestinian Islamic Jihad (hereafter PIJ) was founded in the late 1970s in the Gaza Strip and stood out as an organization with radical Islamic Sunni tendencies. Despite the Islamic Sunni identity of its founders, the organization drew inspiration from the success of the Islamic revolution in Iran, and regarded it as a model for emulation. However, until the late 1989s Iran did not attribute special importance to this Palestinian organization.

In 1988, at the end of the Iran-Iraq war, Iran began actively to disseminate the concepts of the Islamic revolution among the radical Sunni organizations throughout the Muslim world. The Intifada that erupted in Gaza and the areas of Judea and Samaria at the end of 1987 and the fortification of the radical Islamic streams within the Palestinian camp in the form of the Hamas and the Palestinian Islamic Jihad contributed to improved relations between the Palestinian Islamic entities and Iran, which placed itself at the head of the supporters of the Palestinian struggle.[93]

After the expulsion of the PIJ leaders from Israel to Lebanon in 1988, strong ties developed between the PIJ and radical Shiite entities in Lebanon (the Hizballah) and Iran, both on military and ideological levels. The PIJ is the only Palestinian organization that has adopted the Iranian revolution as a model for emulation, the perception of Jihad as established by Khomeini, and the suicide attacks as one of the prominent symbols of Shiite activism, as expressed in the organization's struggle against the state of Israel.[94]

On the ideological level, the PIJ made every effort to play down the basic differences between the Sunna and the Shia, and emphasized the common elements to the entire Islamic nation. The PIJ also identified with the Iranian positions regarding ongoing issues such as the opposition to the peace process between the Palestinians and Israel (Madrid, Oslo). From the end of the 1980s the PIJ began to enjoy Iranian political, financial, and military aid. The assistance was transferred to the organization directly or via Iranian representatives in Syria and Lebanon, including the Hizballah. In an interview that

Fathi Shkaki granted to the *New York Times* in April 1993, he noted that since 1987 his organization had been the recipient of Iranian financial aid. He stated that funds and military equipment had been transferred to Gaza and the areas of Judea and Samaria in order to finance and aid military campaigns, and provide support to the families of the organization's martyrs and prisoners.[95]

In the years 1991-1992, cooperation developed between the PIJ and the Hizballah in Lebanon, which led to the perpetration of several joint attacks by both organizations against SLA and IDF forces in the security zone in south Lebanon. The first joint action took place on July 1, 1991, when the two organizations attacked an IDF patrol in the village of Blida in south Lebanon.[96] In April 1992, an additional joint attack was launched via an ambush set for an IDF force near the Hula village in the security zone.

The PIJ adopted suicide attacks as a central modus operandi in its operational activities, and won the blessings and encouragement of Iran and the Hizballah. The termination of the organization's leader Fathi Shkaki by Israel, and extensive activities initiated by Israeli and Palestinian security entities significantly weakened the organization's operational capabilities in the period between 1993-2000. Nevertheless, since the outbreak of the Al Aksa Intifada in September 2000, the scope of the suicide attacks carried out by the organization is evident, as is the high toll of Israeli victims.

The PIJ continues to be the Palestinian organization closest to Iran from ideological and operative points of view. Proof of the latter can be seen in the following example: In March 1998, a U.S. court ruled that Iran must pay $240 million dollars in reparation to the family of Alissa Plateu—a U.S. citizen murdered in a suicide attack that the PIJ had perpetrated in Gush Katif in April 9, 1995. The court ruled that Iran was responsible for her murder due to the support and encouragement that it provided to the PIJ for the perpetration of attacks.[97]

Notes

1. Zbigniev Brezezinski, *Power and Principle, Memoirs of the National Security Adviser, 1977-1981*, Weidenfeld & Nicolson, London, 1983, pp. 483-489.
2. Edgar O'Ballance, *Islamic Fundamental Terrorism, 1979-95*, New York University Press, 1997, pp. 48-51.
3. David Menashri, *Iran in Revolution*, Hakibbutz Hameuhad Publishing, Tel Aviv, 1988, p. 207.
4. Ibrahim Pourhadi, *Iran and the USA 1979-1981, Three Years of Confrontation*, Library of Congress, Washington, DC, 1982, pp. 12-14.
5. Anthony Parsons, "Iran and Western Europe," *The Middle East Journal* 43, 2 (Spring 1989), pp. 218-229.
6. Muhammad Husnin Hiekal, *The Return of the Ayatollah*, Andre Deutsch, Great Britain, 1983.
7. See elaboration in the chapter addressing attacks in aviation.
8. Anat Kurtz, Maskit Burgin, and David Tal, *Islamic Terror and Israel*, Papyrus Publishing, Tel Aviv University, 1993, pp. 52-55.
9. David Menashri, *Iran in Revolution*, p. 221.

10.   "Hizballah's Activities in Europe Uncovered," *Al Watan al Arabi*, December 9, 1989, pp. 20-21.
11.   *Le Figaro*, December 1989.
12.   Ibid.
13.   *Teheran Times*, January 7, 1990.
14.   *Le Figaro*, May 3, 1990.
15.   Eric Avebury and Robert Wilkinson, *Iran: State of Terror*, Parliamentary Human Rights Group, London, June 1996, pp. 12-16.
16.   Ray S. Cline and Yona Alexander, *Terrorism as State Sponsored Covert Warfare*, Fairfax, VA, 1986, pp. 60-62.
17.   "Hizballah Bases Spread in Africa," *Terror Update*, January 1990, Issue No. 12, pp. 1-2.
18.   Ibid.
19.   *Hizballah*, a Special Collection of Information, the Center for Intelligence Heritage, The Information Center for Intelligence and Terror, March 2003, pp 75-76.
20.   Anat Kurtz and Maskit Burgin, *Inter-International Terrorism*, JCSS, Tel Aviv University, 1987-1989.
21.   Hamshari, Iran, January 24, 1993—an interview with Hassan al Turabi.
22.   *Conflict International*, September 1994.
23.   *Al-Watan alArabi*, Lebanon, December 18, 1992.
24.   *Teheran Times*, December 14, 1991, December 15, 1991, December 14, 1992; *Al-Watan alArabi*, December 18, 1992.
25.   *Conflict International*, September 1994.
26.   IRNA News Agency, Teheran, December 18, 1992; *Al-Watan alArabi*, Lebanon, December 18, 1992.
27.   *Al-Watan alArabi*, Lebanon, December 12, 1992.
28.   *Al-Matzewar*, Egypt, December 2, 1992; *Al-Ahram*, Egypt, December 8, 1992; *Al-Sharq al-Awsat*, London, December 6, 1992; *Conflict International*, September 1994.
29.   *Alkhalma Almamnoa*, Britain, February 1993.
30.   *Alahad*, Jordan, December 21, 1993,
31.   *Al-Watan alArabi*, Lebanon, March 12, 1993.
32.   Reported by the Reuters Agency on January 27, 1993. Reuters was quoting the German Television Network MDR, which reported that some 30,000 Iranians were fighting alongside al Beshir's forces in the war in south Sudan.
33.   *Al-Hayat*, Lebanon, November 27, 1992; *Conflict International*, September 1994.
34.   Hassan al Turabi, *The Islamic Movement in Sudan*, Cairo, The Arab Reader's Publication, 1991; *al-Ahram Almasai*, Egypt, December 3, 1992.
35.   *Al-Hayat*, London, February 10, 1993.
36.   *Guardian*, December 10, 1992; *Conflict International*, September 1994.
37.   *Al-Mahrar*, Lebanon, January 13, 1993—an interview with the Sudanese Information Minister.
38.   Hassan al Turabi, *The Islamic Movement in Sudan*, pp. 251-252.
39.   Yosef Bodansky, *Bin Laden—The Man Who Declared War on America*, Forum, New York, 2001, p. 33.
40.   Ann M. Lecht, "Osama Bin-Laden's 'Business' in Sudan," *Current History* (January 2002).
41.   Peter L. Bergen, *Holy War Inc.—Inside the Secret World of Osama Bin-Laden*, Weidenfeld & Nicolson, London, 2001.
42.   Yosef Bodansky, *Bin-Laden, The Man Who Declared War on America*, pp. 62-64.
43.   Ibid., pp. 65-70.

44. Interview with the Al-Jazeera television broadcasting network, June 10, 1999.
45. Yosef Bodansky, *Bin-Laden, The Man Who Declared War on America*, p. 93.
46. *Hizballah*, , p. 74.
47. Harris Whitbeck and Ingrid Arneson, "Sources: Terrorists Find Haven in South America," CNN.com.
48. Daniel Sobelman, "Israel Takes Special Interest in Triple Border Area," Jane's Intelligence Review, December 2001.
49. Office of the Secretary of State, Office of the Coordinator for Counter-Terrorism, *Patterns of Global Terrorism—2001, Terrorist Activity in Colombia, Peru, Tri-Border Area*, U.S. Department of State Publications, Washington, DC, 2001.
50. Harris Whitbeck and Ingrid Arneson, "Sources: Terrorists Find Haven in South America."
51. Daniel Sobelman, "Israel Takes Special Interest in Triple Border Area," Jane's Intelligence Review.
52. Ibid.
53. Office of the Secretary of State, Office of the Coordinator for Counter-Terrorism, *Patterns of Global Terrorism—2001, Terrorist Activity in Colombia, Peru, Tri-Border Area.*
54. David Menashri, *Iran in Revolution*, pp. 216-221.
55. Magnus Ranstorp, *Hizballah in Lebanon—The Politics of the Western Hostage Crisis*, St. Martin's Press, New York, 1997, pp. 25-26.
56. Anat Kurtz, Maskit Burgin, and David Tal, pp. 52-55.
57. Magnus Ranstorp, *Hizballah in Lebanon—The Politics of the Western Hostage Crisis,* pp. 25-30.
58. Augustus R. Norton, *Amal and the Shi'a: A Struggle for the Soul of Lebanon*, University of Texas Press, Austin, 1987, p. 107.
59. Edward E. Azarand, Paul A. Jureidini (eds.), *The Emergence of a New Lebanon: Fantasy or Reality*, Praeger Publishers, New York, 1984.
60. Yossi Olmert, *The Shiites in Lebanon—From a Marginal Ethnic Community to a Central Factor*, Hakibbutz Hameuhad, Tel Aviv, 1985, pp. 107-110.
61. Fuad Agami, *The Vanished Imam, Mousa Sader and the Shia of Lebanon*, Am Oved, Tel Aviv, 1988, pp. 133-134.
62. Ibid., pp. 193-195.
63. Anat Kurtz et al., *Inter-International Terrorism*, JCSS, Tel Aviv University, 1989, pp. 40-41.
64. Marvin Zonis and Daniel Brumberg, "Khomeini, The Islamic Republic of Iran and the Arab World," *Middle East Papers* 5 (1989), p.75.
65. Martin Kramer, David Menashri, *Ha'aretz*, Tel Aviv, February 3, 1988.
66. *Christian Science Monitor*, July 26, 1989.
67. Edgar O'Ballance, *Islamic Fundamentalist Terrorism*, 1979-95, New York University Press, 1997, pp. 116-117.
68. Small numbers of members of the Revolutionary Guards began arriving in Lebanon already in 1979-1980.
69. Shimon Shapira, "The Origins of Hizballah," *The Jerusalem Quarterly* (Spring 1988).
70. Based upon "An open letter to the Depressed," which was read aloud at a general meeting held by the Hizballah on March 16, 1985. The main points of the document serve as the organization's "political manifesto." These principles are reinforced by repeated statements made by the organization's leaders.
71. Martin Kramer (ed.) *Shi'ism, Resistance and Revolution*, Westview Press, Boulder, CO, 1987, pp. 47-50.

72. Martin Kramer, *The Moral Logic of Hizballah*, Occasional Papers No. 101, The Dayan Center for Middle Eastern Studies, Tel Aviv University, August 1987, pp. 63-66.
73. *Al-Nahar*, May 19, 1985.
74. *Al-Itihad*, September 13, 1988.
75. Anat Kurtz et al, *Inter-International Terrorism*, pp. 55-58.
76. Interview with Fadallah for the periodical *Journal of Palestinian Studies* (Winter 1987).
77. Friday sermon by Fadallah as quoted by the French News Agency. See *Le Figaro*, August 5, 1989.
78. *Al-Muharar*, Lebanon, July 28, 1989.
79. Anat Kurtz, Maskit Burgin, David Tal, *Islamic Terror and Israel*, pp. 52-55.
80. This section is based on Ronen Bergman, "The Terrorist with Nine Lives," *Yediot Aharonot*, October 27, 2000; *Hizballah*, pp 36-39.
81. *Hizballah*, pp. 73-74.
82. Maskit Burgin, Ariel Merari, Anat Kurtz, "Foreign Hostages in Lebanon" (Memorandum No. 25), JCSS, Tel Aviv University, August 1988.
83. Magnus Ranstorp, Hizballah in Lebanon—*The Politics of the Western Hostage Crisis*, St. Martin's Press, New York, pp. 86-88.
84. Ibid., p. 108.
85. Guy Bechor, *Fatah Lexicon*, Ministry of Defense Publication, 1991, pp. 71-73.
86. Ibid.
87. Ibid.
88. Anat Kurtz et al., *Inter-International Terrorism*, pp. 69-71.
89. Davar, Tel Aviv, May 6, 1988.
90. An interview with Ahmed Jibril for the French newspaper, *Lavanman de Jidy*, Paris, October 23, 1989.
91. An interview with Ahmed Jibril for the Lebanese newspaper *Al-Sapir*, Lebanon, January 1990.
92. Anat Kurz, Maskit Burgin, David Tal, *Islamic Terror and Israel*, pp. 86-87.
93. Elie Rekhess, *Justice* 5 (May 1995).
94. Ibid.
95. *New York Times*, April 15, 1993.
96. "Voice of the Oppressed," July 2, 1991, in FBIS-NES, July 2, 1991.
97. *Ha'aretz*, Tel Aviv, March 18, 1998.

3

The Modus Operandi
of Iranian/Shiite Terror

Characteristics of International Terror Activity
Perpetrated by Shiite Terror Organizations

During the years 1980-1999, Shiite terror organizations and Iranian entities perpetrated 260 international terror attacks (this number does not include terror acts performed by the Hizballah against IDF forces in Lebanon and terror attacks perpetrated against Iraq during the Iran-Iraq war).[1] Shiite terror attacks warranted publicity and international acclaim due mainly to two modi operandi that they utilized:

- *Suicide Attacks*—The Shiite organizations were the first to perpetrate suicide attacks against Western targets in Lebanon and Kuwait. Despite the fact that the Shiite organizations carried out a total of only five suicide attacks against Western targets, the impact of these attacks was tremendous—they brought about the evacuation of American and French forces from Lebanon and became the "trademark" of Shiite terror;[2]
- *Kidnapping Hostages*—During the years 1983-1989, the kidnapping of Western hostages in Lebanon became a central method to apply pressure on Western countries and others to change their policies regarding the Iran-Iraq war and the Arab-Israeli conflict, as well as leverage for the release of Shiite terrorists throughout the world.

The Iranian and Shiite terror activities can be divided into four main categories (see Figure 3.1):[3]

- Kidnapping of hostages   67 incidents
  (25.76 percent)
- Hijacking/detonating airplanes   12 incidents
  (4.61 percent)

- Detonating explosive devices and car bombs[4]   82 incidents
  (31.53 percent)
- Assassinations (generally by shooting)   97 incidents
  (37.30 percent)

Assassinations (mostly by shooting the victim) were the most common attack method used by the Iranians, and the majority of the assassinations (85) were carried out against Iranian expatriates and activists of the opposition organization Mujahidin Khalq, and Kurd resistance organizations such as the Iranian Democratic Kurd Party.

International Iranian and Shiite terror took place in thirty-two different countries spread over four continents (see Figure 3.2):

- 57 attacks in Europe;[5]
- 173 attacks in the Middle East;[6]
- 23 attacks in Asia;
- 6 attacks in the United States;
- 1 attack in Africa

Figure 3.1
Iranian and Shiite Terror Attacks according to Categories
(in absolute numbers)

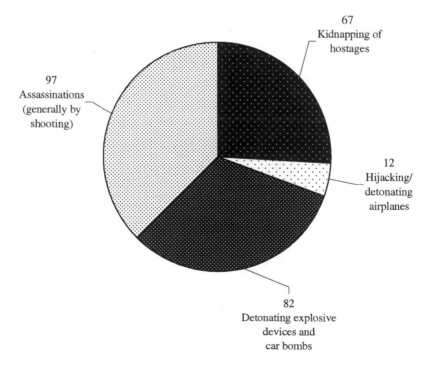

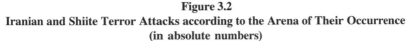

Figure 3.2
Iranian and Shiite Terror Attacks according to the Arena of Their Occurrence
(in absolute numbers)

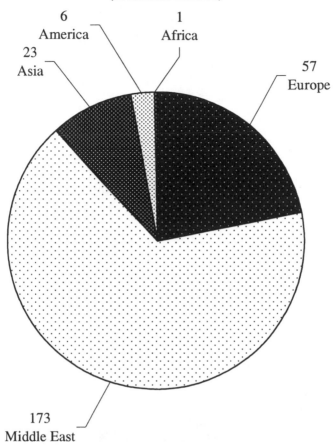

An examination of arenas chosen for the perpetration of Iranian/Shiite attacks indicates that 190 attacks were carried out within the areas of Muslim states (in the Middle East and Asia). It would appear that Muslim states are a relatively convenient arena for Iranian terror activity due to the existence of infrastructures consisting of local collaborators and radical sponsor organizations that perpetrate the attacks or assist the Iranian entities in their perpetration. The countries that served as main attack arenas are as follows:

- In Europe: *France*—21 terror attacks
- In the Middle East: *Lebanon*—73 terror attacks (all of the kidnappings of Western citizens were perpetrated on Lebanese territory).

Iraq—44 terror attacks (mainly against the Mujahidin Khalq and the Kurds).[7]
Kuwait—32 terror attacks.
Turkey—18 terror attacks.

- Asia: *Pakistan*—13 terror attacks

The countries that constituted central targets for the Iranian Shiite terror were as follows (see Figure 3.3):

- *United States*:   40 attacks were perpetrated against American targets.
- *France*:   27 attacks were perpetrated against French targets.
- *Kuwait*:   21 attacks were perpetrated against Kuwaiti targets.
- *Saudi Arabia*:   20 attacks were perpetrated against Saudi targets.

An examination of the terror targets vis-à-vis attack arenas indictates that there is no correlation between the two parameters—the Iranian and Shiite attackers generally chose to attack sites belonging to the target country inside the territory of other states, and not necessarily in the target countries them-

Figure 3.3
Iranian and Shiite Terror Attacks according to Main Target States
(in absolute numbers)

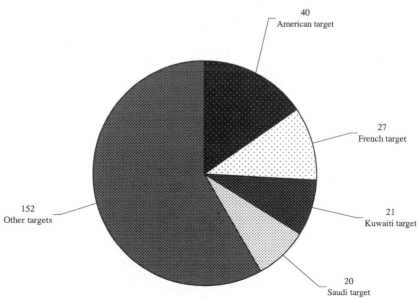

selves. The four countries mentioned above fell victim to 42 percent of the Iranian/Shiite attacks, while the United States and France (The Great Satan and The Small Satan in Iranian terms) together represented the targets for 67 attacks, whereas Saudi Arabia and Kuwait, due to their "reactionary" regimes and their support for Iraq during the Iran-Iraq war absorbed 41 attacks together.

An analysis of the Iranian/Shiite attacks during these two decades indictates several changes and developments in Iranian terror:

- During Khomeini's administration (1979-1989), which included the period of the Iran-Iraq war (1980-1988), Iranian and Shiite entities perpetrated 171 international terror attacks. In contrast, during the term of office of Khomeini's successors (1989-1999), Shiite/Iranian entities carried out only 89 attacks, which represents a decrease of some 50 percent in the number of attacks (see Figure 3.4).
- Since 1990, the kidnapping of Western civilians in Lebanon has ceased and by 1992 all hostages held in Lebanon were released.
- Since 1989 all Shiite attacks against aircraft (the hijacking and detonation of airplanes) have ceased.
- Starting in 1989, attacks were perpetrated against targets connected to the publication of Salman Rushdie's book (*The Satanic Verses*). The death sentence continues to loom over him following Khomeini's fatwa in this matter.
- Since 1990, there was an increase in Iranian activities against Iranian expatriates and opposition organizations (the main arenas were Iraq, Turkey, Pakistan, and France). Most of the Shiite and Iranian attacks perpetrated in the 1990s were directed against these targets, while the amount of their attacks against Western targets dropped significantly (see Figure 3.4).

Suicide Attacks

From the beginning of the 1980s, following the Islamic revolution in Iran, suicide attacks perpetrated by Shiite and Iranian entities became one of the most prominent characteristics of Shiite terror. These attacks took a heavy toll on the states that constituted the main targets, particularly Western countries and Israel, and turned out to have a significant psychological impact on those countries.

Khomeini's philosophy was based on his interpretation of several key issues in Shiite Islam and the adjustment of the solutions to the new reality of the twentieth century. In the center of his philosophy there stands the call to take an activist approach in order to promote the goals of Islam and achieve salvation. Khomeini's philosophy grew and flourished against the background of historical Shiite frustrations, a harsh socioeconomic reality, and the strengthening of the fundamentalist frame of mind in the Muslim world.

Figure 3.4
**Number of Attacks during Khomeini's Administration and during His
Successors' Terms of Office**

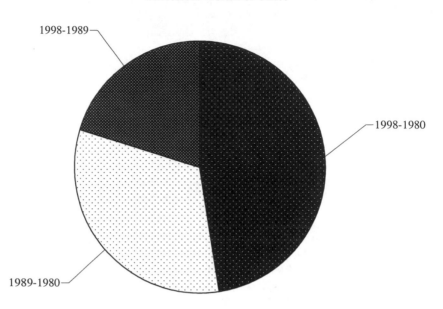

Figure 3.5
**Iranian/Shiite Attacks against Iranian Expatriates and Iranian Opposition
Organizations as well as against Other Targets (in terms of percentage)**

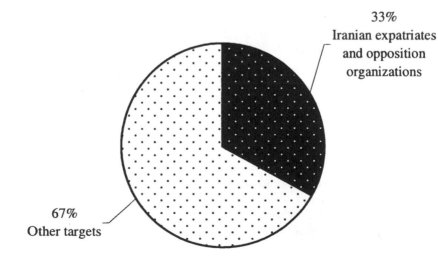

Khomeini regarded "revolutionary violence" as a central tool for the resolution of the problems plaguing Muslim society as well as a solution for the
individual's plight. The struggle concentrated primarily on the purification of
Islamic society from within, starting with the Shiite community and subsequently moving on to the wider Islamic circle. The struggle was not meant to
end in the Islamic arena, but rather was designated to destroy the "root of
evil"—the superpowers that corrupt the world. Therefore, Khomeini's revolutionary message wasis universal, and the Shiites represented the depressed on
earth.

Khomeini presented the religious/ideological and rational justifications
for the use of violence to promote the goals of Islam, and cited the Jihad and
"self sacrifice" at the ideological forefront of his philosophy. This fact gave
the Shia the reputation worldwide of being a fanatical faith that demanded
self-sacrifice of its followers. One of the prominent innovations of Khomeini's
theory was the granting of permission to sacrifice the life of the individual in
order to realize the goals of Islamic society, in contradiction to accepted Islamic law, which bans individual suicide.[8] Khomeini justified his ruling in
this matter through the use of several arguments: First of all, he maintained
that the individual lives in a corrupt society whose main role is to meet material needs. When the individual sacrifices himself, he sacrifices something
physical for a lofty spiritual goal (sacrifice of the "material me" in favor of the
"spiritual me"). Khomeini regarded the incident of the Imam Hussein's death
as the main argument justifying self-sacrifice in the service of Islam. When
Hussein set forth on his long journey from Hájaz to Carbala, according to this
interpretation he already knew that he would not return and that he would die
a horrible death; however, his sacrifice was vital for the Shiite community's
claim to Islam's crown of leadership. Hussein's death is reconstructed every
year at the Ashura rituals; however, Khomeini argued that this was insuffi-
cient, and that it was important to relive Hussein's self-sacrifice in practical
terms through daily self-sacrifice on behalf of Islam.[9]

The issue of self-sacrifice is also closely linked to the concept of Jihad.
According to Islamic religious ruling, there are two types of Jihad: defensive
and offensive. The defensive Jihad refers to the defense of Muslim territory
occupied by infidels. The goal of the offensive Jihad is to impose Islam on
parts of the world that have not yet surrendered to its control. Falling in battle
during a Jihad, including self-sacrifice in the battlefield, is a lofty command-
ment that entitles the martyr to the opening of the pearly gates before him.[10]

According to the customary concept among the Shia, only the "vanished
Imam" is permitted to declare a Jihad, and therefore until his return the duty of
Jihad does not fall upon the Shiite believers. Khomeini negated this approach
and claimed that until the return of the vanished Imam, the responsibility for
the leadership of the devout community fell upon the Mujtahid, who were also
permitted to declare a Jihad.

During the 1980s, the encouragement of self-sacrifice became a major Shiite theme both within the framework of the war in Iraq and in the framework of the struggle waged by radical Shiite organizations against Israel and Western targets in Lebanon. In 1983, Khomeini was fully aware of the considerable attraction that the war had for Iranian youth and issued a religious ruling allowing boys over the age of twelve to volunteer for the front without their parents' permission. The young volunteers became the wards of the Imam and they were promised a place in the Garden of Eden if they died on the battle-field.[11] Tens of thousands of young volunteers received a "key to the Garden of Eden" (made of plastic and manufactured in Taiwan), along with purple headbands bearing the slogan "long live Khomeini," and were then dispatched to the battlefield. The willingness to die "a martyr's death" motivated the Iranians to use special tactics during the Iran-Iraq war such as launching "human waves" opposite the enemy, breaching mine fields by dispatching young boys to run across them, and suicide attacks against fortified targets and Iraqi tanks.[12]

Prior to their departure for the battlefield most of the "volunteers" wrote wills with the help of special couriers sent to the front for this purpose. The wills were written in the form of letters addressed to the Imam or the fighters' mothers. Here is a sample of the wording:

> How worthless, how unfortunate, how ignorant I was in all of my fourteen wretched years, which passed without my knowing Allah. The Imam has opened my eyes…how sweet, sweet, sweet is death; it is like a blessing that Allah has heaped upon his dear ones.[13]

The Iranian press published the shahids' wills daily, in which they expressed their aspirations—before setting out on missions from which they would not return—to claim shelter in the shade of Allah's wings. In many of these wills death is idealized as a lofty value. Many of their titles consisted of verses from the Koran: "Do not think that the shahids are dead: they live and flourish in the shade of Allah's wings." Some bore titles taken from Islamic sources and Khomeini's writings that describe the pleasurable eternal life of the shahids in the Garden of Eden, and promise that this will be the lot of anyone who is killed in a religious war. As to the wounded, Khomenei, for example, addressed them and promised that they would not feel their amputated limbs when they reached the Garden of Eden.[14]

The Shiites in Lebanon and Suicide Attacks

The link between Iran and the Shiites in Lebanon is reflected in the adoption of Khomeini's ideology and religious rulings by the Hizballah's clerics and activists in Lebanon. The operational ties between the Lebanese Shiites and Iran were characterized by the link to spiritual authority and obedience to the Imam on the part of his "soldiers in Lebanon," which was sustained via the Hizballah's religious clerics. The latter were devoted to the interpretation of Khomeini's rulings, which were perceived as operative orders and authorization of violent activities perpetrated by the Shiites against foreigners.[15]

The question of the perpetration of suicide attacks was also examined by the circles of Shiite philosophers in Lebanon. Sheikh Fadallah, the Hizballah's spiritual leader, maintained that in the absence of the vanished Imam the mujtahid was only allowed to declare a defensive Jihad. However, he claims that the struggle being waged in Lebanon and in Palestine was a defensive Jihad whose aim was to liberate occupied Muslim territory, and therefore martyrdom as part of the struggle against the invaders was permitted according to Islamic law. The following was clarified by one of the Hizballah's eligious clerics Sheikh Hassan Trad:

> Lebanon would not be liberated without Iran's Jihad. Lebanon was liberated only through the Istishad (matyrdom) actions, and the only one who gave them his blessing was the Imam Khomeini. Fihatz Bilal, who became a symbol of the resistance, sent me a letter in which he wrote: "I am a *mukalid* (follower) of the Imam Khomeini who instructed to carry out *Istishad* and strike out at the enemy and I answered him (positively) based on the rulings of his *marjia taklid* (source of authority), the Imam Khomeini."[16]

Another religious cleric of the Hizballah, Sheikh Yosef Damush, elaborated on the link between Khomeini and the Shiite suicide attackers in Lebanon:

> The Istishad activities perpetrated by our youth were carried out at our inspiration. Several of them came to consult with me regarding the perpetration of Istishad. I explained to them that this matter requires a fatwa from the supreme authority, meaning the Imam Khowai or Khomeini, as a believer will not carry out an action without taking the principles of religious rulings into account. The martyrs Ahmad Kutsir (a Shiite suicide attacker who detonated the IDF headquarters in Tyre) and Hassan Kutsir (a Shiite suicide attacker who detonated a car bomb near an IDF patrol), perpetrated Istishad on the basis of a fatwa and there are acts of bravery that are still undisclosed and no one knows of their perpetrators."[17]

As state above, in the Lebanese arena the leaders of the Hizballah encouraged the perpetration of suicide attacks. Sheikh Tsubhi Tufeili, one of the leaders of the Hizballah in Lebanon, defined the suicide attackers as "the heroes of the Holy War" acting in the name of Islam. In August 1985, in a memorial ceremony commemorating three members of the Revolutionary Shifts killed in Lebanon, Tufeili said:

> The names of many of the heroes of the mujahidin who acted against foreign targets, including the American Embassy, are still unknown, but their actions were on behalf of Islam. We must remain loyal to their blood and instill in the consciousness of the world and history that it is Islam that will destroy Israel and America."[18]

He explained that the non-exposure of the names "of many of the heroes and fighters who detonated the American Embassy and bombed American, French, and Israeli (targets), was meant to glorify the name of Islam rather than provide personal publicity for anonymous soldiers."[19] And indeed the Hizballah did not publish the names of the terrorists who perpetrated mega attacks against the American, French, and Israeli targets. The reason for this could stem from the desire to maintain confidentiality regarding the perpetrators in order to prevent any possibility of reaching their dispatchers.[20]

Two and a half years after the bombing of the IDF headquarters in Tyre, in November 1985, the Hizballah published details regarding the identity of the Shiite suicide terrorist, Ahmad Kutsir, whom they claimed had carried out the attack.[21] The Hizballah did not provide any explanation for the exposure of the identity of the fifteen-year-old Shiite.

Ahmad Kutsir disappeared about a month before being dispatched on his final mission. He was declared missing and his family published his photograph in the Lebanese newspapers, appealing to the public to help search for him.[22] It is possible that the exceptional exposure of his identity stemmed from the Kutsir family's repeated questions regarding their son's fate. Ahmad Kutsir became a hero in Lebanon and Iran. The *Alahad* newspaper published blowups of the Shiite teenager's picture, with his image rising from the ruins of the Israeli headquarters. The Kutsir family living in Dir Kanon Alnahar, a remote village in Southern Lebanon, received a certificate of esteem from Ka'ad Ulama Al Islamiya (the commander of the Islamic nation—Khomeini).

Hizballah's religious clerics also had followers in the rival organization, Amal, including Fihatz Bilal, who in his short life also served as the bodyguard of Amal leader Nabia Beri.[23] When Fihatz came to the decision to carry out a mission from which there was no return, he knew exactly to whom to turn in order to obtain Khomeini's approval. "The letter written by Bilal Fihatz, which was signed by one of the well-known clerics (Sheikh Hassan Trad) and in which it was stated that the Imam Khomeini had given the plan his blessing, was transferred to Abu Ali (Mustafa Dirani, who served as the director of Amal's operational mechanism), who then issued the appropriate instructions to assist Bilal Fihatz in realizing his wishes."[24]

In the framework of the ruling allowing suicide attacks in principle, the Hizballah leaders established guidelines regarding the conditions under which this activity was allowed. The Shiite setting out on a suicide mission for a just cause (in the service of Islam) is no different than someone who falls in the battlefield during Jihad, and martyrdom in this case is the main weapon of the weaker party in his war against the invaders who have the advantage when it comes to strength and numbers. Khomeini also believed that Shiite martyrdom was a vital and central tool in the struggle of the depressed against their oppressors with their superior strength, and that the human advantage could compensate for the quantitative and technological superiority of the enemy.

One of the guidelines pertaining to the issue of suicide attacks requires that the attack achieve exceptional results, which can be applied as leverage for political or military changes, and inflict significant losses upon the enemy. In addition, the suicide terrorist must carry out his deed out of a sense of complete understanding and recognition regarding the value of his deed and his personal martyrdom. The use of suicide attacks against Israeli and Western targets began in Lebanon in April of 1983, and subsequently spread to Kuwait where several attacks were perpetrated against Western targets.

As a result of the withdrawal of the American and French forces from Lebanon and the deployment of the IDF in the security zone, the scope of suicide attacks decreased, although subsequent suicide attacks were occasionally perpetrated against IDF forces in the security zone of South Lebanon. The major suicide attacks perpetrated by Shiite terror entities against Western targets in Lebanon follow.[25]

November 4, 1983—A car bomb exploded at the headquarters of the IDF forces in Tyre, causing the deaths of sixty-one people (twenty-eight IDF soldiers and thirty-three Lebanese and Palestinian detainees).

From November 1983 to March 1985 the arena for Shiite terrorist attacks expanded from Lebanon to Kuwait:

Examples of Suicide Attacks against Western Targets in Lebanon and Kuwait

Suicide attack against the U.S. Embassy in Lebanon. The Hizballah perpetrated its first suicide attack on April 18, 1983. A van loaded with about 400 kilograms of explosives and driven by a suicide terrorist exploded near the structure of the U.S. Embassy in Beirut. As a result of the explosion, part of the building collapsed, leaving sixty-three dead and 120 wounded, including most of the employees at the embassy and at the branch of the CIA in Lebanon. The Islamic Jihad organization (a cover name for Pro-Iranian radical Shiite entities— the Hizballah) claimed responsibility for the attack (subsequently the Hizballah continued to use this name in order to claim responsibility for attacks).[26]

Suicide attack against the U.S. Marines headquarters in Beirut.[27] On the morning of October 23, 1983, a Mercedes truck loaded with explosives and driven by a suicide terrorist exploded near the building housing the Marines headquarters at the Beirut airport. The truck rammed through the gate and exploded in the courtyard near the headquarters. The four-story building, which served as both the headquarters and barracks for the Marines, collapsed as a result of the explosion. Two hundred and forty-one people were killed and eighty were injured, most of which were U.S. Marines serving in the multinational force in Lebanon.[28] This terror attack took the heaviest toll on the United States prior to the attacks of September 11, 2001. To quote the commander of the U.S. Marines Corp General Kelly: "It was the largest terrorist act in United States history.... When 220 Marines died on October 23, 1983, the day became the Corp's bloodiest since February 1945, when Marines fought to secure Iwo Jima. October 23, 1983 surpasses even the Corp's bloodiest days during the Vietnam and Korean Wars."[29]

Suicide attack against the U.S. Embassy in Kuwait. From November 1983 to March 1985 the arena for Shiite terrorist attacks expanded from Lebanon to Kuwait. On December 12, 1983, a truck bomb driven by a suicide terrorist exploded near the U.S. Embassy in Kuwait. The suicide bomber and four Kuwaiti citizens were killed in the blast. This attack was part of a series of attacks directed partially against Western targets in Kuwait including the French Embassy, the control tower at the international airport, a residential building that housed employees of the U.S. company, Riton and refineries. A total of six people were killed and some eighty were injured in the entire wave of attacks.

The Shiite al Dawa organization was responsible for the attacks, apparently with Iran's bidding and blessings. Following the attacks, the Kuwaiti authorities arrested seventeen members of the al Dawa organization, including a cousin of Imad Muraniya—head of Hizballah's "Special Intelligence Agency" in Lebanon. The demand for the release of the al Dawa detainees became a regular condition in hostage situations initiated by the Hizballah in Lebanon. The seventeen detainees were released by Iraq when it invaded Kuwait in August of 1990.

Suicide attacks perpetrated by the Hizballah against Israeli targets. The first suicide attack perpetrated by the Hizballah against an Israeli target was on November 4, 1983, when a car bomb driven by a suicide terrorist exploded near the IDF headquarters in Tyre, causing the deaths of sixty-one people (twenty-eight IDF soldiers and thirty-three Lebanese and Palestinian detainees). The Islamic Jihad claimed responsibility for the attack, which shared the same characteristics as suicide attacks perpetrated by the Hizballah against "foreign" targets in Lebanon in the months of April and October 1983.

Following the IDF's tightening of security measures surrounding its headquarters in Lebanon, the Hizballah moved its suicide attacks to the roads. On June 16, 1984, a car bomb driven by a suicide terrorist exploded near an IDF convoy south of the Zaharani. Five soldiers were injured in the attack. In the first months of 1985 the Hizballah carried out three similar attacks using the same method:

- February 5, 1985—The explosion of a car bomb near an IDF convoy at al-Burge al-Shimali caused injuries to ten soldiers;
- March 10, 1985—The explosion of a car bomb at the Egel Gate near Metullah caused the deaths of twelve soldiers. An additional fifteen were injured.
- March 12, 1985—The explosion of a car bomb near Ras al-Ayin resulted in no casualties.

At the inspiration of the Hizballah, secular terror organizations in Lebanon began leveling suicide attacks against the IDF in March 1985. These terror organizations displaced the Hizballah as "leaders" in this area through the perpetration of their own attacks during the years 1985-1987 (see specifics below). Beginning in 1985 there was a decline in the number of suicide attacks perpetrated by the Hizballah, with an average of one to two attacks per year. However, between the years 1983 and 2000, the Hizballah definitely perpetrated thirteen suicide attacks, although it would appear that the number of attacks that it carried out in reality was greater because during that period fourteen unclaimed attacks took place, and it is probable that the majority of them were perpetrated by this organization.

The Hizballah focused its suicide attacks against IDF targets, while the secular terror organizations in Lebanon concentrated on the South Lebanon Army (SLA). It appears that this preference stemmed from the need for a religious ruling regarding the perpetration of suicide attacks. This ruling was granted for attacks against IDF targets, but it is doubtful if it was also valid vis-à-vis the South Lebanon Army. Moreover, the organization viewed the IDF as the main enemy, and for skirmishes with this entity it was justified to carry out the kind of attacks involving suicide.

Most of the Hizballah's suicide attacks were perpetrated via a suicide attacker driving a car bomb. As far as can be discerned, there were only two incidents in which the organization attempted to carry out suicide attacks using belt bombs, on August 22 1987 and on August 3, 1992.

With the exception of the 1983 attack against the IDF headquarters in Tyre, all of the attacks were directed against IDF convoys.

During the time that the IDF was stationed in Lebanon, Israeli forces created methods of action and drills to defend against the suicide attacks that came in the form of car bombs driven by a suicide terrorist, which significantly reduced the damage caused. As a result, the Hizballah preferred to adopt different modi operandi, which it found to be sufficiently effective, without resorting to intensive activity in the framework of suicide attacks.

The Hizballah organization acted against Israeli targets, using suicide attacks outside of the Lebanese arena as well. In March 1992, the organization carried out a suicide attack using a car bomb that exploded near the Israeli Embassy in Buenos Aires. Twenty-nine people were killed and 250 were injured. The attack was carried out to avenge the termination of the organization's secretary-general, Abas Musawi, in a raid by IDF attack helicopters. Two years later, the organization carried out another suicide attack in Argentina, this time against the Jewish community's building (AMIA) in Buenos Aires. This attack came in retaliation for a raid by the IDF Air Force against the Hizballah camp in Ein Dardara, which resulted in multiple casualties for the organization.

Hizballah has served as a source of inspiration and instruction for the perpetration of suicide attacks by secular Lebanese organizations, as well as for

Palestinian organizations like the Palestinian Islamic Jihad and the Hamas or the al Dawa organization in Kuwait. Although the Hizballah has carried out a relatively small number of suicide attacks since the 1990s, suicide attacks still remain its threatening "business card."

Iran and the Hizballah supported the Palestinians during the years of the Intifada (1987-1993). However, after the signing of the Oslo Agreements, Iran and the Hizballah positioned themselves at the head of the camp opposing peace and focused their support on Islamic terror organizations—the Hamas and the Palestinian Islamic Jihad—which began to perpetrate suicide attacks (adopting the Hizballah's model) with the aim of torpedoing the peace process between the Palestinians and Israel.

Several examples follow, highlighting Iranian and Hizballah positions in this connection. The Iranian Ayatollah Osama Fadel Lankrani made the following statement in a newspaper interview:

> The Zionists' aggression and oppression express their worldview which seeks to expand the rule of Zionism on to Muslim lands from the Nile to the Euphrates. It is the duty of Muslims in the occupied territories in Palestine and Lebanon and of every Muslim to fight a Holy War (Jihad) in any way possible without any restriction on the means that they use.[30]

In an interview with the Al-Manar[31] television station, Hassan Nasrallah, secretary-general of the Hizballah, stated that if it was the desire of the Palestinians to promote awareness of their problem in world public opinion, the proper way to do so was through suicide attacks that would make bodies of men and women roll in the streets of Tel Aviv and Jerusalem. When asked why the Hizballah refrained from carrying out more suicide attacks, he explained that these activities should be perpetrated only when the goal could not be achieved in other ways.

On September 5, 1997, after a Palestinian suicide attack in Jerusalem, Hassan Nasrallah said on Radio Nur:

> Greetings to the martyrs who carried out the suicide attack yesterday in the heart of conquered Jerusalem, a mission which shocked the enemy and awakened the "devils" in the world. The mission proved the power of our nation yet again, its determination and desire to continue in its struggle and inflict upon the enemy repeated defeats.[32]

Suicide Attacks Perpetrated by the Hizballah against Israeli Targets in Lebanon

Suicide attack against the IDF headquarters in Tyre. On November 4, 1983, a car bomb exploded at the IDF headquarters in Tyre. The car, a Chevrolet, which was driven by a suicide terrorist, was loaded with some 500 kilograms of explosives. The driver rammed through the barrier at the entrance and despite the shooting in his direction managed to come within five meters of the structure. At that point he detonated the bomb. The powerful blast completely demolished one of the buildings and another was partially destroyed. Twenty-eight members of the security forces were killed in this incident and thirty-one were injured. In addition, thirty-three local residents, who were being detained in the building, were also killed.

Suicide attack against an IDF convoy in Lebanon. On March 10, 1985, a suicide attack was perpetrated through the use of a GMC van loaded with some 100 kilograms of explosives. The latter was activated against an IDF convoy only a few hundred meters away from the border control north of Metullah (the Egel gate). Twelve IDF soldiers were killed and another fifteen were injured. This suicide attack claimed the highest toll of fatalities among IDF soldiers in Lebanon. The Hizballah claimed responsibility for the attack under the alias of "the Islamic Opposition."

Suicide attack against an IDF convoy in Lebanon. On October 19, 1988, a suicide attack was carried out using a Toyota pickup truck loaded with some 250 kilograms of explosives against an IDF convoy at the border control in Metullah. Eight soldiers were killed and seven more were wounded. Again, the Hizballah claimed responsibility for the attack under the alias of the Islamic Opposition.

Suicide attack against an IDF convoy in Lebanon. On December 30, 1999, a suicide attack was perpetrated by a car bomb against an IDF convoy making its way from the headquarters of its communications unit in Marj Ayoun (located in the eastern sector) to Fatma gate. As a result of the explosion one IDF soldier and eleven Lebanese citizens were injured, in addition to the driver of the car. Alongside the car a hunting rifle, a cellular phone, a forged identity card, and a copy of the Koran were found. The Hizballah publicly claimed responsibility for the incident, stating that it was perpetrated in commemoration of "Iranian Jerusalem Day" (which fell on December 31 that year), marking the anniversary of the death of the Imam Ali, founder of the Shia (which falls on December 28), as well as "Al-Qader" eve (which falls on the night between January 2-3). This was the first suicide attack carried out by the Hizballah since April 1995 and the last suicide attack before the IDF withdrawal from Lebanon in May 2000.

Suicide Attacks Perpetrated by the Hizballah in Buenos Aires, Argentina

In the beginning of the 1990s, the Hizballah, with Iranian assistance, perpetrated two suicide attacks in Buenos Aires against Israeli and Jewish targets.

- On March 17, 1992, a suicide attack was perpetrated against the Israeli Embassy in Buenos Aires.

• On July 18, 1994, a suicide attack was perpetrated against the Jewish cultural center (AMIA) in Buenos Aires.

Attack against the Israeli Embassy in Buenos Aires. On March 17, 1992, a few minutes after 3 p.m., a powerful explosion shook the Norte Quarter of Buenos Aires; a car bomb was detonated in front of the Israeli Embassy, demolishing the six-story building. Twenty-nine people were killed including four Israelis and five Jews, all embassy employees. Two hundred and twenty-four individuals were wounded, including eight Israelis. The Argentinean government immediately launched an investigation of the incident and the Israeli government dispatched a special team to investigate how the attack had occurred and who bore responsibility for it.

The Islamic Jihad Organization (Hizballah had used this alias to claim responsibility for attacks in the past) claimed responsibility immediately after the attack. However, out of fear of Israeli and international reprisals, the organization retracted its original announcement (on March 19), but subsequently reassumed responsibility for the attack (on March 23).[33] The attack, which was apparently carried out by the Hizballah with Iranian assistance, was launched in retaliation for the termination of Abas Musawi, secretary-general of the Hizballah, by Israeli attack helicopters.[34]

In response to the attack, Syrian President Hafez al Assad announced that his country had no connection to the incident. In contrast, the chairman of the Iranian Parliament announced at a reception in honor of the new leader of the Hizballah, Sheikh Hassan Nasrallah, that Israel would be dealt ongoing blows of revenge in various areas of the world.

The investigation of the Argentinean authorities indicated that Imad Muraniya, chief member of the Hizballah's attack mechanism, stood behind the attack. He had availed himself of the assistance of Iranian intelligence entities in Argentina in order to obtain the required weapons and explosives, as well as papers for the assailants.[35] Argentinean authorities disclosed that they had succeeded in proving that the truck that served as the attack vehicle had been purchased by a Brazilian citizen named Ruberio de Luz, who was suspected of having links with the entities that perpetrated the attack in Argentina via the tri-border (Argentina, Brazil, and Paraguay).[36]

In September 1999 (seven years after the attack), the Argentinean courts issued a warrant for the arrest of Imad Muraniya for suspicion of involvement in the attack. In an announcement published in Beirut, Hizballah denied Argentina's accusations and stated, "the accusation lacks any legal basis; it merely reflects political incitement and is not based on independent judgment. The fact that the judgment is based on information provided by the CIA, whose goals are known in advance, constitutes additional proof regarding the accusation's political nature." Hizballah appealed to the Argentinean government "not to become a victim of the American-Zionist conspiracies."[37]

Attack against the Jewish cultural center (AMIA) in Buenos Aires, Argentina. On July 18, 1994, at about 7:00 a.m., a car bomb exploded near a seven-story building that served as the cultural center of the Jewish community in Buenos Aires, resulting in the structure's collapse. There were ninety-seven fatalities and 230 injuries, most of which were Jewish Argentineans. The "Islamic Commando—Hizballah Argentina" claimed responsibility for the attack.[38]

Already during the start of the investigation launched by Argentinean security entities it became clear that the cultural attaché of the Iranian Embassy, Muhsein Rabani, had been involved in the attack. He had gathered intelligence for the operation and purchased the car that served as the attack vehicle.[39] The investigation also revealed that four retired Argentinean policemen were involved, and had helped the Shiite and Iranian attackers to realize their intent. A short time after the attack, the Argentinean attorney general issued warrants for the arrest of four Iranian diplomats, including Rabani, who had already left the country and never returned. Against the background of Argentina's accusations that Iranian entities had been involved in the attack, both countries recalled their ambassadors and the diplomatic ties between the two countries were reduced to the level of economic attachés.

In 2002, the Argentina Intelligence Service (SIDE) completed a comprehensive report about the attack at the AMIA building.[40] According to the report, the decision in principle to perpetrate another attack in Argentina was made in August 1993, about a year before the attack, at a meeting of Iran's National Security Council. The meeting was attended by the Iranian leader Ali Khamenei, the president at that time Rafsanjani, the erstwhile Foreign Minister Valyati, the person responsible for intelligence and security issues in the office of the Iranian leader Muhammad Hijazi, and the Intelligence Minister Ali Fallahian.

It appears that the decision was based on various considerations including the success of the bombing of the Israeli Embassy in Buenos Aires (in March 1992), the deterioration in relations between Argentina and Iran at that time, and the operational possibilities that were available to Iran and the Hizballah in Argentina. The decision was handed over to Fallahian in the form of a fatwa issued by the leader Khomenei.

The implementation of the attack and the preparation of a "target portfolio" about the AMIA building were placed in the hands of Intelligence Minister Ali Fallahian. He decided that the Hizballah's Special Security Agency headed by Imad Muraniya would carry out the attack as a "contractor" in the service of the Iranians, just as it had perpetrated the attack on the Israeli Embassy in Buenos Aires.

The actual date of the attack was set on the basis of a status evaluation stemming from developments. It appears that the main reason for actually carrying out the attack on the AMIA building was Iran's desire to even the score with Argentina for the chilling of relations between the two countries and for Argentina's decision to break off cooperation agreements with Iran. It is also possible that Iran viewed Israel and Jewish entities in Argentina as those responsible for the negative trend that had developed in relations between Iran and Argentina at that particular time. In addition, the kidnapping of Mustafa Dirani from Lebanon to Israel (on May 21, 1994) and the Israeli attack on the Hizballah training camp at Ein Dardara in Eastern Lebanon (June 2, 1994), were perceived as detrimental to Iranian interests.

Based on the traditional policy dictating the obliteration of any traces of evidence that might lead to Iran's involvement in terror, Iran chose to execute the attack through a Lebanese "implementation contractor" with a worldwide infrastructure and proven operational capabilities—the Hizballah.

The Hizballah had a notable advantage when approaching the Argentinean arena: It availed itself of a network of collaborators made up of expatriate Lebanese who were living in Argentina, particularly community members residing in the "tri-border" area of Argentina, Brazil, and Paraguay, as well as those concentrated in the Floresta neighborhood in Buenos Aires. A small and compartmentalized group of expatriates provided practical assistance in promoting logistic aspects related to the attack.

In this connection it is important to note that in recent years several similar networks of "overseas attack mechanisms" belonging to the Hizballah have been discovered in various global arenas, including Southeast Asia and the Middle East. Thus, this modus operandi appears to be a favored Hizballah method, which is utilized to this very day.

The network of Hizballah collaborators in Argentina was built and tended diligently by the Iranian Embassy in Argentina from the 1980s onwards. Originally, this activity was designated to expand the circle of those supporting the Islamic revolutionary principles in any Muslim community regardless of its location, particularly among the Shiite communities in the world. In practice—and there is ample evidence to this effect in many states worldwide—these networks of collaborators were also exploited for the establishment of dormant terror cells, which could provide assistance in the perpetration of attacks such as those carried out in Argentina.

All of the relevant authorities in the Iranian regime assisted in the AMIA attack. The Iranian Foreign Ministry provided the diplomatic camouflage and the official representations to facilitate the activities, and in actual fact served as a branch of the Iranian Intelligence Ministry. Specifically, close to the date of the attack at the AMIA building (noted after the fact) there appeared to have been a sharp rise in the number of visits of Iranian diplomatic couriers in Argentina. This phenomenon raises the suspicion that those couriers transferred equipment needed for the attack or acted as agents of the Iranian Intelligence Ministry (for example, some of them stayed in Argentina for far longer periods than is customary for diplomatic couriers). Alternatively, it is possible that this activity was meant to disguise the specific operational activity related to preparations for the attack, in which the Hizballah was involved during that entire period.

The Iranian Islamic Guidance Ministry, which acts to cultivate ties with Muslim communities abroad, served as a camouflage for activities of the Iranian Intelligence Ministry, and independently promoted the establishment of an attack infrastructure. In the Argentinean case, its activities were particularly conspicuous because the central axis for the preparation of the local attack infrastructure was the activity of Muhsein Rabani, a representative of this office in Buenos Aires.

Following the decision to prepare the attack in August 1993, all of the relevant entities in Iran and in the Hizballah were asked to promote it; the gathering of intelligence about the target was accelerated, its various operational aspects were examined, a political activity plan was prepared to take advantage of the attack and exercise damage control, and the advance logistical preparations were launched.

Already at the end of 1993, Muhsein Rabani, who was serving at that time in Argentina, explored the possibility of acquiring a Renault Traffic van, which subsequently did in fact serve as the attack vehicle. During that same period Rabani traveled to Iran several times, and when he returned in March 1994 he remained there until the attack.

It would appear that in the summer of 1994 the operational preparations had reached an advanced level. Following an additional status evaluation by Iran and the Hizballah it was decided to activate the plan, and after a final period of preparations, about six weeks, it was indeed executed. During the months of May and June, Hizballah leaders came out with statements about the organization's "long arm" throughout the world, which can be regarded as propaganda-related "groundwork" prior to the attack.

In June 1994 and during the days prior to the attack (after the fact), it was possible to detect several "preliminary signs," which indicated a change in the routine of the entities involved in the preparations. For example, the director of the Iranian Intelligence branch in Buenos Aires left Argentina, and the Iranian ambassadors in Chile and Uruguay were absent from their assigned countries when the attack took place.

Several days before the attack, the suicide attacker arrived in Argentina; he was a member of the Hizballah in Lebanon, named Ibrahim Hussein Bierou. He arrived in Argentina via the "tri-border," accompanied by one of the Hizballah collaborators in the region. It appears that at the same time preparations of the car bomb were being completed somewhere in Buenos Aires. It is known that the vehicle was parked in a public parking facility not far from the AMIA building some three days beforehand. In the days preceding the attack an extensive number of telephone calls between Iranian and Hizballah entities and Hizballah collaborators was recorded between Argentina, Lebanon, and Iran.

On July 18, 1994, several hours before the attack, the suicide terrorist called his family in Lebanon and told them "he was going to commit suicide with his brother," (his brother had been killed in a car bomb attack against IDF forces in Lebanon in August 1989). On the same day, Beru drove the Renault Traffic loaded with hundreds of kilograms of explosives into the entrance of the AMIA building and detonated it.

On September 9, 1994, the Hizballah announced the death of one of its men in action in South Lebanon (on Lebanese Radio Nur, which was under its control). The man's name was reported as Ibrahim Hussein Bierou. The organization apparently chose to announce his demise in this fashion two months later, without any connection to the attack upon the AMIA building.

The Argentinean press reported that the country would ask Interpol to issue arrest warrants for the secretary-general of the Hizballah Hassan Nasrallah, Imad Muraniya, and several Iranian diplomats for their involvement in the attack on the Jewish community building. Jose Galiano, the federal judge in Argentina who was appointed to the case, was quoted in the Saudi international daily *Al-Sharq al-Awsat* as saying that Argentina was requesting the extradition of the Hizballah leaders. Argentinean security authorities were quoted in the local press as saying that the investigation had been conducted in cooperation with the American intelligence agency, the CIA.

In Beirut, the Hizballah responded to these announcements and a source in the organization stated that the Hizballah "does not have branches outside of Lebanon." In the course of 2002, the Shiite organization was forced to deny several times that its activity had a "global dimension." Advocate Marta Narchalas, who represents the Jewish communities, stated "for the first time there are legal cases which contain evidence regarding the links of senior officials in the Iranian government and in the Hizballah, and their involvement in the preparation of the assault."

It is to be noted that to date no one has been arrested as a suspect in this affair despite the prolonged investigation. Based on a key witness report, in July 2000, the *New York Times* published an article stating that Iran had paid former Argentinean President Carlos Menem $10 million in bribes so that he would cover for that country and eliminate any suspicion regarding its involvement in the attack. Menem denied the accusations and announced that he would sue the newspaper for slander. It is noteworthy that immediately following the attack, Menem's government accused the Hizballah and Muslim radicals acting under Iran's sponsorship of being responsible for the attack. This accusation lost steam because of the snail's pace of the investigation, which was impaired by the disappearance of witnesses and unexplained delays and obstacles placed in its way.

The Policy of the Hizballah and Iran vis-à-vis the Issue of Suicide Attacks after the IDF's Withdrawal from Lebanon

In May 2000, the IDF withdrew from Lebanon and redeployed along the line of the international border with Lebanon according to UN resolution 425. The Hizballah claimed credit for the IDF's withdrawal from Lebanon, but declared that this move did not signify the end of the struggle against the State of Israel, as it argued that the latter was still occupying Lebanese land at the "Shab'a." The organization also declared its commitment to assist the Palestinian struggle against the Israeli occupation. Since May 2000, the Hizballah has continued perpetrating attacks against Israel, mainly in the "Shab'a Farm" sector (Har Dov area), but to date no actions have taken the form of a suicide attack.

Although, as stated above, the Hizballah decreased the perpetration of suicide attacks even during the IDF deployment in Lebanon, it still serves as a source of inspiration for Palestinian suicide attacks and encourages them to continue employing this method in the framework of the Al Aksa Intifada. Iran, the Hizballah's patron, also aligned itself alongside the Palestinian Intifada and its leaders provide the Palestinians with military aid (such as the shipment of weaponry aboard the ship *Karin A*), as well as political and moral support. Iranian religious clerics, and its leader Ali Khamenei, grant religious legitimization and encourage the Palestinians to continue carrying out suicide attacks against Israel. Following are several examples of speeches delivered by Hizballah and Iranian leaders encouraging the Palestinians to conduct suicide attacks.

SPEECH DELIVERED BY THE SECRETARY-GENERAL OF THE HIZBALLAH HASSAN NASRALLAH ON JERUSALEM DAY (AL-MANAR TELEVISION—DECEMBER 14, 2001)

Brothers and sisters, children of our nation, in view of the reverberating declarations of the American administration you have no other choice. Do you still have any illusions that by appealing to this great devil you will be able to restore a piece of land or honor? It has been decreed upon us, and this is not only within the bounds of an option, to struggle, to stand firm and hold fast to our rights and weapons. In Palestine the opposition will continue with suicide attacks (in the original: *al-Amaliat al-Istishadia*, meaning sacrificing one's life in martyrdom for the name of Allah—S.S.), and the qualitative actions, and despite the many martyrs it is the only way to defeat these Zionists. Our brothers in Palestine, know that your actions have shaken the enemy from within and it is embroiled in an existential crisis. If these actions were for nothing, without value or benefit then why is there all this anger directed against you by the United States and Europe, and why is there this rage in the Zionist society against you? This rage, this anger, and the concentration of the forces of arrogance constitute proof that your actions are striking at the heart and are laying the foundations for the victory that will not fail to come. What is required is to stand firmly and persevere. We must not make a mistake. On the last Friday of the Ramadan month I say to you: Do not listen to all of these people who tell you that you must not perpetrate suicide attacks. Do not listen to all of those who speak of "civilians and soldiers" in Israel.

The suicide attacks are the shortest way to Allah, may He be exalted and praised. They are the most lofty and wondrous expressions of martyrdom in the name of Allah. It is the weapon that Allah placed in the hands of this nation and which no one can take away from us. They can take away our cannon or a tank or an airplane, but they cannot take away from us the spirit that yearns for Allah or our determination to sacrifice life in the name of Allah. As for the Zionist society, and I know that the words I am going to say to you cost a high price, I tell you with all legitimate, moral and "Jihad" responsibility that there are no civilians there. They are all conquerors, all are land stealers, and all are accomplices to the crime and the butchery. Therefore, we must continue on this road without any hesitation or illusion. As for Israel, it is the will of Allah and His promise, and the will of the believers, the Jihad fighters and suicide attackers (in the original *Istashadin*—S.S), that it will not have any existence and there will be no memory of it among us and among yourselves. Allah will pass judgment between you and us. Peace be with you, as well as Allah's compassion and blessings.[41]

SPEECH DELIVERED BY THE SPIRITUAL LEADER OF IRAN (MAY 1, 2002)

In a speech delivered on May 1, 2002, the spiritual leader of Iran, the Ayatollah Ali Khamenei addressed the Israeli-Palestinian conflict, among other issues, and defined the acts that Israel committed in Gaza and the areas of Judea and Samaria of the Palestinian Authority as occupation, oppression, and crimes against humanity, and justified the martyrdom of the Palestinians as the just and legitimate choice in their struggle against Israel.

...In response to the terrible oppression currently afflicting the Palestinian people there are two solutions. These solutions must be acceptable to everyone. The first solution is to continue with the Intifada. The people in Palestine must continue their opposition, praise to Allah, just as they have persevered with it until now. The climax of this opposition can be seen in the martyrdom seeking operations. Self-martyrdom is the pinnacle and symbol of human dignity: The youth, the boy and girl, who are willing to sacrifice their lives while serving the interests of their country and religion.

This is the supreme expression of bravery and courage, and it is this which casts fear upon the enemy. Therefore, we see that everyone, starting with the President of the United States and down to the last of his officials, have been trying to put an end to the acts of martyrdom and condemn their perpetrators.

Are these not acts of martyrdom when an army demands of its soldiers to sacrifice everything dear to them for the protection of the homeland? Are these not deeds of martyrdom when an enemy invades another country and its inhabitants oppose the conquering army? In such cases, who can condemn acts of martyrdom? Who can criticize these deeds and these values that are being conducted from the depth of their consciousness and awareness as human beings? The martyrdom of the Palestinians is the crowning glory of their struggle. This is the truth, even if there are those who deny fifty years of Palestinian suffering and struggle, and today they are left with no other choice but to sacrifice their blood in order to achieve their rights. The Palestinian people lives and is marching forward and this is the first solution.[42]

Attacks against Aviation

Since 1968, attacks against international civil air transportation have become important in the view of the various terrorist organizations. Civil aviation constitutes a preferred target for terror attacks for several reasons: The main motive apparently lies in the fact that almost every attack against a civil aviation target attracts international attention, because most of these types of attacks involve victims from various nationalities—this factor intensifies the media interest and makes the response to the terrorists even more complex. Another reason is the relatively high level of vulnerability related to aviation targets and the high number of victims when this type of attack is successful. In addition, the attractiveness of civil aviation also lies in the fact that national carriers represent their countries; thus any strike against them is identified as a blow to the state that they serve. And finally, airlines represent an easy target for the gathering of intelligence because their inherent role is to provide a service to the public, including precise information regarding flight times, routes, boarding procedures, etc.

The terror activities directed at civil aviation focus on three main targets: airplanes, airline offices, and airports. From the 260 terror attacks perpetrated during the years 1983-1989 by Shiite/Iranian entities, twenty-four were directed against civil aviation targets (i.e., almost 9.2 percent).

Hijackings were the method of attack most preferred by the Shiite/Iranian terror entities: 42 percent of all the attacks against civil aviation were carried out in this manner (ten hijackings). The main victims of hijackings by Hizballah activists and additional pro-Iranian Shiite entities were France (three hijacked airplanes) and Kuwait (two hijacked airplanes). This type of attack generally did not claim a high toll of victims from among the hijacked passengers, but it did receive considerable media attention and sometimes caused international crises.

This method, much like the kidnapping of hostages, enables the hijackers to achieve maximum results vis-à-vis the "victim" (the country whose aircraft was hijacked) through bargaining and negotiation processes. In addition, the hijackers have the ability to plan the arena and date of the incident, as well as to apply pressure and issue threats in order to achieve their demands, while the victim is forced to make his decision under public pressure and within a deadline. Indeed, some of the hijackings ended in the surrender of the terror victims to the demands of the hijackers.

In many cases it was possible for the terror "patron"—Iran—to fulfill the role of "mediator" between the victim and the hijackers. This position was optimal from Iran's point of view: On the one hand, it could channel the negotiation process towards the achievement of the hijacking goals (in many cases these goals were defined according to Iranian demands and needs); on the other hand, not only was Iran not exposed to the terror victim's condemnation or retaliation, but instead it received gratitude for its "assistance" in resolving crises.

The following examples of airplane hijackings shed light on the various motives at the root of these incidents, on Iran's significant involvement in most of the hijackings, and on the high level of their effectiveness:

June 24, 1983	*Greece*—A Romanian aircraft chartered by Libya was hijacked during a flight from Greece to Libya. The two hijackers, both Amal members, forced the airplane to land in Cyprus and demanded the release of Imam Mousa al Sader from Libya (see elaboration regarding al Sader in chapter two, under the heading "Iranian Terror by Proxy"). Ultimately, the hijackers turned themselves in and the aircraft was released.
August 26, 1983	*Austria*—An Air France airplane was hijacked after taking off from Austria. Its hijackers, apparently Hizballah members, demanded the release of Lebanese detainees being held in France and that military aid to Chad, Iraq, and Lebanon be stopped.
July 31, 1984	*Germany*—An Air France airplane was hijacked after takeoff from Frankfurt en route to France. The plane was forced to land in Iran, where it was detonated by its hi jackers. "The Islamic Organization for the Release of Jerusalem" claimed responsibility for the attack.
December 4, 1984	*Kuwait*—A Kuwaiti plane was hijacked on a flight from Dubai to Pakistan and was forced to land in Teheran. During the hijacking two American passengers were killed. Iranian authorities took over the airplane and rescued the hostages (the hijackers did not offer any resistance).
June 17, 1985	*Greece*—A TWA passenger plane on flight from Athens to Rome was hijacked by four Shiite Lebanese terrorists from the Islamic Jihad organization (a cover name for Hizballah). The hijackers were led by Imad Muraniya, who was also an accomplice in the attacks on the U.S. Embassy and Marines headquarters in Beirut in 1983. The hijackers belonged to a unit that called itself the "Sader Brigades," after the Imam Mousa al Sader. The hijacked airplane was carrying 153 passengers and crewmembers (mostly Americans). On June 18, 1985, the

hijackers released most of the passengers and crewmembers but continued to hold thirty-six passengers and thirteen crewmembers as hostages. The hijackers demanded the release of several hundred Shiites imprisoned in Israel in exchange for the release of the hostages. Israel refused to submit to the hijackers' demands, and the United States did not apply pressure on the former to cave in to the demands.

In order to prove their determination, the hijackers murdered an American passenger (a U.S. army serviceman) and threw his body out on the runway.

The hijacking of the airplane put President Reagan's declarations regarding his resolve not to yield to terror to the test. Therefore, the Americans began to plan a rescue operation to extricate the hostages. The counter-terror "Delta" force was flown to Europe, and the aircraft carrier *Nimitz* was moved forward to the Lebanese coast. Due to the hijackers' fears of a military operation, the hostages were placed in various houses in western Beirut and in the city's suburbs, which were under the control of the Shiite organizations, thereby thwarting any extrication attempt. It was clear to Iran, Syria, and the Hizballah that any harm to the hostages would elicit a harsh American response; therefore, they initiated contact in order to bring the affair to an end. On June 24, 1985, in the throes of the crisis, the chairman of the Iranian Parliament Hashemi Rafsanjani arrived in Damascus and launched mediation efforts in order to resolve the crisis. In a press conference held in Damascus he claimed that his country was not involved in the hijacking and "if we had known the identity of the hijackers, we would have thwarted the hijacking."

On June 25, 1985, Syrian President Assad proposed a for mula that enabled the resolution of the crisis. Assad promised a safe haven to the hijackers and obtained an Israeli commitment to release the Shiite prisoners at a subsequent date, so that it would not appear that the United States and Israel had capitulated to the hijackers' demands. After the United States and Israel had agreed to the proposal, Iran instructed the Hizballah to release the hostages. On June 29, 1985, the hostages were transferred by bus from Beirut to Damascus, and from there they were flown on a special flight to Europe. On July 3, 1985, Israel released 300 Shiite terrorists, thus fulfilling its promise to the United States.

July 24, 1987   *Switzerland*—An Air Afric plane, which was en route from Congo to Paris, was hijacked to Geneva. The hijacker, a Hizballah member named Ali Muhammad Hariri, demanded the release of Muhammad Ali Himadi from Germany, the release of all Shiite terrorists arrested in France since 1986, including the terrorist George Ibrahim Abdallah, and the release of all Arab detainees in Israel. During the hijacking a French passenger was killed, but the hijacking was brought to an end when the crew succeeded in disarming the hijacker.

An unknown organization claimed responsibility in Beirut, and threatened to strike out at Swiss targets if the hijacker was not released. The organization also threatened to execute French and American hostages if the French authorities did not remove their siege from the Iranian Embassy in Paris (a siege imposed due to the exposure of Shiite terror cells and the escape of Iranian terrorist Gorgi to his country's embassy in Paris). The demands made by the organization and the hijacker attest to the involvement of the Hizballah, and possibly Iran as well, in the hijacking.

April 1988   *Kuwait*—A Boeing 747 of the Kuwaiti airline, which was en route from Thailand to Kuwait with 112 passengers on board, was hijacked and forced to land in Mashad, Iran. The hijackers, members of the Hizballah, demanded the release of seventeen terrorists, members of the organization, who had been arrested in Kuwait in 1983.

The person responsible for the hijacking was Imad Muraniya, who had also been involved in many kidnappings of hostages in Beirut, apparently with the encouragement of radical elements in Iran that sought to strain the relations with Kuwait and the West due to the imminent elections for the Iranian parliament.

After three days in Mashad, in the course of which fifty-seven passengers were released, the airplane took off for Larnaca (Cyprus). On April 9, the hijackers executed a Kuwaiti citizen after their demand to refuel the plane was denied. Subsequently one passenger was released as a gesture of goodwill, but at this stage the Kuwaiti government refused to give in to any of the hijackers' demands.

The Cyprus government promised the hijackers unrestricted departure from the country if the passengers were
released, while the chairman of the Iranian Parliament
Rafsanjani promised the hijackers a safe haven in Iran in
exchange for releasing the passengers. After the
execution of another hostage the Cypriots agreed to re
fuel the plane, and following the release of twelve
additional hostages the hijacked plane took off for
Algeria. That is where the hijacking finally came to
an end, but only after another eight days during which
protracted negotiations were held between the hijackers
and the Kuwaiti and Algerian representatives, at the end
of which the hostages and the airplane were released and
the hijackers were transferred to Lebanon.

Other attacks against civil aviation were carried out with the planting of
explosive devices, the detonating of car bombs, and the lobbing hand grenades. There were a total of eight attacks of this kind; four explosive devices,
three car bombs, and the lobbing of one grenade. The main targets were the
offices of airlines and airports. There is an essential difference between planting explosive devices in targets on land (airline offices and aviation facilities)
and planting them in airplanes. Although the first kind may cause many casualties, it is not inherently different than planting a bomb or a car bomb at any
other target on land. In contrast, the planting of a bomb on an airplane necessitates sophisticated planning and performance in order to circumvent security means, which are more exacting when related to aviation. In addition,
when an attack of this type succeeds its consequences are far more deadly.

During the years 1988-1989, two sabotage incidents occurred on airplanes
in which Shiite/Iranian involvement was suspected, although this was never
proven: The detonation on a Pan-Am flight over Lockerbie, Scotland, in December 1988, in which 270 people were killed; and an explosion on board a
UTA flight over the Sahara Desert in September 1989, in which 171 people
perished.

As noted above, attacks aboard airplanes require greater operational so-
phistication than that needed for attacks on the ground. For example, the
smuggling of explosives in such a way that they will not be discovered at the
various inspection points for equipment and passengers; the use of "duped
couriers" (a duped courier is a passenger who boards the airplane without knowing that his suitcase is carrying a bomb that is to detonate him along with the
aircraft), or "suicide attackers" who are carrying the bomb and are intended to
explode along with the passengers; or the use of sophisticated activation systems
for explosive devices through a barometer that detonates when the aircraft
reaches a certain height (like the device that detonated the Pan-Am aircraft).

An investigation of airborne attacks of this sort is particularly complex and necessitates the investment of huge resources as well as intelligence know-how and high technologies. The investigation of the explosion aboard the UTA flight is bogged down in a dead-end to this very day, but the attack aboard the Pan-Am flight was vigorously investigated by Britain and the United States, a fact which ensured that two Libyan agents were brought to trial on suspicion of involvement in the incident. A brief description of that attack follows:

December 1988   *Scotland*—A Pan-Am flight en route from London to the United States exploded in the skies over the Scottish town of Lockerbie. Two hundred and fifty-nine passengers were killed and as a result of the crash eleven town residents perished as well.

It appears that the airplane was detonated via an explosive device triggered by barometric activation. Following an intensive investigation, the United States and Britain came to the conclusion that Libya stood behind the explosion, but suspicions regarding the involvement of Iran and the Popular Front for the Liberation of Palestine—The General Headquarters, headed by Ahmed Jibril, have not been re pudiated to this day. It is noteworthy that on December 30, 1988, an organization called "The Guards of the Islamic Revolution" claimed responsibility for the incident and threatened the United States that additional American targets would be attacked if it did not banish the Shah's son from the country.

On July 7, 1997, the German prosecutor handling the interrogation of the attack declared that Germany was investigating new testimony according to which Iran was behind the attack.[43] This was an apparent reference to the testimony given by Abdul Hassan Masbakhi—a former Iranian intelligence agent who was also a key witness at the trials of the men accused of murder at the Mikonos restaurant in Berlin. According to the *Der Spiegel* news paper, Masbakhi revealed that Iran had planned the incident in retaliation for the downing of an Iranian passenger plane in July 1988 by a U.S. navy ship, and requested Libyan aid in perpetrating the attack. Masbakhi maintained that the bomb had been brought on board the aircraft at the Frankfurt airport and was detonated while the airplane was flying over Lockerbie, Scotland. Iran has tened to deny the accusations and claimed that they were part of an anti-Iranian campaign being waged in the Ger man media following the Mikonos incident.[44]

In any case, in February 2001, following an extended investigation as well as U.S.-British and international pressure on Libya, two Libyan agents suspected of involvement in the incident were brought before a Scottish court in The Hague. One was found guilty while the other was released, but either way the court's verdict points to Libya as the responsible party for the attack.

Table 3.1
A List of Attacks against Civil Aviation Perpetrated by Iranian/Shiite Entities[45]

Date	Venue	Target	Affiliation	Type of attack	Perpetrating organization
March 1982	Lebanon	Airplane	Libyan	Hijacking	Amal
June 1983	Greece	Airplane	Libyan	Hjacking	Amal
August 1983	Austria	Airplane	French	Hijacking	Shiite organization
December 1983	Kuwait	Airport	Kuwaiti	Car bomb	Shiite organization
July 1984	Germany	Airplane	French	Hijacking	Shiite organization
December 1984	Dubai	Airplane	Kuwaiti	Hijacking	Amal
February 1985	Lebanon	Airplane	Jordanian	Hijacking	Amal
June 1985	Greece	Airplane	American	Hijacking	Shiite organization
July 1985	Spain	TWA offices, British Airways offices	American and British	Sabotage	Shiite organization
July 1985	Denmark	Offices of Northwest Airlines	American	Sabotage	Shiite organization
December 1985	Cyprus	Airplane	Swiss	Hijacking attempt	Shiite organization
January 1987	Kuwait	Swissair & Pan-Am offices	Swiss	Sabotage	Shiite organization
July 1987	Kuwait	Air France offices	French	Car bomb	Shiite organization
July 1987	Switzerland	Airplane	French	Hijacking	Shiite organization
March 1988	Malaysia	Offices of the Saudi national carrier	Saudi	Sabotage	Shiite organization
April 1988	Kuwait	Airplane	Kuwaiti	Hijacking	Hizballah + al Dawa
April 1988	Pakistan	Offices of the Saudi national carrier	Saudi	Sabotage	Shiite organization
April 1988	Kuwait	Offices of the Saudi national carrier	Saudi	Sabotage	Shiite organization
May 1988	Kuwait	Offices of the Kuwaiti national carrier	Kuwaiti	Car bomb	Shiite organization
December 1988	Scotland	Pan-Am airplane	American	Sabotage	Libya; possible involvement of Jibril's Front with Iranian aid
September 1989	Niger	UTA airplane	The Central-African Republic (France)	Sabotage	Libyan organization; possible involvement of Jibril's Front with Iranian aid
November 1993	Iran	Air France offices	French	Lobbing hand grenade	Iranian organization

The Shiite terrorists activated car bombs against aviation targets only in Kuwait (three car bombs), due apparently to the existence of a massive Shiite infrastructure in this country, which enabled the preparation of the car bombs, which require technical capabilities, and offered the capability of acquiring a significant amount of explosives. On the other hand, the use of explosive devices was more widespread and was directed mainly against the offices of the Saudi national carrier (in Kuwait, Pakistan, Malaysia, among others).

As stated above, the main victims of aviation terror were France, the United States, Kuwait, and Saudia. The main arena for attacks was Kuwait (six attacks). As to the perpetrating organizations: Amal carried out four attacks—two were directed against Libya to protest the "disappearance" of the organization's leader Imam al Sader in Libya, and the remaining two were designated to release imprisoned members of the organization. The Hizballah was behind at least eighteen attacks against civil aviation, although the claiming of responsibility for these incidents was done under cover names such as "The Islamic Jihad," "The Revolutionary Justice," and others.

Assassinations

During the years 1980-1998, since the revolutionary regime rose to power in Iran, it is possible to enumerate dozens of assassinations carried out by Iranian agents or their representatives (such as the Hizballah) at Iran's bidding, and it is likely that the actual number of assassinations and terminations was even higher.[46]

In contrast to suicide attacks and hijackings, whose aim was to cause maximum damage to the target state while achieving extensive media coverage, which is important for the facilitation of Iran's goals, the area of assassinations was generally covert and was meant to take action against "pinpointed targets" that the regime sought to terminate. In these cases, Iran made significant efforts to refrain from leaving "fingerprints," and tended to blame rival opposition organizations or other countries, such as Iraq, for the incidents. However, in the case of assassinations motivated by retribution, the central element is the sponsored organization, which seeks vengeance for activities against its people, but even in these cases the activity is incorporated within overall Iranian interests.

The main targets for assassinations are Iranian expatriates, heads of hostile underground organizations, and heads of opposition organizations (such as Mujahidin Khalq, the Kurd underground, and others). The attempt to strike out at these elements constitutes a direct continuation of state terror that the regime operates within Iran's boundaries in order to suppress any sign of opposition, and is part of the regime's overall struggle against these entities, many of which are involved in activities meant to undermine the revolutionary regime (including terror activity). Therefore, it is possible to state that this activity constitutes a "boiling over" of the internal Iranian power struggle into the international arena, with Iran striving to eradicate the regime's enemies wherever they may be.

This category includes Iranian figures from the Shah's administration (the Shah's relatives, statesmen such as Shahfur Bakhtiar, and military personnel), expatriates who formerly allied themselves with Khomeini, and the heads of national movements (such as the Kurd leader Kasmelo, and Masoud Rajavi, a former leader of Mujahidin Khalq). There are at least thirty known instances of assassinations of Iranian expatriates, many of which occurred in France, due to the fact that France serves as a land of refuge for Iranian expatriates. This category includes Muslim religious clerics, whose opinions were at odds with Khomeini's philosophies, thus making them a target for elimination. Thus, for example, two Muslim religious clerics who were opposed to Khomeini's death sentence against writer Salman Rushdie were murdered in Brussels. A different type of assassination is carried out due to power struggles with hostile countries. In these cases, the exact identity of the victim is secondary, but for the most part the assassins make sure to emphasize that the victim represents the target country. Thus, in many cases diplomats have been chosen as victims of assassinations, the most prominent example of which would be the series of assassinations of Saudi diplomats worldwide (Turkey, Thailand, Belgium, Pakistan). As to the assassinations of Saudi targets, these attacks were perpetrated due to the ongoing hostility between Iran and Saudi Arabia as well as retribution for the execution of Shiite terrorists that acted as Iranian emissaries and perpetrated attacks in Saudi Arabia. In such cases, Iran and the Hizballah have a double motive—to avenge the death of their members while deterring Saudi Arabia and other states from sentencing Shiite terrorists to death. Another example is the detonation of the car belonging to the wife of the U.S. naval commander who accidentally downed an Iranian passenger plane over the Persian Gulf.

Iranian/Shiite assassination activities are conducted all over the world. The targets are chosen carefully, and the acts themselves are mostly executed "professionally," which makes apprehension of the murderers difficult. The majority of the assassinations are achieved by shootings, but in some cases an explosive device may be used.

To date the use of assassinations has been directed almost solely against Iranian expatriates or targets from Mediterranean countries (only in rare instances were assassinations carried out against Western targets). The struggle to release assassins who were apprehended sometimes brought about additional attacks, mainly taking hostages and hijacking airplanes, while demanding the release of the imprisoned terrorists.

Table 3.2
Prominent Examples of Assassinations Perpetrated by Iranian/Shiite Entities

Date	Description of the incident
July 1980	An assassination attempt against Shahfur Bakhtiar, prime minister of Iran during the Shah's reign, failed in Paris. The assassin (Anis Nakash) was caught and imprisoned.
February 1984	General Gulam Ali Obeisi, commander of the land forces during the Shah's reign, was assassinated in Paris.
May 1985	An assassination attempt against the Kuwaiti Emir (in the form of a car bomb detonated near the convoy in which he was traveling) failed in Kuwait. The Islamic Jihad claimed responsibility and demanded the release of its members from Kuwaiti prisons.
October 1988	The second secretary at the Saudi Embassy in Ankara (Turkey) was murdered. The diplomat was shot near his home. A Shiite organization claimed responsibility.
December 1988	The Saudi Deputy-Consul was assassinated in Karachi (Pakistan). A Shiite organization claimed responsibility for the killing.
July 1989	Abd al Rahman Kasmelo and two additional leaders of the Kurd Iranian Democratic Party were murdered in Vienna (Austria). This entity functioned as an opposition organization to the Islamic regime in Iran.
October 1989	A Saudi diplomat was seriously injured in Ankara when an explosive device detonated in his car. The Islamic Jihad claimed responsibility.
April 1990	Kazem Rajavi, a senior activist in Mujahidin Khalq and brother of the organization's leader Masoud Rajavi, was killed in Kopt (Switzerland).
August 1991	The prime minister during the Shah's reign Shahfur Bakhtiar and his aide Surus Qatib were assassinated in Paris. As noted earlier, an attempted assassination against Shahfur Bakhtiar in July 1980 failed. The French investigation indicated then that Iranian agents were involved in the attack.
September 1992	Four Kurd expatriates were murdered at the Mikonos restaurant in Berlin (Germany).
February 1996	On February 20, two Iranian opposition members were murdered in Turkey—Zahra Rajavi and Abd al Ali Murdi.
March 1996	On March 4, two opposition members were murdered in Pakistan—Malavi Mulazda and Abdel Nasser Jamshadzahi.
March 1996	On March 18, four Iranian opposition members were killed in Iraqi Kurdistan—Othman Rahimi, Taher Azizi, Hassan Ibrahimzada, and Farmkaz Ksharaz.
May 1996	Riza Mazloman was murdered in Paris.

Explosive Devices and Car Bombs

Explosive devices and car bombs were among the main attack means used by Shiite/Iranian terror entities during the review period (1982-1999). Out of a total of 260 attacks perpetrated by these parties, eighty were perpetrated through the use of an explosive device or a car bomb.[47] Most of the attacks were directed against civilian targets in order to cause as many casualties as possible and arouse extensive media interest, thus placing public pressure on governments to meet the demands of pro-Iranian terror organizations.

An analysis of the attack characteristics (as well the interrogation of the terrorists who were caught) indicates an organized and well-planned modus operandi activated at "timing," designed to promote the interests of the Shiite terror organizations and their patron, Iran. In most cases, there was preliminary preparation of an infrastructure for a terror network, which included the infiltrating of weapons into the target country, the preparation of hideaways for housing and absorbing the terrorists, the gathering of intelligence information about the targets, and finally the organizing of the sabotage incidents. The actual perpetration of the attacks began only after the completion of all of the infrastructure preparations.

Prominent examples of this modus operandi can be observed in terror networks exposed in Kuwait, Saudi Arabia, and particularly in the network of Fuad Ali Salah, which was discovered in France in 1989. A"series of attacks" spread over a period of several months was generally perpetrated in order to create a prolonged psychological effect, which would bring the attack victims to their knees. The terror organizations hoped that the exposure of the attack victim's weaknesses and its inability to provide personal security to its residents would lead it to the conclusion that the only way to stop the terror campaign was to yield to their demands. Here are several examples of the use of this type of modus operandi:

- Between February 3, 1986 and March 20, 1986 seven attacks were perpetrated in France.
- Between September 4, 1986 and September 19, 1986 six attacks were perpetrated in France.
- Between January 3, 1987 and January 10, 1987 four attacks were perpetrated in Cyprus.
- Between January 10, 1987 and November 25, 1987 sixteen attacks were perpetrated in Kuwait.

An additional characteristic of Shiite terror is the concentration of a large number of attacks in the target state in the course of one day, thus achieving a more impressive effect:

- On December 12, 1983 six attacks were perpetrated in Kuwait.

- On June 19, 1986 four attacks were perpetrated in Kuwait.
- On April 21, 1988 eight attacks were perpetrated in Kuwait.
- On April 18, 1988 two attacks were perpetrated in Germany.

Most of the attacks were perpetrated through the use of explosive devices, and the minority—twenty-two incidents—was accomplished with bombs. In connection to attacks in this category it is impossible to prove direct Iranian involvement because in practical terms they were perpetrated by sponsored organizations, such as the Hizballah, or by organizations under cover names, such as the Islamic Jihad. Several examples of attacks using car bombs follow.

Car Bomb Attacks in Saudi Arabia

On November 15, 1995, a car bomb parked near the fence of a training base of the Saudi National Guard in Riyadh exploded. The explosion demolished a three-floor building that housed the offices of American military consultants and trainers. Seven people were killed in the attack, five of which were American, and forty-two were injured. The Saudi security forces arrested four terrorists suspected of perpetrating the attack, and brought them to trial before an Islamic court. The four—Saudis—confessed to perpetrating the deed and stated that they had been sent to carry out the attack by a pro-Iranian Islamic group. The court sentenced them to death by decapitation and they were executed at the beginning of June 1996.[48]

On June 25 1996, at about midnight, a car bomb exploded near an American air force base in al-Khobar in Daharan. Nineteen people were killed in the explosion and over 500 were wounded. Investigations launched by U.S. and Saudi security entities revealed that the terrorists had loaded an empty oil tanker with some 2,300 kilograms of explosives, and eluded the control barriers set up by Saudi soldiers on the roads leading to the base, which is situated in the al-Khobar section. The guards reported a suspicious looking tanker to the Saudi authorities, but the Saudi National Guard car that arrived on the spot did not make it in time, and its passengers were greeted by the sight of a demolished tanker underneath which a huge crater (eleven meters deep and twenty-six meters wide) had been gouged. Eyewitnesses said that after the explosion they saw two people who had parked the tanker near the base's fence fleeing rapidly towards the town in a white car.

Following the attack, the Saudi security forces conducted extensive investigations and made arrests in order to apprehend those parties involved in the incident. Saudi Arabia submitted extradition requests to Afghanistan and Lebanon, the countries to which the twelve Shiite Saudis suspected of involvement in the attack had fled. The suspects had undergone military training in Iran and in Hizballah camps in Lebanon, and returned to Saudi Arabia to complete the preparations for the attack and perpetrate it.

Table 3.3
A List of Sabotage Attacks Perpetrated by Iranian/Shiite Organizations

Date	Venue	Attack target	Type of attack	Perpetrator
18.4.1983	Lebanon	American	Car bomb	Shiite organization
23.4.1983	Lebanon	American & French	Car bomb	Shiite organization
12.12.1983	Kuwait	Kuwaiti	Car bomb	Shiite organization
12.12.1983	Kuwait	Kuwaiti	Car bomb	Shiite organization
12.12.1983	Kuwait	American	Car bomb	Shiite organization
12.12.1983	Kuwait	Kuwaiti	Car bomb	Shiite organization
12.12.1983	Kuwait	French	Car bomb	Shiite organization
12.12.1983	Kuwait	American	Car bomb	Shiite organization
21.12.1983	Turkey	Iraqi	Bombing	Shiite organization
4.3.1984	Lebanon	French	Bombing	Shiite organization
11.7.1984	Lebanon	Libyan	Bombing	Amal
20.9.1984	Lebanon	American	Car bomb	Shiite organization
3.2.1985	France	French	Bombing	Shiite organization
19.5.1985	Saudi Arabia	Saudi	Bombing	Shiite organization
25.5.1985	Kuwait	Kuwaiti	Car bomb	Shiite organization
1.7.1985	Spain	American	Bombing	Shiite organization
22.7.1985	Denmark	American	Bombing	Shiite organization
22.7.1985	Denmark	American	Bombing	Shiite organization
4.2.1986	France	French	Bombing	Shiite organization
5.2.1986	France	French	Bombing	Shiite organization
17.2.1986	France	French	Bombing	Shiite organization
20.3.1986	France	French	Bombing	Shiite organization
20.3.1986	France	French	Bombing	Shiite organization
19.6.1986	Kuwait	Kuwaiti	Bombing	Shiite organization
19.6.1986	Kuwait	Kuwaiti	Bombing	Shiite organization
19.6.1986	Kuwait	Kuwaiti	Bombing	Shiite organization
19.6.1986	Kuwait	Kuwaiti	Bombing	Shiite organization
4.9.1986	France	French	Bombing	Shiite organization
8.9.1986	France	French	Bombing	Shiite organization
12.9.1986	France	French	Bombing	Shiite organization
14.9.1986	France	French	Bombing	Shiite organization
15.9.1986	France	French	Bombing	Shiite organization
17.9.1986	France	French	Bombing	Shiite organization
3.1.1987	Cyprus	Cypriot	Bombing	Shiite organization
7.1.1987	Cyprus	Cypriot	Bombing	Shiite organization
8.1.1987	Cyprus	Cypriot	Bombing	Shiite organization
8.1.1997	Cyprus	Cypriot	Bombing	Shiite organization

Table 3.3 (cont.)

10.1.1987	Cyprus	Cypriot	Bombing	Shiite organization
19.1.1987	Kuwait	Kuwaiti	Bombing	Shiite organization
24.1.1987	Kuwait	Kuwaiti	Bombing	Shiite organization
6.3.1987	Austria	Austrian	Letter bomb	Shiite organization
21.4.1987	Kuwait	Kuwaiti	Eight bombs	Shiite organization
26.4.1987	Kuwait	Kuwaiti	Car bomb	Shiite organization
11.5.1987	Kuwait	Kuwaiti	Bombing	Shiite organization
15.7.1987	Kuwait	French	Car bomb	Shiite organization
24.10.1987	Kuwait	American	Bombing	Shiite organization
3.11.1987	Kuwait	Kuwaiti	Car bomb	Shiite organization
25.11.1987	Kuwait	American	Bombing	Shiite organization
8.3.1988	Malaysia	Saudi	Bombing	Shiite organization
28.3.1988	Saudi Arabia	Saudi	Bombing	Shiite organization
9.4.1988	Kuwait	Kuwaiti	Bombing	Shiite organization
10.4.1988	Pakistan	Saudi	Bombing	Shiite organization
18.4.1988	Germany	Jewish	Bombing	Shiite organization
27.4.1988	Kuwait	Saudi	Bombing	Shiite organization
7.5.1988	Kuwait	American	Bombing	Shiite organization
18.5.1988	Kuwait	Kuwaiti	Car bomb	Shiite organization
21.7.1988	Turkey	Saudi	Bombing	Shiite organization
18.9.1988	Turkey	Iraqi	Bombing	Shiite organization
10.3.1989	United States	American	Bombing	Shiite organization
28.3.1989	Pakistan	British	Bombing	Shiite organization
10.4.1989	Malaysia	British	Bombing	Shiite organization
23.4.1989	Saudi Arabia	Saudi	Bombing	Shiite organization
10.7.1989	Saudi Arabia	Saudi	Bombing	Shiite organization
17.7.1989	Saudi Arabia	Saudi	Bombing	Shiite organization
3.8.1989	Britain	British	Bombing	Shiite organization
17.10.1989	Turkey	Saudi	Bombing	Shiite organization
28.10.1991	Turkey	American	Bombing	Shiite organization supported by Iran
12.3.1992	Turkey	American	Car bomb	Turkish organization supported by Iran
17.3.1992	Argentina	Israeli	Car bomb	Hizballah
18.7.1994	Argentina	Jewish	Car bomb	Shiite organization
13.11.1995	Saudi Arabia	American	Car bomb	Saudi organization supported by Iran
14.2.1996	Bahrain	Bahraini	Bombing	Shiite organization
26.6.1996	Saudi Arabia	American	Car bomb	Saudi organization supported by Iran
12.11.1996	Bahrain	Bahraini	Bombing	Shiite organization

Canada extradited to the United States another man—Hanni al Sayakh—suspected of involvement in the attack. The latter stated in his interrogation that his job had been to signal to the car bomb driver where to place the vehicle. In exchange for non-extradition to Saudi Arabia, the suspect gave information about the others involved in the incident.[49] To date, the American and Saudi authorities have been unable to apprehend the other individuals involved in the attack.

Kidnapping Hostages

The kidnapping of foreign hostages in Lebanon as a political bargaining tool mainly characterizes the Shiite organizations in that country, although Palestinian organizations, such as Abu Nidal's organization, made successful use of this tactic as well. Between 1982 and 1988, ninety-six foreign citizens of various nationalities were kidnapped in Lebanon, mainly citizens of Western countries, in sixty-seven different kidnapping incidents. The Hizballah was responsible for fifty-five kidnappings, Amal for eight, and the remainder was perpetrated by various organizations, some of which were probably Palestinian. The Hizballah, much like other terror organizations worldwide, justified the use of terror against the West by claiming that terror constitutes a self-protection measure against the greater power of imperialism. As an organization with a religious orientation, the Hizballah needed moral arguments to justify the kidnapping of innocent civilians according to Muslim religious law, because from the moral aspect there is a difference between terror attacks against Israeli, American or French military targets, which are defined as part of the struggle against foreign forces, and the kidnapping of hostages. The basic justification for kidnappings was generally the accusation that the hostages had been spying for a Western country.[50]

In any event, the issue of religious justification for kidnapping hostages remained controversial: radical leaders, like Hussein Musawi, supported the kidnappings while the Hizballah's spiritual leader, Sheikh Fadallah, publicly condemned the kidnappings and claimed that they contradicted the spirit of Islam and were detrimental to the Muslim image. Nevertheless, Fadallah himself never took any steps to prevent the kidnappings, probably due to his fear of a confrontation with Khomeini and radical circles within the Hizballah.[51]

Hizballah turned the kidnapping of hostages (those mainly of Western origins) into a central bargaining tool to achieve political and military goals set by the organization and its patrons in Iran. The organization's leaders knew how to exploit Western sensitivity regarding the welfare of its citizens as well as the fanfare of the media and public opinion in these countries in order to apply pressure on decision-makers in those states.

An example of shrewd exploitation and an attempt made by the Hizballah and Iran to influence the political system in a Western country in order to promote their interests was discernible during the presidential election campaign in France in 1987. President Mitterand declared that he was opposed to negotiating with the kidnappers of hostages, and that France would continue supplying weapons to Iraq despite the terror threats.[52] The response of the kidnappers from the Hizballah was dispatched to the French opposition leader Jacques Chirac. The kidnappers demanded that Chirac publish an announcement expressing his concern regarding the president's declaration about terror within forty-eight hours. In addition, the message stated that if Chirac failed to do so, a French hostage would be executed. By preferring Chirac over Mitterand and by fanning the internal political struggle in France, the Hizballah kidnappers served Iranian interests, as the latter preferred to negotiate with Chirac rather than Mitterand.[53]

The Hizballah consistently denied any connection to the kidnapping of hostages, and instead placed the blame for the perpetuation of the problem and its complications upon the United States and the West, while calling for the release of all of the kidnapped Lebanese, Palestinians, and Iranians incarcerated in Israeli prisons. On May 3, 1990, in response to an announcement made by the U.S. administration, the organization claimed:

> The American attempt to blame the Hizballah in the matter of the foreign hostages and to conceal the real reasons for this problem will not prevail…. It is the United States that supports the method of holding civilians in captivity by covering for the crimes perpetrated by the Zionists against the Palestinian people and supporting them…the Zionist entity was founded on the basis of kidnapping innocent civilians and massacring them, and it still adheres to this method. The kidnapping of Sheikh Obeid from his home is the most prominent example of this Zionist method, a method which is protected, supported and covered up by the American administration.[54]

These examples and others indicate that alongside the Hizballah's ideological-religious motives, the organization is also motivated by practical and rational considerations, and is equipped with full knowledge of the weaknesses and vulnerabilities of Western democracies.

Recognition of the sensitivity of these regimes to the media and public opinion, familiarity with the various political entities in these countries, and awareness of the crucial timing within internal political frameworks in various countries (elections, political crises, and more)—all of these factors were shrewdly manipulated by the organization to increase its bargaining leverage and to derive propaganda-related benefits by maneuvering the "bargaining card" of the hostages that it was holding.

Following is an elaboration on the approaches of various countries to the hostage issue, and how these states contended with the Shiite/Iranian entities in this matter.

The United States

The United States' basic approach to the hostage issue avers that under no circumstances should there be any surrender to the kidnappers' demands.[55] In actual practice, the administration was often forced to take the influence of various power factors into account, which made it difficult to implement its declared policy, such as hostages' families' who generated public pressure for their release, as well as the extensive influence of the media. At times, the public pressure was directed towards political channels by opposition entities that criticized the administration's policies. For example, in June 1986, in contrast to the declared policy of the administration at that time, 247 congressmen signed a letter sent to President Assad in which they prevailed upon him to use his influence to liberate the American hostages.

In fact, during most of the hostage situations, the United States conducted secret negotiations with the kidnappers through Syrian, Iranian or Algerian mediators; the public pressure was harmful to these delicate contacts and made it difficult for the administration to take action. A prominent example of American willingness to conduct secret negotiations in order to liberate hostages is the "Irangate" affair, which involved the sale of U.S. arms to Iran in exchange for the release of hostages.

In August 1985, the American administration received a message regarding the intention of entities within the Iranian administration to improve Iran's ties with the United States.[56] These "signals" alluded to the possibility of opening a new communication channel to solve the problem of the American hostages in Lebanon. In the negotiations with the Iranians, the American's primary goal was to achieve the release of William Buckley, head of the CIA branch in Beirut who had been kidnapped by the Hizballah, as well as the release of the remaining U.S. hostages in exchange for the transfer of weapon consignments to Iran. According to the agreement achieved between the two countries at the end of August 1985 and at the beginning of September of that year, the first consignment of "Taw" anti-tank missiles arrived in Iran, while at the same time, on September 14, 1985, the Hizballah in Lebanon released an American hostage named Benjamin Weir. The United States expected the release of additional hostages according to the agreement, but this didn't happen. Moreover, a month later the Islamic Jihad announced that William Buckley had been executed.

On July 26, 1986, another hostage was released in Lebanon, Lawrence Martin Jenky. The Islamic Jihad announced that this was a gesture of "goodwill," but in actual fact it is known that on July 3-4, 1986, a short time preceding the hostage's release, Iran had received an additional consignment of weapons. According to unverified information, the release of the two hostages also involved the payment of ransom money, the amount of which is unknown, which was transferred to the kidnappers through the Catholic Church.

The final consignment of weapons reached Iran in October 1986, after which the hostage named David Jacobs was released on November 2 1986. This was the third and last hostage to be released in the framework of the "weapons for hostages" deals. The United States concealed the details related to this issue until their exposure in the form of the "Irangate" affair at the end of 1986.

At the time that these transactions were being conducted with the Iranians, a British minister named Terry White was acting as an intermediary in Lebanon in the issue of the Western hostages. Initially, the prevalent belief was that the release of the three hostages was the result of White's efforts, and only later did it become clear that in actual fact they had been released as part of the arms deals between the United States and Iran, while White had unwittingly served as "camouflage...for these deals."[57]

Ostensibly, the arms deals with Iran, which had brought about the release of the three hostages, had been successful; however, the findings of the investigation committees that dealt with the affair (for example, the Tower Committee) indicated that this approach was a dismal failure vis-à-vis the basic policy and long-term interests of the United States in its struggle against terror and its international relations. Only three hostages had actually been released although the basic aim of the negotiations had been to liberate all of the foreign hostages. It turned out that William Buckley, who was the main reason for America's willingness to enter into these types of agreements, had been killed long before the beginning of the negotiations for his release. Moreover, in September and October 1986, in the midst of the negotiations between Iran and the United States, the Hizballah kidnapped three additional American hostages in Beirut: Frank Reed, Joseph Cicippio, and Edward Tracy.[58] These kidnappings patently proved that the method of giving in to extortion and the willingness to consent to the supply of weapons to Iran in exchange for the release of hostages was not the right way to deal with this issue, even in the short term. Moreover, this approach had severe negative repercussions on the overall campaign that the West devised against terror and against states that support terror.

It would be just to say that an important offshoot of these deals was the exposure of Iran's involvement in the issue of the kidnapping of hostages as well as its ability to control these sponsored organizations. Also noteworthy is the fact that in December 1986, a short time after the realization of these arms deals, talks were launched between the United States and Iran regarding the freeing of frozen Iranian assets in the United States, and it would appear that this process was also aimed at liberating the hostages, but the contacts were severed without yielding any results.

France

France dealt with the hostage problem via two parallel channels: The first, through direct talks with Iran, the Hizballah's patron; and the other, through mediators vis-à-vis the Hizballah itself, with the help of Syria, Algeria, and Saudi Arabia. One of the mediators who acted in the service of France was Dr. Raad, a French doctor of Lebanese origin who had maintained close contact with the Shiite community in Lebanon. In the course of 1985, Raad made two trips to Lebanon and Syria in an attempt to liberate the four French hostages who had been kidnapped in March and November 1985, but his efforts were unsuccessful.[59]

In 1986, following the kidnapping of four members of a French TV crew in Lebanon, another mediator was sent to Damascus—a Syrian businessman named Amran Adham, in order to deal with their release. At the same time Prime Minster Jacques Chirac, who had just recently been elected, began to contend with the issue of the hostages through other emissaries including Dr. Raad. In June of that year, two of the kidnapped TV crewmembers were released. The French prime minister thanked Syria, Algeria, and—ironically enough—Iran, for their assistance in freeing the hostages.[60] Two weeks after the release of the hostages, France expelled several hundred activists of the anti-Iranian underground Mujahidin Khalq, including the organization's leader Masoud Rajavi; this was France's form of payment to Iran for releasing the hostages.[61]

In November 1986, another French hostage was released in Lebanon, and this time as well the French prime minster thanked Syria, Algeria, and Saudi Arabia for his release. A short time later, France announced its intention to return part of the Iranian loan given to France during the Shah's reign, involving a sum of about a billion dollars, while the French actually paid Iran a sum of approximately $330 million. A short time after the transfer of the money to Iran another hostage was released.[62] Through these actions, Iran not only succeeded in having Iranian opposition members expelled from France but also regained the Iranian funds frozen in France since Khomeini's Revolution.

The release of the two remaining TV reporters on November 27, 1987 was also the result of French capitulation to Iranian demands: France agreed to withdraw all of the charges against Wahid Gorgi, an Iranian terrorist who was involved in a terror network that had perpetrated a series of attacks in France in the course of 1986. Gorgi found asylum in the Iranian Embassy in Paris, and the French authorities surrounded the embassy and demanded that he be turned over to them. The Iranians took similar action in Teheran: They accused the French Consul Paul Toure of espionage and placed a siege on the French Embassy. The French surrender in the matter of Gorgi put an end to the "Embassy War" between the two countries. France repeated its declaration regarding its intention to continue paying back the country's financial debts to Iran, and the third gesture towards Iran was the expulsion of additional Iranian opposition members from France. Some sources claimed that France had also agreed to supply Iran with spare military parts, but French authorities denied this accusation emphatically.[63]

On May 4, 1988, the last French hostages were released, and, subsequently, on June 16, 1988, the countries renewed diplomatic ties. France undertook to act for the release of Anis Nakash (the terrorist who assassinated Shahfur Bakhtiar, the prime minister during the Shah's reign who was in exile in France), and agreed to pay the Hizballah a ransom of about $30 million. There were several reports regarding the intention to reduce the size of arms consignments to Iraq and renew weapon supplies to Iran via Syria. The release of Muhammad Mukhajar, a Hizballah activist arrested in France a year earlier, was apparently also connected to the deal relating to the release of the hostages in Lebanon.

Regarding the deal between Iran, the Hizballah, and France, it is interesting to quote Sheikh Fadallah, who stated in March 1986 that "their release was the outcome of the deal between France and Iran," and "only a similar deal between Iran and the United States may bring about the release of the U.S. hostages."[64] The meaning to be derived from this declaration was that Iran was the entity that stood behind the Hizballah's activities, and it was Iran that could bring about the release of the hostages in exchange for achieving its political objectives.

In summary, it is obvious that France's repeated acquiescence to Iranian demands encouraged Iran and the Hizballah to activate terror against it until realizing most of Iran's political, economic, and military demands vis-à-vis France.

Britain

For the most part, the British approach was refusal to submit to the kidnappers' demands or even to enter negotiations with terror organizations for the purpose of liberating hostages.[65]

The Hizballah was involved in a relatively small number of kidnappings of British citizens in Lebanon, and most were released within a relatively short time. An exception was the kidnapping of Minister Terry White, who was visiting Lebanon in a mediation attempt to release the hostages and was kidnapped himself in 1986. Britain refused to meet the ransom demands posed by the kidnappers and condemned France and Germany for their surrender to the kidnappers' demands in order to free their hostages. According to information which was never officially verified it appears that in late 1987 Britain conducted talks with Iran in order to achieve White's release, but the discussions were discontinued when Britain refused to pay ransom. White was finally released together with other Western hostages in 1991.

Kuwait

Many incidents of kidnappings of Western hostages were perpetrated in Lebanon in order to apply pressure on Kuwait to release seventeen Shiite terrorists who were incarcerated there, some of whom had been sentenced to death. Kuwait's fixed policy not to give in to the kidnappers' demands under any circumstances stood firm during the entire period, despite the considerable pressures under which it was placed, probably due to the Kuwaitis' understanding that the kidnapping of hostages in Lebanon was only a single component of an overall and broader Iranian threat against Kuwaiti interests.[66]

Switzerland

Eric Werley, who was kidnapped by the Hizballah on January 3, 1985, was released in exchange for the release of a Hizballah member, Hussein Talaat. The latter was arrested at the Zurich airport on November 18, 1984, in the possession of explosives designated for an attack against the U.S. Embassy in Rome.[67] Additional kidnappings perpetrated in order to free the hijacker of the Air Afric airplane, Ali Muhammad Hariri, who was imprisoned in Switzerland, were to no avail. Subsequently, the kidnapped Swiss citizens were released during the years 1991 and 1992.

Germany

The first kidnappings of German citizens in Lebanon occurred in 1987. These kidnappings were connected to the arrest of two Shiite terrorists—the Hamadi brothers—in Germany. A few days after their arrest a German citizen was kidnapped in Lebanon, and several days later another one was kidnapped. As mentioned above, the objective of the kidnappers was the release of the Hamadi brothers. Shortly after the kidnappings Germany appealed to Syria and Iran to help obtain the release of the hostages. The German ambassador in Beirut even met with the Hizballah's spiritual leader, Sheikh Fadallah, with the knowledge that the latter had consistently opposed the kidnapping of foreign hostages. The dilemma faced by the German government was that, on the one hand, the Americans were demanding the extradition of Muhammad Ali Hamadi on the charge of hijacking a TWA plane in 1985 and murdering an American passenger, while on the other hand, the kidnappers had declared that if Hamadi were extradited to the United States the hostages would be executed. The German resolution was that Hamadi would not be extradited to the United States, but would be brought to trial in Germany and charged with hijacking and murder. On September 7, 1987, the Hizballah freed one of the hostages—Alfred Schmidt—and announced that his release was in exchange for the release of the Hamadi brothers in Germany.

Germany thanked Syria and Iran for their assistance in liberating the hostage but denied any kind of deal with the kidnappers. British sources claimed that Schmidt's release had been part of a deal according to which Muhammad Ali Hamadi would be sentenced to a short prison term after which he would be deported to Lebanon, while his brother would be liberated after serving an even shorter sentence.[68]

The second German hostage, Rudolph Kords, was also released shortly afterwards. There were reports in the press that Germany had paid the Hizballah $3 million through the mediator Rashid Makrum, a German businessman of Lebanese origin. The German Siemens Company, which employed Kords, was also involved in the deal and it appears that the company closed the deal in Damascus with Syrian arbitration.[69]

On May 16, 1989, two German citizens were kidnapped in Germany— Heinrich Sturbig and Tomas Kamptner. No organization claimed responsibility for the kidnappings. On May 30, 1989, Hussein Musawi, one of the leaders of the Hizballah in Lebanon, was interviewed by the German DPI News Agency in Baal-Bek, Lebanon.[70] In the interview, Musawi stated, "Germany has no conflict with anyone in Lebanon, not even with the Hamadi family. The government in Bonn agreed to release Hamadi in exchange for the two hostages Alfred Schmidt and Rudolph Kords." However, when this promise was rescinded, and Hamadi was sentenced to life imprisonment, the Hamadi family apparently carried out the kidnapping in a new attempt to achieve his release. In the beginning of the 1990s, the German hostages were released and the members of the Hamadi family were set free before finishing their sentence, after which they returned to Lebanon.

During the kidnapping campaign of hostages in Lebanon at least eight hostages were executed by their captors, but the rest of the hostages were released over the years through negotiations that the countries held with Shiite terror organizations and Iran.

From 1989 onwards no Western hostages were kidnapped in Lebanon, although Shiite terror organizations continued to hold several hostages captive until the end of 1991. The hostage campaign ended with the release of the last of the Western hostages in December 1991, apparently due to Iran's desire to improve its ties with the West.

Notes

1.   Office of the Secretary of State, Office of the Coordinator for Counter Terrorism, Patterns of Global Terrorism, U.S. Department of State Publications. Most of the data are based on these official American reports.

2. In addition to these suicide attacks, additional suicide attacks against IDF forces in Lebanon were also perpetrated (see subsequent elaboration).
3. There are additional attacks that are not included in these categories such as the lobbing of hand grenades and Molotov cocktails. These attacks constitute 0.8 percent of all attacks and are therefore not presented in the data.
4. Suicide attacks were statistically included in this category.
5. Turkey was included in the category of the Middle East.
6. This category includes Lebanon, Cyprus, Iraq, Iran, Saudi Arabia, Dubai, Kuwait, and Turkey.
7. These data relate solely to the period after the end of the Iran-Iraq war, i.e., from 1989 and onwards.
8. Martin Kramer (ed.), *Protest and Revolution in Shiite Islam*, Hakibbutz Hameuhad, Tel Aviv, 1985, pp. 11-15.
9. Ibid.
10. Emanuel Sivan, *Islamic Extremists*, Am Oved, Tel Aviv, 1986, pp. 196-197.
11. *Kihan*, October 26, 1983.
12. Amir Taheri, *The Holy Terror—Inside Story of the Islamic Terrorism*, Sphere Books, London, 1987, pp. 85-86.
13. David Menashri, *Iran in Revolution*, Hakibbutz Hameuhad, Tel Aviv, 1988, pp. 237-238.
14. Ibid.
15. Shimon Shapira, *Hizballah between Iran and Lebanon*, Hakibbutz Hameuhad, Tel Aviv, 2000, pp. 167-169.
16. Ibid.
17. An interview with Sheikh Yosef Damush, *Alsapir*, Beirut, August 14, 1986.
18. *Al-Sapir*, August 25, 1985.
19. *Alahad*, Beirut, August 15, 1985; *Al-Nahar*, Beirut, August 15, 1985.
20. Shimon Shapira, *Hizballah between Iran and Lebanon*, pp. 167-169.
21. *Alahad*, Beirut, May 24, 1985.
22. *Al-Sapir*, Beirut, November 10, 1982.
23. Mark Juergensmeyer (ed.), *Violence and the Sacred in the Modern World*, Frank Cass, London. 1992, pp. 30-47.
24. Shimon Shapira, *Hizballah between Iran and Lebanon*, p. 72.
25. Ibid.
26. Ibid.
27. http://www.Beirut-Memorial.org/history.
28. The United States, Italy, and France were members of the multinational force.
29. The eulogy delivered by General Kelly on the eighteenth anniversary of the attack against the U.S. Marines headquarters.
30. *Jamhuri Islami*, April 20, 1996.
31. The Al-Manar television network, August 29, 1997.
32. Radio Nur, September 5, 1997.
33. Reuters, March 19, 1992, March 23, 1992.
34. Shaul Shay, *Terror in the Service of the Imam 1979-1999*, Mifalot Publishing, the Interdisciplinary Center, Herzliya 2001, p. 86.
35. *Ma'ariv*, Tel Aviv, September 5, 1999.
36. Ibid.
37. *Ha'aretz*, September 7, 1999.
38. AP, July 18, 1994.
39. The Argentinean attorney-general in an interview with the local radio, quoted by Reuters, May 5, 1999.

40. "Iran as a State that Supports and Activates Terror," a special collection of information, the Center for Intelligence Heritage, The Information Center for Intelligence and Terror, April 2003, pp. 53-59; and *Ha'aretz*, Tel Aviv, October 2, 2002.
41. The Al-Manar television network, December 14, 2001.
42. Muslimedia International, Islamic Movement, May 26, 2002.
43. *Der Spiegel*, July 7, 1997.
44. AP, Teheran, July 7, 1997.
45. The attacks in July 1985 and January 1987 are counted as two attacks each, because they were directed at different targets simultaneously.
46. The data regarding the assassination are based on: Office of the Secretary of State, Office of the Coordinator for Counter Terrorism, *Patterns of Global Terrorism*, U.S. Department of State Publications—as well as the following publications and lists distributed by opposition circles and Iranian expatriates: "Report in the Islamic Republic's Terrorism Abroad: Summary of the Khomeini Regime's Terrorism—1979 to the Present" (1996).

    Eric Avebury, Robert Wilkinson, *Iran: State of Terror*, Parliamentary House Rights Group, London, June 1996.
47. The data are based on the following sources: Office of the Secretary of State, Office of the Coordinator for Counter Terrorism, *Patterns of Global Terrorism*, U.S. Department of State Publications; Anat Kurtz et al., *International Terrorism*.
48. *Washington Post*, June 24, 1996.
49. *Ma'ariv*, Tel Aviv, June 26, 1996.
50. Martha Kramer, *The Moral Logic of Hizballah*, Occasional Papers No. 101, The Dayan Center for Middle Eastern Studies, Tel Aviv University, August 1987, p. 13.
51. Magnus Ranstorp, *Hizballah in Lebanon—The Politics of the Western Hostage Crisis,* St. Martin's Press, New York, 1997, pp. 41-49.
52. *International Herald Tribune*, March 12, 1987 (quoting AFP).
53. *Le Monde*, May 6, 1988. In one of its declarations, the Hizballah condemned the Socialist Party for its ties with Zionism. In March 1986, the organization's periodical *al-Ahad* wrote that the safety of French citizens worldwide depends upon the defeat of the Socialist Party in the upcoming elections.
54. The declaration made by Sheikh Yizbakh of the Hizballah, as it appeared in *al-Anuar*, July 12, 1990.
55. R. K. Ramzani, "Iran's Foreign Policy Contending Orientations," The Middle East Journal 43, 2 (Spring 1989), pp. 204-206.
56. Shmuel Segev, *The Iranian Triangle—The Secret Ties between Israel, Iran and the United States*, Sifriat Ma'ariv, Tel Aviv, 1981, pp. 126-127.
57. Maskit Burgin, Ariel Merari, Anat Kurtz, "Foreign Hostages in Lebanon," (Memorandum No. 25), JCSS, Tel Aviv University, August 1988.
58. Magnus Ranstorp, *Hizballah in Lebanon—The Politics of the Western Hostage Crisis*, pp. 98-99.
59. *Le Monde*, May 6, 1988.
60. *Jerusalem Post*, March 27, 1986 (quoting Reuters).
61. *Newsweek*, June 23, 1986.
62. *International Herald Tribune*, December 26, 1986 (quoting Reuters).
63. *Ma'ariv*, November 12, 1986.
64. *Al Nahar*, March 24, 1986.
65. *Times*, June 23, 1990, quoting an interview with British Prime Minister Margaret Thatcher.
66. Shahram Chubin, "Iran and Its Neighbors: The Impact of the Gulf War," *Conflict Studies,* 204 (1986), pp. 12-14.

67. *Yediot Aharonot*, June 20 1986, quoting *The Daily Express*.
68. *Ha'aretz*, September 11 1987, quoting *The Times*.
69. *Ma'ariv*, September 20 1987, quoting *The Times*.
70. *Times*, May 30, 1989, quoting the DPI German News Agency.

4

Targets of the Iranian/Shiite Terror

Israel

Israel was one of the most loathed states by Khomeini and his regime, although not the most despised. This approach stands—like in other policy areas—in complete contrast to the close and special ties that developed between the two countries during the Shah's reign. Suffice to say that from the early 1960s all Israeli prime ministers visited Iran. Also, there were strong military ties, including mutual visits paid by the most high-ranking officers, in addition to highly developed economic relations; Iran exported oil to Israel and in return acquired security equipment and technologies for industry and agriculture.

Khomeini had already expressed an anti-Israeli and anti-Zionist stand during his period of exile in the 1960s. At that time, his links with Arab and Palestinian nationalist circles grew stronger and his animosity towards Israel increased. Khomeini attributed gross injustices to Israel and Zionism, which in his eyes turned it into the source of all evil on earth. His accusations relate to three main axes:[1]

- Accusations pertaining to anti-Islamic policies adopted by Israel and Zionism: hostility towards Islam, joint attempts with the Great Satan (the United States) to cause dissension in the Arab world, invasion of the sites holy to Islam, and the burning of the Al Aksa mosque;
- Accusations related to aspirations for expansion and Israel's imperialist nature—the invasion of Palestine, oppression of the Palestinians, the invasion of Lebanon, and perpetual wars against the Arabs with the aim of realizing the Zionist vision of a "world kingdom";
- Accusations against Israel that it is partner to economic exploitation of Iran and to a policy crafted to perpetuate Iran's dependency upon the United States and Israel.

Thus, it is not surprising that Palestinian Liberation Organization (PLO) chairman Yasser Arafat was the first foreign leader who came forward to congratulate Khomeini upon his victory on February 18, 1979. At the same time, Khomeini said:

> The Iranian revolution will reward the Palestinian revolution for the help that it gave in ousting the Shah, and Iranian volunteers will participate in the struggle to eradicate the Zionist conquest and liberate Jerusalem.

Subsequently, an official announcement was published regarding the severance of relations, and the cessation of oil exports and aviation ties between the two countries. Following that announcement—and in the presence of Prime Minister Bazargan, Foreign Minister Karim Sanjabi, and member of the Revolutionary Council Dr. Ibrahim Yazdi—Arafat waved the Palestinian flag over the Israeli Embassy building in Teheran.

From the day that the Islamic regime came into power, its leaders never missed an opportunity to condemn Israel and criticize most of the Muslim states for their lack of determination in the struggle against it. Khomeini promised aid to anyone willing to fight Israel, and on June 8, 1981, the Iranian Majlis (Parliament) passed a resolution to allow Iranian "volunteers" to enter the war against Israel in South Lebanon. The resolution was approved by the Supreme National Security Council and by the Revolutionary Guards headquarters. A year later, the Lebanon War presented Khomeini with a golden opportunity to prove his dedication to the war against "imperialism and Zionism," and thus, despite the war with Iraq, Iran opened "another front" against Israel and the United States in Lebanon, and dispatched forces from the Revolutionary Guards, which positioned themselves in Lebanon.

The Hizballah, which was established in Lebanon under Iranian patronage, adopted the hostility and hatred towards Israel that characterized the Khomeinist ideology. One of the fundamental principles of the organization's ideology, which is derived from the vision of the leader of the Islamic revolution in Iran, Khomeini, is the ongoing and uncompromising struggle against the State of Israel until its eradication and the liberation of Jerusalem. On the basis of this fundamental principle, and in order to bring it to fruition, the organization believes that it is ideologically and practically obligated to strive for an ongoing struggle against Israel using any means and at every sector.

The Hizballah's terror activity is accompanied by malicious propaganda, which includes blatant anti-Semitism. For example, Hassan Nasrallah, secretary-general of the organization, stated in his speech on May 7, 1998:

> I wish to draw attention to the danger related to this entity growing in Palestine, an entity which has no boundaries, which spreads to any place where Israelis go, to any place where there are remnants of the Talmud or where a Jewish rabbi once lived. The hope to realize the divine promise regarding the destruction of this cancerous affliction grows in everyone.[2]

In another interview that took place on April 9, 2000, Nasrallah said:

The source of all of the great disasters that have troubled this region is the existence of Israel. As long as there is a state named Israel, these disasters will continue. This is a malignant body in the region. If we ignore the fact that our body has cancer, we may discover this when it is too late…there are those who view cancer as the flu…. When cancer is found it must be dealt with bravely and extracted from the roots. Part of this body and its blood must be sacrificed so that the body will be healthy and whole.[3]

The hostility against the State of Israel is accompanied by a hatred for the Jewish people. The organization's leaders have often made sharp anti-Semitic statements that not only revile Israel as a state, but also the entire Jewish people, while using themes taken from classic and Muslim anti-Semitism. This, for example, is how Hassan Nasrallah expressed himself in speeches delivered in Beirut:

What do the Jews want? They want security and money. Throughout history the Jews have been Allah's most cowardly and avaricious creatures. If you look all over the world, you will find no one more miserly or greedy than they are.[4]

This year, unfortunately, the tenth day of the month of Muharam (the *Ashura* holiday) falls near the fiftieth anniversary of that bitter and tragic historical disaster of the establishment of the state by the descendants of monkeys and pigs, meaning the Jewish Zionists.[5]

If we gathered the blood spilt and money spent in Iran, in Iraq and in the nation during eight years of war, they would suffice to liberate Palestine scores of times and to eradicate Israel dozens of times. Is that correct or not?[6]

Based on the way it views Israel, the Hizballah negates any possibility of a future agreement with the former, which would include recognition of its existence as a national entity in the region and coexistence. The organization makes a point of expressing its unshakable opposition to any efforts to reach an agreement in the region, and sharply criticizes those negotiating with Israel, with the aim of increasing the pressure in the Arab street. During recent years special emphasis has been placed on the prevention of negotiations and agreements between Israel and Palestine, and on maintaining the level of violence and terror in Gaza and the areas of Judea and Samaria.

Iran's status in Lebanon, as it has developed in the last twenty years, is important to the regime in Teheran. Iran's ties with the Shiite community in Lebanon, the bolstering of this community's status within the Lebanese system, the use of the Lebanese arena for the struggle against Israel (and in the past the United States, too), and most importantly the establishment of the Hizballah—all of these factors constitute the most successful model for exporting the Islamic revolution, Iran style. Iran's status in Lebanon is also important for the purpose of expanding its influence throughout the Middle East, particularly in connection to the Arab-Israeli conflict and the peace process.

The fundamentalist Islamic ideology which motivates the regime in Iran and Lebanon's importance dictate to Iran the following interests vis-à-vis the issue of South Lebanon:[7]

- Strengthening the status of the Shiite community in general, and the Hizballah in particular, in the Lebanese system. Although Iran has ties with other Shiite Lebanese organizations and entities, Hizballah serves as its main arm in Lebanon. On the ideological level, the fortification of the Hizballah is a stage in the realization of the long-term objective of establishing an Islamic arrangement in Lebanon.
- Preserving the alliance with Syria, while ensuring that controversies that erupt from time to time with that country regarding the Lebanese issue do not impair this alliance. Iran is aware of the fact that its status and influence are largely dependent on its cooperation with Syria. It also regards Syria as a central strategic ally in the Arab world. Therefore, if disputes develop between Iran and Syria regarding the Hizballah's modus operandi, Iran will prefer to acquiesce if it believes that the controversy may cause a rift in its ties with Syria. It appears that according to Iran's point of view, strategic alliance with Syria is more important than inflicting damage on Israel via the Hizballah.
- Ideological support of the struggle against Israel until it is eradicated as a political entity.

To date there has been no essential conflict between Iran's various interests pertaining to South Lebanon. The encouragement to act against Israel was in keeping with the strengthening of the Hizballah's status and with Syrian interests in Lebanon. Since 1982, the operational infrastructure of the Hizballah has mostly been built with extensive Iranian assistance, which included funding, the transfer of large amounts of weaponry (mostly through Damascus), and the training of the organization's activists. All of this, alongside Syrian political and military aid, which has grown significantly since President Bashar alAssad rose to power.

From Iran's point of view, the Hizballah is the forerunner of the "terror weapon" in general and its focus against Israeli targets in particular. Iran also regards the Hizballah as a central source of inspiration for the armed Palestinian struggle against Israel, and in a broader connection—an important instrument in the Islamic struggle against Israel.

Iran regards the fortification of the Hizballah in Lebanon as the greatest success (and the only one to date) of the "export of the Islamic revolution." Even after Israel's withdrawal from Lebanon, Iran continues to regard Lebanon as its most forward front against Israel, and the Hizballah as a key factor in leading the struggle. Based on this concept, Iran persevered in strengthening the Hizballah's military capabilities. Iran has consistently expressed its support for the continuation of Hizballah's terror activity along the border between Israel and Lebanon and calls for the "liberation" of additional Lebanese land, which it claims is still invaded by Israel.[8]

The "Al Quds Force" ("Jerusalem Force"), which belongs to the Iranian Revolutionary Guards and is deployed in Lebanon, is an Iranian entity that leads Iranian activity in the region and its aid for the Hizballah. The force deals in the channeling and provision of various forms of military and financial aid for terror activity against Israel, particularly that of the Hizballah and Palestinian organizations—both religious and secular.

Iran transfers airborne military aid to the Lebanese arena via the Al Quds Force. This aid passes through the international airport in Damascus and constitutes the Hizballah's almost single supply pipe of weapons. The Iranians, who are aware of the fact, are careful to maintain the continuity of the aid, with Syrian consent, thereby perpetually enhancing the organization's operational and military capabilities. Over the years, large quantities of qualitative weapons have been transferred to the organization by air including anti-tank missiles, Katyushas, cannons with different diameters, SA-7 and SA14 shoulder missiles, naval combat equipment, motorized hang gliders, and sophisticated weaponry including long-range land-to-land Fager3 rockets (with a range of forty-five kilometers) and Fager5 missiles (with a range of seventy-five kilometers).[9]

The Al Quds Force plays a central role in establishing the operational plans of the Hizballah in the event of scenarios of conflict escalation with Israel, their realization in the field, and the determination of the Hizballah's response levels in the course of the developments. This means that the Iranians constitute a key factor in the organization's operational-terrorist guidance, and it is in their power to trigger a regional deterioration if they choose to do so.

The Hizballah enjoys not only Iranian aid, but Syrian aid as well. In the framework of the "Syrian arrangement" in Lebanon, Syria turned the Hizballah into the central Lebanese militia organization that is still armed, in blatant contravention of the Taaf Agreements (1989). While other ethnic militias were disarmed, the Syrians enabled the Hizballah to maintain a broad military infrastructure and to conduct operational activity against Israel from South Lebanon without disruption.

Since Bashar al Assad's rise to power (in July 2000) there has been a significant change in the pattern of relations between the Syrian regime and the Hizballah, which consists mainly of the organization's upgrading from an instrumental toy and aid in managing Syria's policy against Israel and Lebanon to a strategic partner ("a front arm") and a central actor, which has significant influence on Syria's policy in this matter.[10] The setting for this change is rooted in the special and close relationship that has developed between the inexperienced Bashar al Assad and the leader of the Hizballah, Hassan Nasrallah, which is particularly conspicuous when one recalls the distance and suspicion with which Assad Sr. treated the organization. Two main developments have contributed to the rapprochement process between the parties and to the formation of the current relationship pattern:[11]

- A change in the balance of forces between Syria and the Hizballah due to the change of government in Damascus and Hizballah's success in forcing the IDF to withdraw from Lebanon in the summer of 2000. In the initial stages of the stabilization of Bashar al Assad's government, Syria's position was weakened considerably, while the Hizballah was reaching the pinnacle of its glory and power due to its successes in Lebanon.
- A coinciding of Syrian and Hizballah interests due to the failure in the channel of the Syrian-Israel negotiations (March 2000), the Israeli withdrawal from Lebanon (May 2000), and the fear of what was interpreted as Israel's attempt to force new "game rules" by attacking Syrian targets in response to attacks in South Lebanon (April and July 2001).

Syria offers the Hizballah political support in the internal-Lebanese and international arenas, as well as wide maneuvering space for its fortification in Lebanon and the continuation of its activities in South Lebanon: This activity is directed at preventing the Israeli-Lebanese border from turning into a quiet one, and maintaining controlled tension. Expressions of this approach can be observed in the Shab'a Farms, in the firing of anti-aircraft shells at Israel Air Force flights aimed at pestering and frightening the civilian population along the border, and attacks—sometimes under Palestinian cover, outside of the Mount Dov sector (such as the Matsuba incident on March 12, 2002).

On the propaganda and informational level, Syria and the Lebanese administration under the former's control are acting to create an international defense umbrella for the Hizballah, by presenting it worldwide as a legitimate "resistance organization" rather than a terror organization. Syria offers the organization military aid, which supplements the Iranian support, and is willing to deviate from the aid patterns that were customary during the period of Assad Sr. For example, during the past year Syria has given the Hizballah Syrian-made long-range 220 mm. rockets.

As mentioned above, the Hizballah strives to preserve a controlled level of tension along the border with Israel, while finding various excuses for raising the tension level even in matters unrelated to the military. For example, when controversy rose between Israel and Lebanon regarding the drawing of water from the Vazani, the head of the southern sector in the Hizballah Sheikh Kauk stated, "the issue is not open for discussion or negotiation." Similarly, the head of the Hizballah faction in the Lebanese Parliament Naim Ra'ad stated, "the world is trying to force negotiations upon us regarding the waters of the Vazani springs.... It is our right to use the water as we see fit, in any way that we deem appropriate, and no one has the right to interfere with this right."[12] This example illustrates Hizballah's uniqueness as a terror organization that takes upon itself the authority to represent the interests of the central administration in Lebanon and to state in its name whether or not negotiations will take place.

Although since the mid-1990s neither the Iranians nor the Hizballah have carried out attacks against Israeli targets abroad, the operational infrastructures of the Hizballah and Iran can be used for these types of attacks in the future, if the Iranians should decide to do so. These capabilities were reflected during the years 1990-1994, in the course of which six attacks were perpetrated against Israeli and Jewish targets in the world (see Table 4.1). Two of these attacks were perpetrated in Argentina and were discussed intensively in chapter 3 (in the section discussing suicide attacks).

Table 4.1
Attacks against Israeli and Jewish Targets Abroad in Which Iran and the Hizballah Were Involved

Date	Description of the attack
February 4, 1990	A bus of Israeli tourists, which was making its way from Ismailiya to Cairo, was attacked. Nine Israelis were killed and nineteen were injured. One of the factions of the Palestinian Islamic Jihad (the Mahana faction) was responsible for the attack and acted with the full knowledge and support of the Revolutionary Guards in Lebanon.
February 14, 1991	The firing of an RPG missile at David Golan, an Israeli diplomat in Istanbul, Turkey. No one was injured. The attack was perpetrated by a local group of activists operated by the Iranians.
March 7, 1992	The detonation of a car belonging to Ehud Sadan, a security officer at the Israeli Embassy in Ankara, Turkey. Sadan was killed. It appears that the attack was perpetrated by local entities directed by the Iranians. The attack came in retaliation for the termination of Abas Musawi, secretary-general of the Hizballah, by Israel.
March 17, 1992	A car bomb driven by a suicide terrorist exploded near the Israeli Embassy in Buenos Aires, Argentina, and caused its collapse. Twenty-nine people were killed in the attack and 242 were injured. The Hizballah is responsible for the attack, and acted on the basis of an Iranian resolution and with Iranian aid.
January 28, 1993	An assassination attempt was made against the leader of the Jewish community and one of the richest people in Turkey, Jack Kimche, by shooting a rocket at his car. The attack was perpetrated by local entities directed by the Iranians.
July 18, 1994	The building of the Jewish community in Buenos Aires (AMIA) was destroyed as the result of a car bombing. Ninety-seven people were killed and 230 were wounded. The attack was perpetrated by the Hizballah following an Iranian resolution and with Iranian aid.

Hizballah and Iran's Policy following the IDF's Withdrawal from Lebanon (May 2000)

The Hizballah and its patron Iran regard the IDF's one-sided withdrawal from Lebanon as a victory and proof that through armed conflict it is possible to defeat Israel. This message is emphasized repeatedly in speeches delivered by Hassan Nasrallah, secretary-general of the Hizballah, who called on the Palestinians to break off negotiations and launch an armed struggle, which did indeed occur in September 2000 with the outbreak of the Al Aksa Intifada.

The Hizballah does not regard the IDF withdrawal from Lebanon as the end of the conflict. Moreover, it views the continued conflict against Israel as a central component of its ideology and a central justification for its perpetuation as an armed power in the Lebanese arena. The organization claims that the struggle against Israel must continue for the following reasons:

- Liberation of the remaining Lebanese soil, which the organization claims is still under Israeli occupation. This refers mainly to the Shab'a Farms (the Mount Dov region), but also to additional areas like the "Seven Villages." (These areas are located beyond the line of the international boundary and since 1949 have been included in the area of the State of Israel.)
- Defense of Lebanese sovereignty and citizens – The organization regards itself as obligated to respond to what it perceives as Israeli actions that violate Lebanese sovereignty. The organization believes that any harm caused to the Lebanese population or infrastructure by Israel must be countered by an attack against Israeli civilian targets.
- The release of Lebanese prisoners and detainees being held in Israeli prisons: The organization demands the release of detainees and prisoners, particularly Dirani and Obeid.[13] The Hizballah claims that the kidnapping of three IDF soldiers on October 7, 2000 and the kidnapping of Israeli citizen Elhanan Tanenbaum were perpetrated in order to bring about the liberation of the organization's prisoners and those affiliated with Palestinian organizations.
- In January 2004, Israel and Hizballah reached an agreement for exchange of prisoners, abductees and bodies. (The mediator was the German Ernest Uhrlau).
- Israel released 424 prisoners, including sheikh Abdel Karim Obeid and Mustafa Dirani.
- Hizballah released the Israeli civilian Elhanan Tannenbaum and the bodies of the three Israeli soldiers whom the Hizballah had kidnapped in October 2000.
- Aid and support for the Palestinian armed struggle and a demand to solve the problem of the Palestinian refugees, while placing emphasis on those living in Lebanon.

With the aim of perpetuating the struggle against Israel after its withdrawal from Lebanon, the Hizballah has been acting on several levels with Iranian and Syrian aid:

- Deployment of the organization's infrastructure along the border with Israel, which enables defensive alignment on the one hand, and the perpetration of offensive terror activities, on the other;
- Perpetration of terror activity mainly in the Mount Dov (Shab'a Farms) sector, which is perceived by the organization and by Syria and Lebanon as a "legitimate" sector for activity;
- The development of a "strategic arm" of long-range rockets as a strategic deterrence component in the hands of the organization and Iran vis-à-vis Israel;
- The development of an intelligence infrastructure for the perpetration of attacks inside Israeli territory.

Until the outbreak of the Al Aksa Intifada, the Hizballah perpetrated sporadic attacks in the Mount Dov sector. However, since September 2000, following the beginning of the Intifada, the Hizballah has escalated its attack policy with the aim of dragging Israel into confrontation on an additional front, thus aiding the Palestinians and increasing the pressure on Israel.

Throughout the entire period (since its withdrawal from Lebanon) the Israeli government has adhered to its policy of restraint in order to prevent the opening of a second front in the north, in addition to the confrontation with the Palestinians, and based on the knowledge that the Lebanese arena contains the risk of deterioration to the point of overall war in the region. But due to the policy of restraint, the IDF's deterrent power has eroded, since the Hizballah has interpreted this restraint as Israeli weakness and raised the level, frequency, and scope of the attacks.

Escalation in the Hizballah's attacks peaked during the Defense Shield Campaign (March 28 to April 13, 2001), when it initiated a series of massive shooting attacks on the northern border; the attacks included the firing of about 1,000 anti-aircraft missiles and nearly a 1,000 mortar shells, rockets, and artillery shells. This was the most severe and intensive activity since the IDF's withdrawal from South Lebanon in May 2000, and it went on continuously for a two-week period. The IDF responded with artillery fire and airborne attacks, and, simultaneously, Israel issued a warning through diplomatic channels to Syria and Lebanon regarding the grave consequences of continued Hizballah activity.

The Israeli warnings, backed up by the mobilization of the reserves, had the desired effect and the Hizballah ceased shooting. Since April 2002, the Hizballah has reverted to its previous modi operandi, that is, focusing relatively infrequent attacks on the Mount Dov area, and the shooting of anti-aircraft missiles allegedly against the Air Force but actually with the aim of harassing the settlements near the northern border.

Table 4.2
Hizballah Attacks against Israel after the IDF's Withdrawal from Lebanon
(May 2000)

Date	Description of the attack
October 7, 2000	The Hizballah shot anti-aircraft missiles at IDF outposts at Mount Dov. At the same time an explosive device was activated and light weapon fire was directed at an IDF patrol jeep in the Mount Dov region. Three IDF soldiers were kidnapped from the incapacitated jeep.
October 15, 2000	Hassan Nasrallah, secretary-general of the Hizballah, announced that his organization was holding an Israeli citizen named Elhanan Tanenbaum (a colonel in reserves).
November 16, 2000	Three explosive devices were activated against an IDF convoy that was moving in the Mount Dov area. Two soldiers were slightly wounded by the explosions.
November 26, 2000	Six explosive devices were detonated against an IDF patrol at the Sion River. One soldier was killed and two others were wounded.
January 2, 2001	An Israeli laborer working on the roof of an observation post on the Lebanese border was shot and injured.
January 3, 2001	The Hizballah fired several mortar shells into Israeli territory near the Mount Dov and Sion River regions.
January 26, 2001	An IDF observation post identified a unit of three terrorists crossing over the Lebanese border fence. IDF forces fired at the unit and as a result of the gunfire two of the terrorists were killed and one was wounded. It would appear that the cell was made up of Palestinian terrorists.
February 16, 2001	The Hizballah launched two anti-tank Taw missiles at an IDF supply convoy at Mount Dov. One soldier was killed and three others were wounded in the attack.
April 14, 2001	The Hizballah fired two anti-tank missiles at an IDF tank at Mount Dov. One IDF soldier was killed and the tank was damaged. In retaliation, IAF (Israel Air Force) planes attacked a Syrian radar base at Dahr al Bider near the Beirut-Damascus road on April 14.
May 14, 2001	The Hizballah fired two Sager anti-tank missiles at an IDF outpost on Mount Dov. No one was hurt but the building was damaged.
June 29, 2001	The Hizballah fired missiles and mortar shells at IDF outposts at Mount Dov. One IDF soldier was seriously injured in the attack. In response, IAF airplanes attacked a Syrian radar station in Bakaa in South Lebanon on July 1. The Hizballah retaliated with mortar fire towards the Mount Dov IDF outposts.

Table 4.2 (cont.)

October 3, 2001	The Hizballah fired missiles and mortar shells at IDF outposts at Mount Dov. No one was hurt but damage was caused to one of the outposts.
October 22, 2001	The Hizballah fired missiles and mortar shells at IDF outposts at Mount Dov. One soldier was wounded and damage was caused to the outpost.
January 15, 2002	The Hizballah fired anti-aircraft missiles at IAF airplanes cruising in the air.
January 23, 2002	The Hizballah fired an intensive barrage of anti-tank missiles and mortar shells at IDF outposts at Mount Dov. One soldier was slightly wounded and damage was caused to the outposts. In retaliation, IAF planes attacked Hizballah targets in South Lebanon, and IDF tanks and artillery also fired at terrorist targets.
January 31, 2002-March 11, 2002	Nine events of anti-aircraft fire by Hizballah.
March 12, 2002	Two terrorists crossed over the border fence into Israeli territory from Lebanon (using a ladder). The terrorists situated themselves in the Metsuba region and opened fire at vehicles driving down the Shlomi-Metsuba road. Five civilians were killed in addition to an IDF officer. Five civilians and two soldiers were injured. The two terrorists were eliminated by IDF fire.
March 30 – April 13, 2002	During the intensified Israeli combat against the Palestinians (the Defense Shield Campaign), the Hizballah escalated its attacks from the Lebanese border in order to trigger overall deterioration and the opening of another front against Israel as an expression of its solidarity with the Palestinian struggle.
August 29, 2002	The Hizballah fired anti-tank missiles towards IDF outposts at Mount Dov. One soldier was killed and two were injured.
December 9, 2002	An explosive device was planted near an IDF outpost. Two soldiers were wounded in the explosion.
January 12, 2003	The Hizballah fired mortar shells and anti-tank missiles at IDF outposts at the Mount Dov sector. No one was injured.
August 8, 2003	The Hizballah fired anti tank missiles and mortar shells at mount Dov, One soldier was injured
October 27,2003	The Hizballah fired anti tank missiles and mortar shells at mount Dov, One soldier was injured.
November 5,2003	Seven explosive devices were found by an IDF patrol near the border fence in the western sector of the Lebanese Israeli border
December 10, 2003	Five explosive devices were found by an IDF patrol near the border fence in the Western sector of the Lebanese Israeli border.

Table 4.2 (cont.)

January-December 2003	53 events of anti aircraft fire by the Hizballah.
January 4,2004	An explosive device was found by an IDF patrol near the border fence
January 19,2004	The Hizballah fired anti tank missile at IDF D-9
March 24,2004	The Hizballah fired anti tank missiles and mortar shells at mount Dov.
May 7,2004	The Hizballah fired anti tank missiles and mortar shells at mount Dov, One soldier was killed and fourteen were injured.
July 20, 2004	Snipers of Hizballah fire at an IDF position in the western sector of the Lebanese Israeli border. Two soldiers were killed.
January-November 2004	Two incidents of anti-aircraft fire by the Hizballah.

The Hizballah's Strategic Branch[14]

With the help of Iran and Syria, the Hizballah developed a strategic cache of various rockets, some of which are long-range and pose a strategic threat against the population of northern Israel. According to various reports, the Hizballah has more than 10,000 rockets of various sorts, with the aim of creating a strategic deterrence balance that will tie Israel's hands in its battle against the organization's terror activity. The organization possesses the following rockets:

- Short- and medium-range Katyushas (107 and 122 mm.);
- Fager3 rockets with a range of forty-five kilometers;
- Fager5 rockets with a range of about seventy-five kilometers;
- Syrian rockets with a 220-mm.

The long-range rockets enable Iran and the Hizballah to attack deep inside Israeli territory, thus expanding the circumference of the threat and deterring Israel from harsh retaliation against the Hizballah attacks at Mount Dov. Messages that reflect this perception can be found in the words of Secretary-General Hassan Nasrallah:

> We are well acquainted with the north, we know the villages, the small settlements, the orchards, the places where the 1948 Arabs lived, where the Jews live, the factories and the airport—it is all in our hands, and all that is needed is to press a few buttons and nothing will fall in vain. (Radio Nur, March 22, 2001)

> When you return to your homes, take a map and mark the area from Haifa, meaning the coastal plain, to Tiberias. This entire area is in the grasp of the resistance fighters in Lebanon. (Radio Nur, March 22, 2001)

...The targets that will absorb the retaliation have already been chosen and are well defined, and our brothers know how to act. They do not require any more than a two-second telephone call." (Al-Manar television network, October 15, 2002)

On the November 8, 2004, Hizballah launched for the first time an un-manned aerial vehicle (UAV) for a surveillance mission over the northern part of Israel. The UAV crossed the border near the sea and flew over the city of Nahariya and on its way back crashed in Lebanese territory. The UAV "Mirsad 1" was produced by Iran as a part of the Iranian UAV program. Hassan Nasrallah claimed that the UAV can be used for surveillance missions or to attack targets in Israel with a payload of about 40 Kg. The introduction of the UAV to the weapons arsenal of Hizballah has strategic significance and creates a new type of threat to Israel.

The Hizballah—Espionage and Attempts to Perpetrate Attacks Inside Israel

Following the IDF withdrawal from Lebanon, the Hizballah focused on intelligence gathering and the establishment of terror infrastructures that would act against targets inside Israeli territory. In the years 2000-2003, two types of Hizballah activities were exposed:

- The establishment of espionage rings to gather intelligence in Israel;
- The infiltration of terrorists into Israel in order to establish terror infra-structures and perpetrate attacks.

Espionage Rings in the Service of the Hizballah

Since the IDF's withdrawal from Lebanon several espionage affairs on be-half of the Hizballah have been exposed:[15]

- Nissim Nassar, a thirty-six-year-old Jew from Holon, was arrested in July 2002 and charged with contact with a foreign agent and handing over information to the enemy with the aim of impairing state security. Nassar, who had arrived in Israel in the 1990s, was activated by a Hizballah member through his brother who resides in Lebanon. Nassar was suspected of giving the Hizballah photographs and maps of sensi-tive sites inside Israel, mainly in the Tel Aviv area.
- In August 2002, two Arab residents of the Rajar village were arrested under the suspicion that they had handed classified intelligence mate-rial over to the Hizballah in exchange for drugs and weaponry. The interrogation revealed that the two had mediated between the organi-zation and drug dealers in Israel, and had received a large amount of drugs in exchange for maps, computer software, books about Jerusa-lem and hiking trips with route markings. In exchange for their ser-

vices, the two received fifty kilograms of hashish, three hand grenades, and two handguns.

- In October 2002, another espionage episode was released for publication. The main suspect was Lieutenant Colonel Omer al Haib, a handicapped IDF officer who was a Beit-Zarzir resident and a member of a bereaved family. Nine other Bedouins were arrested along with him. They were suspected of handing over information to the Hizballah about the IDF deployment, which included information about the location of ambushes and outposts.
- In February 2003, a mixed network of Jews and Arabs from northern Israel was arrested; its members were suspected of supplying the Hizballah with weapons, maps, and photographs of northern Israel in exchange for large amounts of drugs. The network included twelve members from the village of Rajar and from Kiryat Shmona. The suspects included a Jewish woman from Kiryat Shmona as well as two soldiers who were stationed at the roadblock south of Rajar; the latter cooperated with the smugglers in exchange for drugs.

Attack Attempts by the Hizballah Inside Israel[16]

The Hizballah's terror activity against Israel includes the use of the organization's terror infrastructures worldwide. The global activity of the terror cells is supervised by the headquarters in Lebanon while maintaining a high level of compartmentalization so that the arrest of one member will not result in the arrest of other activists. The recruited agents are to enter Israel and help gather intelligence about targets in Israel for the purpose of perpetrating attacks.

The advantage of activists recruited abroad is that they carry foreign passports which enable them unrestricted entry into Israel and freedom of movement. The probability that these people will be suspected of being Lebanese citizens is low, and it is easier for them to adapt their personality to the cover story.

To date, four activists who were sent to Israel in this manner have been apprehended. The first, a member of the Hizballah's "foreign unit," was Hussein Mukadad, who arrived in Israel in 1996. On April 12, 1997, Mukadad exploded in a hotel room at the Lawrence Hotel in East Jerusalem as he was negligently handling a bomb. The hotel records identified him as a British citizen, Andrew Jonathan Charles Newman, an accountant from London. The passport was checked and found to be a professional forgery. This was the first time that someone from the Hizballah had infiltrated Israel. He was recruited into the Hizballah in September 1995, when one of Muraniya's men contacted him and introduced himself as the director of a department in the organization's security agency. Hussein Mukadad, who was gravely wounded in the "work accident," had intended to detonate an airplane or a crowded site in Israel. He was released in the framework of prisoner exchanges with the Hizballah.

On November 28, 1997, a German citizen named Stefan Smirk was arrested upon arrival at Ben Gurion Airport following a flight from Amsterdam. Smirk was charged with membership in a terror organization and planning a suicide attack in Israel. Smirk had converted to Islam in 1994, taken on the name Abd al Karim, and two years later contacted the Hizballah. According to the charge sheet, Smirk was in Lebanon between August and November of 1997,where he underwent training in the use of weapons and explosives. According to Israeli claims, he arrived equipped with a video camera and instructions to gather information about targets in Tel Aviv and Haifa. Subsequently, he was supposed to fly to Turkey in order to receive final instructions from Muraniya regarding the perpetration of a suicide attack.

Jihad Shuman was arrested in East Jerusalem in January 2001. During his interrogation he revealed that he was a Hizballah activist who had entered Israel a few days previously with a British passport. His mission was to perpetrate attacks inside Israel.

The last one on the list for the time being is Fauzi Ayub, who was arrested during the Defense Shield Campaign in Hebron. Ayub, a thirty-eight-year-old Lebanese Shiite, had lived in Canada in recent years, where he accepted various missions imposed upon him by Hizballah leaders. Upon his return from Canada to Lebanon senior members of the organization, with whom he had developed close ties since his earlier involvement, contacted him and recruited him for a mission in Israel. He was sent to attend a series of training sessions, which were to prepare him for his mission. In the course of his briefings, Ayub was instructed to use his real passport to travel from Lebanon to a European state, leave his passport there, and receive a forged passport from another member of the organization in order to gain entry into Israel. Ayub was also instructed to purchase new luggage and destroy any evidence of his Lebanese origins. Subsequently, he was to arrive in a third European country, from which he would set out for Israel, with the aim of covering up any traces of his original identity. Ayub was briefed to adhere to very strict rules of behavior during his stay in Israel, which included using only the English language and denial of his Arab identity. Ayub was dispatched to Israel with a forged U.S. passport immediately after the outbreak of the Al Aksa Intifada, and stayed at a hotel in downtown Jerusalem. He later moved to Hebron where he joined another man who was to aid him with his task. Ayub's task was to teach members of the Islamic Jihad and the Hamas how to prepare sophisticated explosive devices and perpetrate attacks (according to the models that the Hizballah developed during the fighting in Lebanon). Prior to that, Ayub gathered weaponry from various places of concealment for his use in the course of the mission. At the time of his arrest he was caught with two glider parachutes that had been smuggled into Hebron at the Hizballah's initiative in order to perpetrate a large attack in Israel.

Parallel to the Hizballah's attempts to infiltrate terrorists and set up infrastructures in the Palestinian Authority, it also began to found "dormant cells" among Israeli Arabs. Initially, several Hizballah activists penetrated Gaza and the areas of Judea and Samaria who then recruited activists and sent them for training at Hizballah camps. Massoud Ayad, a lieutenant colonel in "Force 17"—Arafat's presidential guard—became head of the Hizballah's organization in the Gaza Strip. In this framework, he was responsible for the firing of mortars, the smuggling in of heavy weapons, and the planning measures to kidnap IDF soldiers and transfer them to Lebanon. Iyad was issued instructions by the Hizballah headquarters in Beirut. Two Apache gunships following his car as it traveled along Salah a-Din Street towards the Jibaliya refugee camp, fired missiles at the vehicle and killed him on February 13, 2001.

But this was only the beginning. Gradually, the Hizballah's involvement in Gaza and the areas of Judea and Samaria became more systematic and organized. In September 2001, in the framework of covert negotiations between the Palestinian Authority and the Iranian leadership, the Iranians consented to help supply weaponry upon the *Karin A* arms ship, but made a stipulation in exchange for the support: They demanded that the Palestinian Authority refrain from interfering with Hizballah activity in the areas of Judea, Samaria, and Gaza. Yasser Arafat, who was eager to acquire Katyushas, hastened to dispatch his agreement to Teheran. The Iranian-Palestinian connection, which began to develop in April 2001, thus peaked with the *Karin A* gunship affair. From the point of view of the Iranians, Nasrallah and his men are the most effective spark to ignite the fuse and undermine stability, without the tracks leading to Teheran.

The Iranian Intelligence Ministry and the Revolutionary Guards do indeed supply consultancy services and logistic aid, and in many cases also send dollars, but the contractor in the field is the Hizballah.

The Iranians also recruited wounded Palestinians who came to Iran from the Palestinian Authority for medical treatment. The wounded Palestinians departed from Gaza and the areas of Judea and Samaria for Jordan, and from there were flown on military and passenger flights to Iran, without stamping their passports, and were then transferred to military hospitals in Teheran. During their stay in Iran, contact was made via official Iranian entities, which were supposedly motivated by their desire to offer humanitarian aid. The wounded Palestinians underwent a process of intensive indoctrination—official receptions that were held for them were attended by senior Iranian leaders; they were brought in contact with various "popular committees"; and were taken to a movie theater where they were shown an Iranian propaganda film about the war against Israel and the Jews. Some of the wounded even underwent military training during their stay in Iran.

After the return of the wounded Palestinians to Gaza and the areas of Judea and Samaria, Iran began to utilize them as a pool of activists that could be operated in order to perpetrate acts against Israel while serving Iranian interests. These acts included the gathering of intelligence, the recruitment of an infrastructure of collaborators in Gaza and the areas of Judea and Samaria in order to perpetrate terror attacks, and the smuggling of weaponry into Gaza and the areas of Judea and Samaria under the camouflage of business. These activists were operated by the Hizballah or other terror organizations in Gaza and the areas of Judea and Samaria, and sometimes even directly by Iran. In this way, Iran clearly augmented its foothold in Gaza and the areas of Judea and Samaria.

The utilization of drug dealers has also become a regular useful vessel for the Hizballah. The organization's forces, which are deployed along the border with Israel, make sure to block dealers trying to infiltrate into Israel. Only those who promise to cooperate with the Hizballah by smuggling weapons, gathering intelligence about IDF bases and Israeli sites, and transmitting messages to Hizballah supporters functioning in the northern area are allowed to cross the border. This is how the drug market in the north came to be controlled by local Hizballah commanders, and this is also how it came about that experienced drug dealers also offer their services to smuggle weaponry for large sums of money. Indeed, Israeli security entities have issued numerous warnings that the Hizballah may flood Israel with drugs or even plant large amounts of poisoned drugs in its cities.

The Hizballah makes every effort to exploit vulnerabilities that it identifies in Israeli society. In this framework, the organization views the Israeli Arabs as a potential pool from which activists may be recruited to act among the organization's ranks. The Hizballah understands that the State of Israel trusts the Israeli Arab population, therefore they search for those who have had criminal dealings in the past, mainly those who deal in or use drugs, and try to recruit them.

Iranian Involvement in the Al Aksa Intifada[17]

Iran is one of the few countries in the world that openly declares its intentions to bring about the annihilation of the State of Israel. It not only makes this declaration openly, but also believes in its ability to implement it and acts to achieve its goal through the use of terror.

Iran, which is defined by the U.S. State Department as a state that supports terror, maintains a consistent policy involving the encouragement and fanning of the Palestinian Intifada through the provision of political and informational support as well as practical aid for terror attacks against Israel. This strategy is geared to achieve a variety of goals: weakening Israel by creating rifts and cracks in its society and impairing the Israeli economy; bolstering radical Islamic forces in the Palestinian Authority; and torpedoing any chance of renewing the momentum of the political process and achievement of an Israeli-Palestinian agreement. All of this falls within the framework of the overall use that Iran makes of the "terror weapon," as a tool to promote its national interests (see Figure 4.1).

This Iranian strategy fits in well with the use that Arafat makes of violence and of "the terror weapon" as leverage to advance his strategic goals, particularly since the launching of hostilities. That is the reason why until this time no real controversy has arisen between Iran and the radical Islamic opposition that it supports, and the Palestinian Authority. On the contrary, when confrontation occurs, the Iranians have presented the Palestinians with direct assistance (see the *Karin A* episode) and indirect aid for the Fatah and the Martyrs of the Al Aksa Brigades, which are under Arafat's command (via Munir al Makdakh, a former Fatah member acting from Lebanon and Hizballah).

From time to time, Iran denies the military-operational nature of the support that it gives to the organizations defined by the United States and the international community as terror organizations, and portrays it as political, humanitarian, or informational aid. However, findings from the interrogation of senior terrorists that fell captive to the IDF during the Defense Shield Campaign, along with Palestinian Authority documents that were confiscated during the campaign, and information accumulated during the Intifada, all supply unequivocal proof as to the falseness of these Iranian denials.

The method for implementing the Iranian terror strategy is by encouraging and fanning the flame of terror inside Israel, Gaza, and the areas of Judea and Samaria via the Palestinian and Lebanese terror organizations, radical Islamic organizations and leftwing organizations sponsored and controlled by Syria or Iran. These organizations, which participate in Palestinian terror or abet it, can be divided into four categories:

- Organizations with radical Islamic leanings—the Hamas and the Palestinian Islamic Jihad;
- Leftwing Palestinian organizations—Jibril's Front, the Popular Front for the Liberation of Palestine (*Habash*), the Democratic Front (*Hawatma*), the Palestinian Liberation Front, the Fatah faction headed by Abu-Mussa and the extremist faction of the "Popular Struggle Front";
- Terror organizations acting from Lebanon—the Hizballah and the 13th of Black September Brigades, a terror faction led by Munir al Makdakh, who split away from the Fatah.
- Fatah infrastructure such as the Tanzima Al Aksa Brigades (see details on following pages).

This Iranian and Syrian support has been supplemented during the Intifada by indirect and direct Iranian aid provided to the Martyrs of Al Aksa Brigades of the Fatah due to the fact that they have joined the circle of violence and terror.

Among these organizations, three organizations with the role of central "implementation contractors" serving Iran and Syria stand out:

- The Palestinian Islamic Jihad;
- The Hamas and its military branch—the Az al Din al Kassam Brigades;
- The Popular Front for the Liberation of Palestine—The General Command (Ahmed Jibril's organization).

These three entities are defined by the United States as terror organizations. The Palestinian Islamic Jihad and the Brigades of Az al Din al Kassam are also defined as terror organizations by the European Union.

Based on all of the sources specified above it appears that the Iranian aid supplied to Palestinian terror in Gaza and the areas of Judea and Samaria is diverse and is reflected in five areas:

1. *Propaganda and political support*—The Iranian media systematically support the perpetuation of the Intifada and praise the acts of violence and terror attacks. At inter-Arab and international forums, Iran stresses the alleged legitimacy of Palestinian terror ("national resistance"), and hosts conferences designated to support continued terror. It opposes agreements and arrangements that strive to put an end to terror, and criticizes the United States and the Arab regimes (Egypt, Jordan, and Saudi Arabia) that are trying to stop the terror and open up communication and negotiation channels.
2. *Directing the terror*—The Iranians fosters ongoing efforts to prevent calm in the "territories" and increase the acts of terror. Iran achieves this through the Palestinian organizations acting under its patronage, mainly the Palestinian Islamic Jihad, the Hamas, and Jibril's Front. This guidance includes coordination and briefings vis-à-vis terror attacks (through telephone calls, the Internet, and summoning activists), as well as assistance in preparing mega attacks (the intention to detonate the Azrieli Towers, for example). The directions to escalate and increase terror attacks are sometimes replaced by instructions to suspend terror activity temporarily when it is in Iranian interest (following the September 11 attacks in the United States, for example).
3. *The use of financial leverage*—Financial leverage constitutes a vital tool for the establishment of terror infrastructures and the momentum of terror activity. Findings from the interrogation of detainees during the Defense Shield Campaign indicate the existence of a systematic and organized method for the transfer of large sums of money from Iran through its sponsored organizations, via the Syrian banking system and that of Gaza and the areas of Judea and Samaria (the Arab Bank appears to serve as a central axis for the transfer of funds to terror organizations). The interrogation of the prisoners exposed the transfer of large sums to the Palestinian Islamic Jihad, to the Hamas, and indirectly to the Fatah's Martyrs of the Al Aksa Brigades (in addition to funds that the Fatah received from the Palestinian

Authority). These funds encouraged and promoted the perpetration of murderous terror attacks in Gaza and the areas of Judea and Samaria as well as Israel, whose execution was the condition for the transfer of financial support for the terror activists in the "field."

4. *Instruction and training*—Syria enables terror organizations sponsored by itself and Iran to maintain a training infrastructure on its soil and in Lebanese territory. Interrogations of terror activists from the Hamas, Palestinian Islamic Jihad, and Jibril's Front reveal that Syria operates a widespread training system for terror activists at Syrian army bases and in the Jibril Front's bases. Sometimes this training is undertaken in the course of academic studies in Syria or in other Arab countries. These training courses include designated professional training in the preparation of explosive devices, installing electrical circuits, and the production of belt bombs. Professional training in these matters is distributed to terror activists in Gaza and the areas of Judea and Samaria via the Internet and possibly via videocassettes. During the Defense Shield Campaign, a professional videocassette was found in Nablus containing detailed explanations given by an instructor from the Brigades of Az al Din al Kassam (the Hamas) regarding the preparation of explosive devices, including instructions on how to detonate a bus and the location of its weak points.

5. *The transfer of qualitative weaponry to Gaza and the areas of Judea and Samaria*—Iran strives to facilitate the Intifada by transferring qualitative weaponry to Gaza and the areas of Judea and Samaria both directly from within its own boundaries (the *Karin A* episode) and indirectly through Lebanon, via Jibril's Front and the Hizballah, whether by land (through Jordan to Gaza and the areas of Judea and Samaria) or sea (the *Santorini* episode). Interrogation of the crewmembers of these ships revealed Iran's role, the involvement of Jibril's Front and the Hizballah, and Syria's connections to the smuggling episodes. There is no doubt that if this qualitative weaponry, including Katyushas and antiaircraft missiles, had reached Gaza and the areas of Judea and Samaria, it would have significantly improved the terror organizations' abilities to attack densely populated areas in Israel (including large cities) as well as civil and military aviation, thus creating a "balance of terror" a la Lebanon.

Iranian Aid to the Palestinian Authority[18]

Up to the beginning of the Intifada, Iran mainly supported the Palestinian Islamic Jihad. The termination of the organization's leader Fathi Shkaki in Malta in 1995, and his replacement by Ramdan Shalakh, who is considered weaker and far less independent, only served to reinforce Iran's control over the organization.

To illustrate, a confidential and internal document of the General Security Agency of the Palestinian Authority, dated June 1, 2000, states that immediately prior to the IDF's withdrawal from Lebanon, Dr. Shalakh participated in a meeting with Sheikh al Islam, the Iranian ambassador in Damascus. In the course of the meeting, the Iranian ambassador demanded that the Islamic Jihad and the Hamas perpetrate terror attacks "inside Palestine" without claiming responsibility for them. Up until September 2000, Iran regarded the Palestinian Authority as a traitorous entity striving to reach a political agreement with Israel. The change in the line taken against Arafat and the agencies under his command came into being a short time after the outbreak of the Al Aksa Intifada. In October 2000, Iran's spiritual leader Ali Khamenei stated on television:

> We regard Palestine as a limb of our body, and the support for the Palestinian nation is a source of pride for the Iranian people.... The Palestinian people must continue with the blessed Jihad and take a stand against the enemies of Islam...the forces of the Hamas, the Islamic Jihad and the Fatah must continue in the struggle in a unified manner...and indeed, the solution (to the crisis in the region) is only one: withering the roots of the crisis, i.e., the Zionist regime forced upon the region.

Khamenei even published a religious ruling that permitted cooperation with the Palestinian Authority and the Fatah.

Iran expresses ongoing and open support for the suicide attacks. The Iranian Foreign Minister Kamal Kharazi stated that the attack at the dolphinarium in Tel Aviv was not a terror attack because Israel is a "conquering force." The Ayatollah Osama Fadel Lankrani, one of the leading religious leaders of the Shiite world, who resides in the city of Qum and is identified with the conservative camp, published a religious ruling stating that as the Palestinian people have no other possibility than to risk their lives in suicide attacks in order to protect their homeland, there is nothing to prevent them from perpetrating these acts.

Iran draws considerable encouragement from the Authority's decision to adopt the direction of terror, and regards it as an historical window of opportunity to weaken Israel. Since September 11, the fanning of the flames of confrontation serves Iran from an additional aspect: President Khamenei's adviser, Moktashemi Pur, claimed that the United States would not attack Iran and Iraq as long as the Palestinian crisis continued. Therefore, Iran must "increase the strength" of the Palestinians, and "prevent Israel from finding any possibility of resolving the crisis in the Middle East." Obviously, this claim was refuted when the United States and the Coalition forces invaded Iraq in April 2003.

From 2003 onward Iran directly and through the Hizballah was the main sponsor of the Palestinian terror.

Iranian Aid to the Organization of Munir al Makdakh[19]

Additional indirect support that Iran grants to terror within the area of the Palestinian Authority is passed through the organization of Munir Khalil al Makdakh—the 13th of Black September Brigades—which is based in Lebanon. The organization was founded in 1993 to commemorate the day of the signing of the "agreement in principle" between Israel and the Palestinians. Although the former member of the Fatah, al Makdakh, is considered an archrival of Yasser Arafat, it appears that he regularly transfers large sums of money to the activists in the Tanzim and the Martyrs of the Al Aksa Brigades in Gaza and the areas of Judea and Samaria. Iran provides considerable financial support to al Makdakh's organization via the "martyrs' fund," which also supports the Hizballah. Thus, Iranian funds reach the organizations affiliated with the Fatah and which are identified with Arafat.

Nasser Avis, a resident of the Balata refugee camp near Nablus and formerly an activist in the Palestinian Authority's General Intelligence Agency, stood out in the months prior to the Defense Shield Campaign as a senior military figure in the Fatah, the Tanzim and the Martyrs of the Al Aksa Brigades. He was involved in a series of brutal terror attacks in Israel in which dozens of Israelis were killed and injured. In his interrogation by the General Security Services (GSS), Avis fingered Munir al Makdakh as a source of financing for the attacks of the Fatah and the Martyrs of the Al Aksa Brigades. According to his testimony, around June 2001 he made contact with al Makdakh in Lebanon. The latter offered him financial aid for the perpetration of terror attacks. The contact between them was over the telephone (conversations every three or four days) and via the Internet. Avis would report to al Makdakh regarding attacks that his people had perpetrated, and al Makdakh transferred some $7,000 a week to cover expenses. Avis estimated that all together he received between $40,000 and $50,000. Similarly, funds were transferred to members of the Martyrs of the Al Aksa Brigades in the Jenin area. The interrogations indicated that al Makdakh was willing to invest generously in any terror cell that expressed the willingness to carry out attacks in Israel, even if the cell was small and inexperienced.

The *Santorini* Episode[20]

On May 6, 2001, the Israeli Navy intercepted a Lebanese ship, the *Santorini*, which was attempting to smuggle weaponry from Lebanon to the Gaza Strip and transfer it to the Palestinian Authority. The charge sheet submitted to the military court of the Gaza Strip in case 51/02 against four members of the Palestinian naval force (the *Bakhriya*) indicates that the four were also involved in several previous attempts of the Palestinian Authority to smuggle weapons into Gaza and the areas of Judea and Samaria on the *Santorini* and *Calypso 2*.

The suspects' interrogation revealed that up to the apprehension of the *Santorini*, four smuggling attempts had been accomplished successfully, which had included a wide assortment of weapons. The latter were placed in sealed casks, which were transported by the smuggling vessel, dropped at a regular spot north of Sinai, and from there were to have been collected by entities who would convey them to Gaza.

Interrogation of the *Santorini* crewmembers also revealed several important aspects related to Syrian cooperation with the Hizballah in smuggling weapons from Lebanon to Gaza and the areas of Judea and Samaria. One of the crewmembers, a Lebanese citizen named Dib Muhammad Rashid Awita, disclosed the following in his questioning:

- In the framework of the search for a ship to be used for the smuggling of weaponry to Gaza and the areas of Judea and Samaria, a ship called *Abd al Hadi* was found at the Aruad port in Syria. Under the sponsorship of members of Jibril's Popular Front, Awita went to Syria to examine the ship. When it was found to be suitable, its purchase was agreed upon at the Shahin restaurant in the city of Tartus in northern Syria. The ship was transferred to Lebanese registration, and its Syrian registration was obliterated. Thereafter, the ship was transported from Syria to the port of Tripoli in Lebanon by Syrian crewmembers, where its name was changed to *Santorini*.
- Awita overheard a discussion regarding the transfer of the weaponry from Syria to Lebanon for loading onto the ship in one of the smuggling cycles from Tripoli. The weaponry was placed in casks in Syria, loaded on a passenger bus with Syrian license plates from which the seats had been removed, and was transported on the Beirut-Damascus highway to Zahla and from there to Tripoli in northern Lebanon.
- The loading of the weaponry onto the *Santorini*, in a third smuggling attempt, was run by the Hizballah as a military campaign, with twenty-five organization activists participating in the operation. Some secured the coast and the roads leading to it, and others helped to load the ship.

In its last voyage, the *Santorini* set out from Tripoli in Lebanon and was supposed to unload its cargo opposite the coast of northern Sinai. However, it was stopped by the Israeli Navy on May 6, 2001, about one hundred and fifty miles west of Tyre. The ship was found to be carrying a wide range of weaponry, including Katyushas, anti-aircraft missiles (Sa7), anti-tank missiles, mortars, light weapons, and ammunition.

In the initial stages of the investigation, and in light of Ahmed Jibril's declarations emanating from Damascus, it was believed at first that the source of weapons was Jibril's organization, but an in-depth investigation revealed that the Hizballah was the driving force behind the operation, and Iranian fingerprints were discovered at every stage of the operation.

In his interrogation, the ship's captain revealed how strong behind the scenes ties were between the Hizballah and the Palestinians. According to his testimony, two days before the ship sailed with forty-five sealed casks of weapons, all of the parties involved in the smuggling episode assembled in his living room. Among those present were the Fatah's naval officers, a Palestinian video photographer from a nearby refugee camp, the Hizballah's smuggling officer called Abu Allah, and a well known drug smuggler from Beirut named Mustafa Karum. A Syrian truck brought the equipment, and the Hizballah activists loaded it onto the ship. Abu Allah and the Hizballah invested tens of thousands of dollars in the *Santorini* operation. At that time, the

Israeli prime minister sent a message to the U.S. administration regarding the interception of the weapons ship in which he emphasized that it was "a severe violation of the agreements that Arafat had signed with Israel—an attempt to acquire weapons through grave and devious means which could cause grievous harm to Israeli citizens." This message was conveyed by the finance minster at that time, Silvan Shalom, who met in Washington with National Security Advisor Condoleeza Rice.

The *Karin A* Episode[21]

Towards dawn on January 3, 2002, the Israel Navy intercepted a ship in the Red Sea carrying fifty tons of weapons—arms and ammunition—designated for the Palestinian Authority. The Israeli "Seals" commando force, in a joint operation with Israeli Navy units, IAF helicopters and aircraft, took over the *Karin A* some five hundred kilometers southeast of Eilat. The ship entered Israel's territorial waters on the evening of January 4 and was transferred to an Israeli naval base in Eilat.

The ship had been purchased in Lebanon by Adel Mugrabi, the individual responsible for transactions and projects for the Palestinian Authority. It had sailed for Sudan manned by a crew of Egyptians and Jordanians, who were not let in on the secret and were unaware of the voyage's purpose. Adel Mugrabi and four Palestinian crewmembers who had assumed responsibility for the operation awaited the ship in Sudan. They were headed by the ship's commander Omar al Ahawi, an officer with the rank of colonel in the Palestinian Authority's naval police. In Sudan, innocent general cargo was loaded on the ship, which was unloaded in Dubai, from whence the ship continued on its way to the Iranian island of Kish. There it joined an Iranian ferry, which was carrying members of the Iranian Intelligence Agency and representatives of Hizballah leader Imad Muraniya, who served as liaison between Iran and the Palestinian Authority. The men on the ferry loaded the weapons onto the ship; these were packed in special floating containers manufactured in Iran (for the purpose of smuggling weapons, it was necessary to use special sealed floating containers which were produced only in Iran).

The ship was supposed to reach the port of Alexandria, where the weapons were to be unloaded and reloaded onto three smaller ships. These ships, which had been purchased specifically for this purpose, were to have cast the containers into the sea opposite the coast of the Gaza Strip, where they were to have been collected by Palestinian boats and brought to shore. The cost of the Palestinian-Iranian weapons deal was about $15 million, not counting the $400,000 paid for the ship.

Initially, the Palestinian Authority denied any connection to the weapons ship and its spokespersons accused Israel of making up the episode in order to torpedo the initiative headed by General Zinni, the U.S. emissary. Jibril Rajub said, "The Israelis planned to use any way to impede Zinni's visit here, whose aim is to prevent Israeli aggression." Yasser Abd Rabu called the weapon ship "a fabrication," but nevertheless stated that the chairman of the Palestinian Authority had expressed his willingness to set up an investigation committee with the participation of a third party "in order to expose the false Israeli claims."

Hamid Rezah Asfi, spokesperson for the Iranian Foreign Ministry, denied Israel's declaration according to which his country was involved in the attempt to smuggle weapons to the Palestinian Authority, and argued that Iran maintained no military cooperation with the Palestinian Authority. He called upon the international community not to remain indifferent to the "crimes" that Israel perpetrates against the Palestinians. Nevertheless, the interrogation of the crewmembers of the *Karin A* indicates that Iran was directly involved in the supply of qualitative weapons to the Palestinian Authority. The Iranian connection was reiterated in the interrogation of Omar al Akawi, captain of the *Karin A*, and in the questioning of other sailors on board.

In his testimony, Al Akawi disclosed that he was to have visited Iran in July 2001 for "special arrangements," apparently in order to organize instruction about the floating containers for Palestinian Authority members. However, he claims that he did not go to Iran as planned, due to instructions he received according to which the Hizballah would handle that side of the arrangements.

The crewmembers of the *Karin A* recounted the ship's arrival at the Iranian shores, in the vicinity of the Island of Kish (on December 9, 2001), and described the loading of the containers with the weapons by the Iranian entities. Salim Mahmud al Sankari, an officer with the rank of *Nakib* (captain) in the Palestinian navy, who in the past had participated in an attempted naval attack, was on the *Karin A* when it was intercepted. In his testimony, he disclosed that an Iranian had filmed the loading of the ship in Iran. He also stated that in September 2001 he had undergone specialized training in deep-sea diving and in the "operation" of the floating containers. The training had been conducted by the Hizballah. He maintained that one of the Hizballah trainers had been present during the loading of the weapons opposite the Iranian coast.

Riad Abdallah, a crewmember, said that in July 2001 he went to Syria in order to purchase a boat. In Syria, he met with a Hizballah liaison named Haj Bassam, who gave him a down payment in order to purchase the boat.

It is to be noted that part of the weaponry discovered on board had been manufactured in Iran (with 2001 the year of production), including RPG-7 anti-tank rockets, YM3 anti-tank mines and YM1anti-personnel mines. The markings on most of the weapons had been changed and their serial numbers had been scratched out, so that their source could not be identified.

The cost of the weapons found on the *Karin A* was estimated at some $2 million. Interrogation of the captain and crewmembers revealed that the money for the purchase of the weapons and the ship came from the Hizballah. However, it appears that the Hizballah lacks resources of its own to finance projects of this scope, and that the project was actually funded by Iran, even if it was conducted under the cover of the Hizballah. The expenses for operating the ship (payment of salaries, insurance, etc.) were covered by the Palestinian Authority. Obviously, the Hizballah denied any involvement in the matter and refuted the Israeli claims.

The chief of staff at that time, Lieutenant General Shaul Mofaz, held a press conference on January 4 in which he stated that the link between the ship's crewmembers and the Palestinian Authority was unequivocal and clear—the ship belonged to the Authority, and senior Palestinian entities were involved in the smuggling. He noted that the operation had revealed a strong link between the Palestinian Authority, Iran, and terror entities affiliated with it that were interested in the annihilation of the State of Israel. He defined the operation of intercepting the ship as "a milestone in the war against terror."

Egypt reacted cautiously to the news, and President Mubarak's political advisor, Osama el Baz, said: "If it is proven beyond any doubt that the weapons ship is connected to the Palestinian Authority, or that the entire operation was conducted with its knowledge, this will constitute a hard blow to the peace process which must be condemned without hesitation."

On January 6, a press conference was convened in Eilat during which the confiscated weapons were put on display. Prime Minister Sharon said: "The Palestinian terror ship, which was on its way to the coast of Gaza, transported what was to have threatened each and every one of you...the type of weaponry caught on board the ship proves yet again that the Palestinian Authority is directing all of its efforts towards terror and is preparing the offensive infrastructure for the coming waves of terror."

At first, even the administration in Washington was skeptical that the large stock of weapons was meant for the Palestinian Authority, and they thought that it was actually designated for the Hizballah in Lebanon, rather than Palestinian organizations in Gaza and the areas of Judea and Samaria. Immediately, upon the interception of the ship, the initial impression was that the United States was not accepting the Israeli version vis-à-vis the Palestinian responsibility for smuggling the weapons. Only following Israeli pressure, the dispatch of senior intelligence officers to the United States, and proof presented by Israel, did the United States change its position, and the American announcements in this matter were modified. On January 10, almost a week after the ship was intercepted, President Bush stated: "I am beginning to suspect that these weapons were designated for the promotion of terror. The moment the proof is decisive, those responsible must be punished." Secretary of State Colin Powell said: "The information we have received and found ourselves clarifies that there is a connection with the Palestinian Authority." The spokesperson for the State Department stated: "This mandates a full explanation from Arafat. There is convincing evidence that senior members of the Palestinian Authority and the Fatah were involved. There is also compelling proof that Iran and the Hizballah were involved in the smuggling operation."

Table 4.3
Weaponry Found Aboard the *Karin A*

Type of weapon	Amount	Technical data
High trajectory weapons		
Launchers and 122 mm. rockets	62 rockets	Launching range about 20 km. Weight of battle head 18.3 kg. Weight of explosives 6.4 kg.
Launchers and 107 rockets	283 rockets	Range of 5.8 km. Weight of battle head 6.4 kg.
Mortar 120 mm. and mortar shells	10 mortars Approx. 700 mortar shells	Range of about 6 km. Weight of explosives 2.5 kg.
Mortar 81 mm. and mortar shells	19 mortars 686 mortar shells	Range of 2.5 km. Weight of explosives 550 grams.
Mortar 60 mm. and mortar shells	10 mortars 159 mortar shells	Range of 1.7 km. Weight of explosives 250 grams.
Anti-tank weapons		
Sagger launchers and missiles	6 launchers 10 missiles	Anti-tank missiles with a range of 3.5 km. 450 mm. penetration
RPG7 rockets	119 RPG rockets Tandem	Effective range of 300m. Penetration ability is unknown.
RPG7 rockets	209 PG7 rockets	Maximum range 400 m. Penetration ability about 300 mm.
RPG7 launchers	15	
Antitank RPG18 rocket + launchers	346	200 m. range. Penetration ability about 375 mm.
Mining and sabotage means		
Iranian MY3 antitank landmines	211	Generation one landmines Weight of explosives some 5.5 kgs.
Iranian anti-personnel MY1 mines	311	Weight of explosives some 50 grams.
Demolition blocks and standard explosives in large packages.	Total – about 2,200 kgs.	C-4 blocks. TNT blocks 10-kg. packs of C-4
Light weapons		
Dragonov sniper rifles	30	Effective range about 1000 m. with a PSO-1 telescope.
PK machine guns	18	
AK-47 assault rifles (Kalachnikovs)	212	Some are used and others are made in China.
Ammunition for light weapons 7.62	407,800 291,400	Kalachnikov bullets Bullets for the Dragonov and PK machine guns.
Hand grenades	735	
Naval equipment		
Zodiac boats with external motors—"Yamaha" 25 horsepower	2	
Oxygen tanks and diving equipment		
Sophisticated floating containers for smuggling weapons	80	Concealment of weapons in a maritime medium.

Ultimately, even Egypt was convinced of Arafat's involvement in the smuggling attempt, and it was clear that the matter caused "embarrassment and considerable chagrin." Not only was the Palestinian Authority planning on using an Egyptian port for the smuggling, but it also awarded the Iranians—Egypt's enemies—a foothold in the Egyptian arena of influence.

The decision that was made in Israel following the ship's interception was to cut off discussions with the Palestinians until Arafat arrested those people involved in the operation. Due to the pressure placed upon it, the Palestinian Authority announced that it had appointed a committee of inquiry, and following its findings the entities responsible for the smuggling were arrested:

- Fathi Razem—Deputy commander of the Palestinian naval police
- Fuad Shubaki—The entity responsible for the financial mechanism in the Palestinian Authority
- Adel Mugrabi—The entity responsible for transactions and projects in the Palestinian Authority.

The subsequent interrogation of the *Karin A* detainees and the exposure of the weapons caught on board ultimately provided unequivocal proof vis-à-vis the Palestinian Authority's involvement in terror and the growing cooperation between the Authority, the Hizballah, and Iran in this matter.

The *Abu-Hassan* Episode[22]

On the night of May 20, 2003, the Israeli navy caught an Egyptian fishing boa, *Abu-Hassan*, as it was attempting to smuggle weaponry, teaching manuals, and a Hizballah sabotage expert into the Gaza Strip. Interrogation of its crewmembers indicated that the boat had left Egypt on May 16, 2003, and sailed for Beirut. Opposite the shores of Beirut, the ship was met by a Hizballah rubber boat carrying weaponry, teaching manuals, and the sabotage expert. It is not yet clear how the smuggling operation was to be performed but there are two possibilities:

- Joining up with a sea vessel from Gaza and transferring all of the ship's contents over the sea;
- Smuggling the contents from Egypt via the Rafiah tunnels.

The Hizballah in Lebanon was involved in the smuggling attempt as well as entities in the Palestinian Authority including Adel Mugrabi and Fatkhi Razem, deputy commander of the Palestinian police. The two had been involved in previous smuggling attempts to the Palestinian Authority in connection with the *Santorini* and the *Karin A*.

The following means were found on board the *Abu-Hassan*:

- Fuses for 122 mm. rockets;
- Electronic timing units for explosive devices;
- Wireless activating systems for explosive devices;
- Training material including thirty-six computer disks, containing detailed information on how to prepare devices, landmines, and belt bombs, and tactical guidelines on how to perpetrate attacks (including where the suicide attacker should position himself on a bus in order to cause maximum damage).

It appears that the infiltration of the Hizballah sabotage expert along with training material was geared toward helping the Palestinians improve their capabilities in the area of preparing devices and attacks, benefiting from the experience and skills developed by the Hizballah in Lebanon.

The Hizballah, on the one hand, and the Palestinian Authority, on the other, hastened to deny any connection to the *Abu-Hassan* vessel or the smuggling attempt.

To summarize this section, following are several examples of confiscated documents that testify to Iran's involvement in Palestinian terror:[23]

Document A:
The National Palestinian Authority
Command of the Thwarting Security Agency
General Headquarters

Date: 31.10.2001
Ref. No. 2001/10/1200

For our brother the President Abu Amar (Yasser Arafat), may Allah preserve him.

With greetings from the homeland.

Re: The opposition parties are acting vigorously to increase joint activity.

According to the information in our possession it appears that intensive meetings are being attended by leaders from the Hamas, the Islamic Jihad, the Popular Front and the Hizballah in Damascus in order to increase the joint activity "inside" with the help of Iranian funding. This comes in the wake of an Iranian message for the leaders of the Hamas and the Islamic Jihad according to which there should be no lull in the situation at the current time. The financial aid will be transferred by the Hizballah in order to escalate the situation in the coming days. What is needed from the opposition parties is the perpetration of suicide missions against Israeli targets in Gaza, the West Bank and inside Israel. For your review.

Revolutionary greetings,
Your brother,
Jibril al Rajub

Document B:
PLO
The National Palestinian Authority
The President's office

10.12.2000

To His Honor the President, the Commander General (Yasser Arafat) may Allah preserve him.

Dear Sir,
We hereby attach for your perusal reports from the brother Amin al Hindi (Head of General Intelligence) which were received from the Lebanese arena by the Hamas Movement (Az al Din) al Kassam. Their content:

1. The Brigades of Az al Din al Kassam have received only $400,000 since the outbreak of the Intifada to date. The brigades are ready to carry out attacks against Israeli targets, but the money sent by Mussa abu Marzouk (a member of the Hamas's political bureau) did not arrive at its destination.

2. The Hamas in Syria published instructions for the Brigades of Az al Din al Kassam "inside," according to which an immediate financial status report and an evaluation report regarding military cells "inside" must be submitted. The leadership of the Hamas in Syria gave a "green light" to the headquarters of the military branch to perpetrate military activities against Israeli military targets without being bound by any decision of the military branch "inside." In addition, the brigades were requested to maintain a distance from the Hamas leaders who are coordinated with the Authority.

3. Ismail Abu Shenab (one of the Hamas leaders in the Gaza Strip) and Ismail Hanya (one of the senior leaders of the Hamas in the Gaza Strip and head of Sheikh Yassin's bureau) are in contact with Mousa Abu-Marzouk (a member of the Hamas's political bureau. At the time that the letter was written he was living in Syria). In addition, Sheikh Jamal Salim (one of the Hamas leaders in Nablus who died in an IDF thwarting operation in July 2001) is holding discussions with Imad al Almi (head on the "interior" committee in the Hamas and the Hamas representative in Syria). There is a real crisis within the Hamas due to lack of coordination and earlier organizational controversy.

4. The Muslim scholars, al Jama'a al Islamiya, Afif Nabulsi and the Hamas agreed that this year's charitable donations ("al Zaka") will be given to the Palestinian people, and that the Hamas will distribute it "inside" far away from the Palestinian Authority.

5. The money that will be collected (the "al Zaka" funds) will not be sent to Gaza and the areas of Judea and Samaria of the Authority, but will rather be placed in the accounts of Osama (Abu) Hamdan (the Hamas representative in Lebanon) and Khaled Mashal (head of the Hamas's political bureau, who resides outside of Gaza and the areas of Judea and Samaria). In addition, some of these funds will be allocated for the support of the military branch of the Hamas on the "inside."

6. The Iranian check for $700,000 reached the Palestinian opposition factions. This sum was included in the general budget of the factions. Iran agreed to allocate sums of money for the Al Aksa Martyrs which belong to these factions that will die the death of a martyr in the course of military attacks against Israel.

The document bears the following stamp:

The general department of the police
The Bethlehem District Police
Administration and Organization
12.12.2000
ref. mr 2140/

A handwritten notation appears in black ink: "Security of the police."
Also handwritten: "Important! Distribute to all police stations, administrations and departments."

Here follows a collection of Iranian statements supporting terror and calling for the annihilation of Israel (beginning January 2001):[24]
Speaker: Akhtari, advisor of the Iranian leader regarding international matters.

Background: A conference about the Intifada (January 10 2001)—ISNA—the Iranian Students Society.

Quotation: "Iran will never under any circumstances recognize even the existence of the State of Israel. Israel, with all its strength and satanic methods, will not be able to prevent the Palestinian people from continuing its Intifada."

Speaker: Iranian leader Khamenei

Background: A meeting with the organizers of "the international conference for support of the Intifada" (January 15, 2001 on Iranian television):

Quotation: "The foundation of the Islamic regime is the opposition to Israel, and Iran's perpetual issue is obliterating Israel from the region. Palestine is Islamic land that was conquered by the anti-Islamic enemy, and according to the ways of Islam we must oppose the Zionist regime. Support for the Palestinians is a religious command."

Speaker: Mukhtashemi-Pur, the president's advisor and head of "the international committee for support of the Intifada."

Background: A conference about Jerusalem that took place in Lebanon (January 29, 2001, Teheran Radio).

Quotation: "The Islamic nations must support the Palestinian people by supplying weaponry and money, and taking care of its Jihad needs."

Speaker: Mukhtashemi-Pur, the president's advisor and head of "the international committee for support of the Intifada."

Background: January 29, 2001, Teheran Radio.

Quotation: "The Zionist entity is a dangerous malignant growth in the body of the Islamic and Arab nation, which through its metastasis threatens world and human peace, and therefore it must be extracted at the root."

Speaker: Foreign Minister Kharazi
Background: An interview during a trip to Lebanon (March 21, 2001), *Al Sapir*, Lebanon.
Quotation: "The Lebanese people suffered terribly from the Israeli invasion, and we in Iran stood beside this people and alongside the Islamic resistance in the campaign to liberate the land, and will always stand by it until the full liberation and the annihilation of Israel.... Iranian-Syrian-Lebanese cooperation that brought about the withdrawal of the IDF from South Lebanon will also bring about the liberation of Palestine."

Speaker: Iran's President Khatami
Background: a speech at the "Palestine Conference" (April 24, 2001, IRNA News—Iranian News Agency).
Quotation: "The dangerous phenomenon of Zionism is what stands behind the military confrontations and the current political conflicts.... Zionism has turned Moses' pure religion into a game serving its satanic desires...the Zionist establishment, which is based on self-glorification and treading on others, created a state that is the greatest of historical tyrannies from the aspect of its violence and brutality and from the aspect of trampling on the most basic human principles...the stories of bravery of the Intifada are a basis for faith and courage of the people and a basis for expelling the government of power and violence...he who desires the spreading of liberty, justice and protection of the rights of humanity and its dignity...has no choice but to support the Intifada. ...the Islamic revolution in Iran, from the time of its conception until the various stages of its triumph and establishment, believed in the slogan: Today Iran and tomorrow Palestine—this is the eternal cry of our shahids...
"The stories of bravery in South Lebanon and in the second Intifada refuted the myth that the Zionist regime is unbeaten, and opened a clear future of struggle and victory before the Palestinian people."

Speaker: Iranian leader Khamenei
Background: A meeting with leaders of the Palestinian opposition organizations (April 25, 2001, Iranian television).
Quotation: "It is forbidden to think that the eradication and destruction of the Zionist regime, despite the support of the superpowers and its sophisticated weapons, are not impossible."

Speaker: The Iranian ambassador to Lebanon
Background: August 9, 2001, Iranian television.
Quotation: "There is no doubt that the existence of Israel and its behavior are clearly contradictory to the national interests of Iran."

Speaker: Iranian leader Khamenei
Background: Friday sermon (December 7, 2001, Iranian television)

Quotation: "The world of Islam must cease its negligence, it must use all of the means at its disposal in order to defend Palestine.... The Zionist regime is currently so deep in the mud that it has no idea what to do. It is clear that the tyrant, falsehoods and murder will not meet a good end. Hard times can be anticipated for the Zionist regime.... Thanks to the participation of young Palestinians in the struggle against the invaders, the honorable flames and fire of the Intifada will continue to grow, and after the imminent or subsequent destruction of the conquerors of Palestine, this piece of land will be ruled by the Palestinians.

Speaker: Rafsanjani, head of the "council to establish the interest" and former president.

Background: Friday sermon (December 14, 2001, the Khaber television network, Iran).

Quotation: "The Jews should expect a 'reverse Exodus' because one day the growth will be removed from the body of the Islamic world and then millions of Jews who moved there will again be homeless. When will this come to be? We will have to discuss this at another time.... If one day—which is of course very important—the Muslim world will also be equipped with the types of weapons that Israel now possesses, then the imperialist strategy will hit a dead-end. That is because the use of one atomic bomb inside Israel will leave no memory of it, and will not only hurt the Islamic world. It is not illogical to study this possibility.... Those people who have no choice but to volunteer for martyrdom will not be frightened by the (Israeli) violence.

"After all, they have nothing to lose. How could a person lose something when he believes that through his explosion one moment he is in the materialistic world and a moment later he is about to enter the divine Garden of Eden on the wings of God's angels. And when he is there he will sit near the Prophet and God's children in a reception given in honor of the shahids."

Speaker: Iranian leader Khamenei

Background: "Defense of the Palestinians" conference (December 31, 2002, the Khaber television network, Iran).

Quotation: "The current generation will witness the liberation of Palestine... many of the problems of the Islamic world stem from the malignant growth in the body of the world of Islam—the Zionist regime—any compromise in the matter of Palestine is in complete contradiction to national Iranian interests, and our prestige, our honor and our national interests are now based on our determined stand against the cancerous growth."

Speaker: Mukhtashemi-Pur, the president's advisor and head of "the international committee for support of the Intifada."

Background: A conference of Muslim religious scholars in Beirut (January 9, 2002, the Al-Manar television network).

Quotation: "The Palestinian people is left only with the possibility of suicide attacks against the conquering army, as the single weapon of this people in its struggle against the Zionist enemy. This, so that the international community will know that the Intifada and the Palestinian resistance constitute a legitimate right which this people is realizing in self-defense, and that the people will continue the struggle and resistance, regardless of the American pressure and the arbitrary steps that the Zionist army takes against the Palestinian Intifada. …it is the duty of each of us to terminate the malignant cell by using the soul, the money and all of the existing resources. …the duty falls upon the sons of the Palestinian people and all Muslims to go forth and fight the Zionist enemy until freeing Palestine through the Jihad and the resistance and through all of the existing possibilities."

Speaker: Muhamadi Rishhari, head of the Haj organization in the leader's bureau.

Background: A rally in support of the Intifada held in Mecca (February 18, 2002).

Quotation: "If the Islamic states unite in order annihilate Israel, they will achieve this goal easily."

Speaker: Radio Teheran

Background: March 9, 2002.

Quotation: "In order to perpetuate the Palestinian resistance it is important to coordinate between all of the entities managing the Jihad, and to cease all security and political initiatives and meetings. The only just and possible solution is the disappearance of the Zionist entity."

Speaker: Valyati, advisor of the Iranian leader regarding international matters.

Background: April 13, 2000, Iranian Television.

Quotation: (He called for the continuance of suicide attacks and emphasized that):"The gravest damage inflicted on Israel is the destruction of its security, as, to differentiate from the first Intifada, suicide attacks may also occur within the "areas of 1948," a fact that causes fear in Israel…. The Intifada causes emigration from Israel, which constitutes the countdown for the lifespan of the Israeli regime."

Speaker: Iranian leader Khamenei

Background: A speech delivered on May 1, 2002 (Radio Teheran in Persian).

Quotation: "Actions involving suicide and martyrdom for national and practical interests and for religion constitute the pinnacle of honor, bravery and courage of every nation…the Palestinian nation is alive and well and will continue on its path…. All Islamic governments, particularly the Arab ones, must bestow practical aid upon the Palestinians."

Figure 4.1
Iran and the Arab-Israeli Conflict

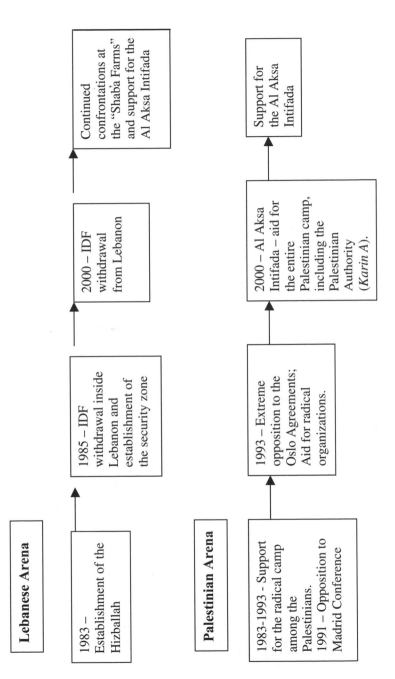

Speaker: Sheikh Hussein al Salam, Iranian Ambassador to Syria

Background: May 23, 2002, the official Iranian news agency, IRNA News.

Quotation: The only way to liberate Palestine from the clutches of the Zionist regime is to continue with the suicide attacks and the Intifada.... Iran believes that Palestine belongs to its original owners, and the Zionist conquerors have no right to it.... Khomeini's message regarding the need to destroy Israel has proven to be true now more than ever. And all Arab and Islamic states must make this thing happen..."

Western Targets

The United States

The United States was perceived by the revolutionary regime as the Great Satan and was accused of four "cardinal sins":

1. Its imperialist character and its manipulatory and oppressive involvement vis-à-vis Third World countries;
2. Its support of the Shah's tyranical regime and its exploitation of Iran;
3. Its support of "reactionary regimes" in the Muslim Middle East in general, and specifically in the Persian Gulf;
4. Its support of Zionism and Israel against the Islamic nation in general and against the Palestinians in particular.

At the outset, the "moderate" circles in the Iranian leadership[25] attempted to establish a normal relationship between the two countries, and it is to be noted that even before the ousting of the Shah some of these leaders had already initiated contacts with the Americans, particularly to prevent U.S. support of a counter-revolution on the part of Iranian generals. Thus, President Carter's announcement (February 12, 1979), according to which the United States would "respect the wishes of the Iranian people" vis-à-vis the replacement of the regime, was welcomed by the government, and the Iranian foreign minister hastened to announce that Iran was ready for "friendly relations" with the United States and the West.

In the course of 1979, Iran withdrew from "The Central Alliance" and canceled the "adminsitrative agreement for economic cooperation" with the United States, which had been valid since 1959, but at the same time the moderate elements in the regime still maintained diplomatic ties with the United States to the chagrin of the "Revolutionary Council" and the radical circles in the regime.

At the outset of the revolutionary regime in Iran, an ambivalent policy was conducted towards the United States, reflecting the controversy and internal power struggles in Iran. Khomeini and radical circles within the regime attributed no importance to maintaining ties with the United States, doubted the sincerity of its intentions and were contemptful of its ability to impair the revolution. These facts were reflected in Khomeini's words according to which "the United States cannot undertake any foolishness, because if it could it would have saved the Shah." After the American condemnation of executions in Iran, Khomeini said (on May 19, 1979) that the United States was an "injured and defeated snake," and compared the ties between Iran and the United States to the relationship between "the robbed victim and its plunderer."[26]

In Khomeini's view the Shah's hospitalization in the United States constituted decisive proof that nothing had changed in U.S. policy, and this step served as a catalyst for radical parties to put an end to Bazargan's government (which had adopted a moderate pro-Western line) shortly after his meeting with Brzezinski in Algeria (November 1, 1979). During the month of November, radical circles initiated "the student takeover" at the U.S. Embassy in Teheran, thus causing the severance of Iranian ties with the United States and the toppling of Bazargan's regime.[27]

The overtaking of the Embassy constituted an important milestone in Iran's political path—from that time on the relations with the United States deteriorated and terror became a major tool for the achievement of Iran's objectives on the international level.

In a speech delivered on November 1, 1979, Khomeini called on the revolutionary students to intensify their demonstrations against the United States and set November 4 (the memorial day for students who had been killed in anti-Shah demonstrations the previous year) as an appropriate day to take action against it. On that day, "the students who walk along the line of the Imam" implemented their leader's recommendation, overtook the embassy and seized the American diplomats (who were defined as "spies") as hostages.

The hostages affair turned into an "ongoing festival" (444 days) of demonstrations and anti-American incitement. The helplessness that the United States demonstrated in this affair, its inability to organize a coordinated Western response (even economic sanctions), combined with the emotional reaction of the American public only fueled Iranian's feeling of triumph. The failure of the American rescue operation in April 1980 constituted the climax of this euphoria.

The American Embassy affair in Teheran had several characteristics that can be observed in the Iranians' subsequent actions:[28]

1. The takeover was carried out by "students" (actually members of the Revolutionary Guards) as part of a defined plan and followed instructions issued by the authorities.
2. This "technique" enabled the Iranian regime allegedly to adopt the "neutral" stand of a go-between, who admittedly identified with and understood the feelings of the students but was not actually responsible for their acts.

3. This incident signaled Iran's willingness to break the most basic international "rules of the game"—honoring diplomatic immunity and extraterritorial sovereignty of a foreign embassy on Iranian land.
4. On the other hand, Iran demanded that the United States act according to international conventions and renounced the latter for its subversive activities which contravene international law, particularly for the activation of American military strength against Iran during the evacuation attempt.

The outbreak of the Iran-Iraq war (September 22, 1980) and the elections in the United States (November 4, 1980), in which Reagan triumphed, served as impetus for Iran to bring the incident to a close. Iran came to the conclusion that the propaganda benefits had been fully extracted on the inner Iranian level, and that it was necessary to focus on the war against Iraq, that is, to concentrate all of the country's resources on this war and divert the revolutionary fervor that had previously been focused on the struggle against the United States to the fight against Iraq.[29]

On September 12, 1980, Khomeini first set forth his conditions for an agreement (already during Carter's administration), based on the assumption that immediately prior to the imminent elections the administration would acquiesce to the Iranian conditions due to its desire to demonstrate achievements for the voters. Iranian stipulations for resolving the crisis included:

1. Handing over the Shah and the return of his property;
2. Cancellation of the American monetary demands vis-à-vis Iran;
3. An American promise to refrain from interfering in Iran's internal concerns;
4. Freeing the Iranian assets frozen in the United States.

On January 20, 1981, an agreement was signed between the United States and Iran in Algeria, according to which the Shah's property in the United States would be frozen, but the administration would not block Iranian legal efforts to reclaim ownership. Iranian assets valued at $11 billion were freed, but only half was returned to Iran and the rest was kept to defray Iranian debts to American banks. An additional billion dollars was kept in a special fund as guarantees vis-à-vis possible American claims against Iran.[30] Iran regarded the hostage affair as a triumph and proof of its ability to "bring the U.S. to its knees." The Iranian rulers stressed that the conclusion of the affair did not signal a change in their attitude towards "the Great Satan," and from that time on Iran left a single official channel open for discussions with the United States—the international court in The Hague, which handled thousands of reciprocal claims.[31] The clash between Khomeini's regime and the United States became an ideological and strategic struggle, with Khomeini presenting the United States as "the main enemy," and the battle against it as "a confrontation between Islam and the infidels."

It is possible to indicate several main areas of friction with the United States during the years of Khomeini's regime,:

1. The U.S. refusal to meet Iranian financial claims in the court of The Hague;
2. U.S. support for Iraq during the Iran-Iraq war (according to the Iranian version, the U.S. encouraged Iraq to start the war);
3. Continued U.S. support of "reactionary regimes": the supply of sophisticated weapons to Saudi Arabia, its military presence in the Persian Gulf and its willingness to "banner" Kuwaiti oil tankers to ensure their passage through the Gulf (1987);
4. U.S. support for Israel, particularly during the war in Lebanon.
5. The American presence in Lebanon, which hindered the establishment of an Islamic republic in this country.

The positive conclusions drawn by the Iranians from the hostage episode in Teheran encouraged them to make repeated use of terror to achieve their political goals vis-à-vis the United States. One of the first goals that Iran attempted to achieve via terror directed at the United States related to the issue of the American presence in Lebanon. As stated above, according to the Iranian view, this presence constituted one of the main stumbling blocks hindering the establishment of an "Islamic republic" in Lebanon. As there was not even the faintest chance of motivating the United States to willingly relinquish its policy and presence in Lebanon, the Iranians turned to the weapon of terror, which had aready proven to be an effective means in the past when dealing with the United States.

During the years 1983-84, a series of suicide attacks was perpetrated against American targets in Lebanon and Kuwait (the American embassies in Lebanon and Kuwait and the marine headquarters in Beirut; see further details in chapter 3). The high toll of American victims and public pressure in the aftermath of the attacks ultimately brought about the withdrawal of the American forces from Lebanon, a fact that constituted another impressive achievement for Iranian terror.[32]

Even after U.S. withdrawal from Lebanon, America continued to constitute a central target for Iranian terror against the background of its policies in the Persian Gulf and vis-à-vis the Palestinian-Israeli conflict, not to mention the fundamental ideological hostility of the Khomeini regime towards the Great Satan.[33] Due to the lack of "available" U.S. military targets in Lebanon, the Iranian/Shiite terror activity against the United States focused on the kidnapping of Americans as hostages and the hijacking of airplanes, like the hijacking of the TWA passenger plane on June 7, 1985 (see elaboration in chapter 3). In these cases once again, through its sponsored organizations, Iran proved that the United States and its allies could be forced to bend to Iranian dictates via terror.

A slightly different example testifies to the pragmatic side of Iranian foreign policy, which when taking temporary needs into consideration integrates compromise with radical ideology and terror as a bargaining tool. This aspect can be observed in the arms deals between the United States and Iran. Despite a fundamental ideological animosity towards the United States, already in 1982-83 Iranian allusions were floated regarding its willingness to reconsider the renewal of diplomatic relations due to its increasing difficuties in the war against Iraq. In a Friday sermon delivered on May 13, 1983, Rafsanjani appealed directly to the American people and noted that in principle his country was willing to maintain relations with all countries "that are willing to sustain proper relations with us, on the condition that they respect our revolution."[34] The only countries to which this rule did not apply, according to Rafsanjani, were Israel and South Africa. In 1983-84, Rafsanjani referred to his country's need and willingness to purchase Western weapons several times: "Iran will not refrain from buying U.S. weapons, preferably from a third party, but if there is no other alternative, then directly."[35]

During the second half of the decade, the Iranians attempted to signal their willingness to enter into negotiations with the United States in order to improve relations between the two countries, but these messages were not welcomed in the United States. As an alternative the Iranians turned to Israel through two mediators—Gurbanifer and Adnan Khashoggi—in the hope that Israel might intercede between them and the United States.[36] The first meeting between Khashoggi and the Israeli representatives (Nimrodi and Schwimmer) took place in March 1985. It should be noted that this initiative reflected the buds of a pro-American turnabout among certain circles in the Iranian regime, in the framework of an internal Iranian power struggle regarding the character of the regime.

In talks that were held between 1985 snd 1986, the Iranians stressed that American military aid was essential for the continued battle against Iraq and that it would contribute to the strengthening of moderate elements in Iran, a fact that would lead to a more positive attitude towards the United States. They also emphasized the joint danger shared by Iran and the United States in the form of the Soviet Union and Communism. In practice, the actual Iranian proposition that stood at the basis of the talks was a deal that would entail the release of U.S. hostages in return for the supply of American weapons and spare parts.[37] In the framework of the contacts that developed during the years 1985-86, through Israel's intervention and with its active involvement, several covert arm shipments were sent to Iran, and three hostages were released in exchange. The affair came to an end upon its exposure by the U.S. media, where it received massive coverage under the title of "Irangate" (see elaboration in chapter 3).

Despite the release of the three hostages, ultimately this move was doomed to failure—if the basic aim was the release of all of the hostages, particularly William Buckley (head of the CIA branch in Beirut), in the end only three were released, while Buckley had been killed by his kidnappers even before the negotiations had begun. Moreover, during the period of the negotiations three additional U.S. citizens were kidnapped. These results clearly proved that the path of acquiescence to terror only gives rise to more extortion and impairs the West's ability to contend with Iranian terror in the long run.[38]

Severe deterioration in Iranian-U.S. relations occurred in 1987 in connection to the "oil tanker war" in the Persian Gulf, when the dispatch of the U.S. Navy to ensure unrestricted sailing in the Persian Gulf triggered several incidents between U.S. and Iranian forces, in the course of which Iranian targets and vessels were damaged. The Iranian reaction was to threaten and retaliate with terror attacks against U.S. targets, including the kidnapping of hostages.

On July 3, 1988, a U.S. destroyer inadvertantly shot down an Iranian passenger plane over the Persian Gulf; this incident presented additional cause for the direction of Iranian hatred at the United States and inflamed aspiration for vengeance. The Iranian retaliatory actions apparently included an attempt to organize a series of attacks against U.S. and European airplanes through the Jibril Front's terror network (the Delckamony Affair), the detonation of the car belonging to the wife of the destroyer's commander who had shot down the plane, and maybe even involvement in the downing of the Pan Am airplane over Lockerbie. Although since the beginning of the 1990s it has been impossible to identify Iranian terror activity against U.S. targets, radical Islamic organizatioins that are supported by the Iranians continued to act against U.S. targets at two main focal points:

- Turkey—On March 12, 1992, a car bomb was discovered and neutralized near the American Consulate in Istanbul.
- Saudi Arabia—On November 13, 1995, a car bomb detonated near the consultancy headquarters of the Saudi National Guard in Riyadh. Seven people perished in the attack (including five American citizens) and forty-two were wounded. Two unknown organizations claimed responsibility for the incident. The interrogation of those involved in the incident, some of whom were apprehended and stood trial, indicated that the attack was initiated by an extremist Islamic Saudi group, which was sponsored by the Iranians.

On June 25, 1996, a car bomb exploded near a U.S. military camp in al Khobar, Daharan. Nineteen people were killed and over 500 were wounded. The investigation was never concluded, but an interrogation of some of the detainees indictated that the perpetrators were a Saudi terror organization sponsored by Iran.

Although the United States was considered Public Enemy Number One of the Islamic revolution, as a rule Iran refrained from carrying out terror attacks inside the United States (in contrast to France or Kuwait, which absorbed extensive terror activity upon their own soil). Nevertheless, it is possible to indicate several incidents connected to Iranian terror that did occur on U.S. soil:

- An Iranian expatriate was killed in Washington in 1981.
- In 1985, a ring of Hizballah activists, which was exposed in Seattle, was collecting intelligence information and intended to strike out at Iranian expatriates.
- In 1987, the Americans acquired information according to which, due to the entrance of the U.S. Navy into the Persian Gulf on an escort mission of the Kuwaiti oil tanker, Iran instructed its agents in the United States to gather intelligence information about potential targets for attack. However, as stated earlier, no attacks were actually perpetrated.
- In 1989, several attacks were perpetrated against book shops in America that sold Salman Rushdie's book. *The Satanic Verses*, and, as stated earlier, an attack was carried out against the wife of the commander of the U.S. destroyer who accidentally downed an Iranian passenger plane.

During the Gulf War (1991), Iran took a neutral stand. On the one hand, it condemned the aggressiveness of the American coalition against Iraq, but on the other, it refrained from supporting Iraq, its strategic foe. Iran derived the most benefit from the Gulf War, which significantly weakened Iraq and imposed a regime of supervision and sanctions upon it, and as a result of the war Iran's status in the Persian Gulf grew as the central power factor in the arena.

Nevertheless, the changes in the world arena as a result of the collapse of the Soviet Union and the new world order dictated by the United States as the sole superpower, posed a complex challenge for Iran that necessitated the re-evaluation of its policy vis-à-vis the United States in a new geopolitical reality.

The era of Khomeini's successors was characterized by an Iranian attempt to minimize the friction with the United States and the West. This trend was reflected in the significant reduction of Iranian terror activity worldwide (with the exception of the Israeli connection) and in the moderation of the Iranian rhetoric vis-à-vis the United States. Nevertheless, in spite of this trend, on the ideological level the hostility towards the "Great Devil" persevered, mainly in the conservative circles.

In the aftermath of the September 11 terror campaign and the U.S. declaration of war on terror, Iran sided with the coalition against global terror. This was an additional expression of Iran's consistent policy involving the public denouncement of terror on the one hand, while covertly using terror for its needs, on the other.

The American war in Afghanistan (2001) and the ousting of the Taliban regime to a large extent also served Iranian interests, as the Taliban regime was hostile towards Shiite Iran and inflicted serious damage upon the Shiite community in Afghanistan, which was granted Iranian sponsorship.

However, although Iran enjoyed the fruits of the two wars that the United States fought along its borders—against Iraq (1991) and against Afghanistan (2001)—the U.S. method of dealing with the Taliban regime in Afghanistan and the continued presence of Iran at the top of the U.S. State Department's list of states that support terror constituted a warning sign for the future.

Indeed, U.S. President George Bush included Iran in the "Axis of Evil" (Iran-North Korea-Iraq) with all of the inherent ramifications. In the aftermath of the American coalition's war in Iraq (2003), it became clear to the Iranian regime that perseverance of the policy regarding the support and utilization of terror, and continued development and acquisition of non-conventional weapons would propel it into a sharp confrontation with the United States, whose forces were already located at its borders both in Afghanistan and in Iraq.

The Hizballah, which acts under Iranian patronage, appears as one the most prominent on the U.S. State Department's list of terror organizations, and Imad Muraniya, as well as several other activists, appear on the list of the most wanted terrorists by the United States. While Iran cautiously weighs its declarations regarding the United States, the Hizballah continues to openly express its hostility and hatred for the United States. This loathing constitutes one of the central components of the Hizballah's ideology, and is an offshoot of adopting the worldview of revolutionary Iran, which defined the United States as the Great Satan. The ideological animosity towards the United States was expressed in practical terms on the level of attacks perpetrated in the past against U.S. targets, in which hundreds of Americans were killed in military and civilian facilities in the Middle East (Lebanon, Syria).[39] The animosity towards the United States is reflected in statements issued by the organization's leaders, headed by Hassan Nasrallah, for example:

> If Albright and Clinton and the American gang thought that if they will someday attack the Hizballah from Washington, we will tremble with fear, then they should know that we will rejoice because their political, media, and military attack against us only boosts our conviction and belief that the truth is on our side. When Satan curses us it means that we are with Allah.[40]

The organization regards the United States as an "imperialist country," and claims that the goal of its policy is to take over the enire region and steal the Arab's natural resources, with Israel serving as a means to realize this policy. Thus, at a conference held in Damascus (January 25-27, 2003), with the aim of encouraging a boycott of American products, Nasrallah called on his listeners:

> All contact with the United States and the Amercian people should be severed and we must adhere to the Arab boycott against Israel....The Arabs must understand that Israel is a regiment of the U.S. Army and nothing more, and the United States is the main enemy.[41]

The organization exploits random incidents in order to fan incitement against the United States and issue threats. For example, in response to the intention to transfer the U.S. Embassy in Israel from Tel Aviv to Jerusalem, Nasrallah declared:

> The response of the Palestinian people must be as follows—you can move your embassy to Jerusalem and bring your diplomats, but the honorable people can turn

your embassy into ruins and return your diplomats to you in coffins. That is the only language that America and Israel understand.[42]

It is noteworthy that these declarations were distributed to the Arab media throughout the Arab and Muslim world, and they contribute to the fanning of hatred towards the United States within them. Since the United States launched its campaign against international terror in the aftermath of the September 11 attacks, the organization has significantly increased its incitement and propaganda against America. An example of this can be observed in a speech that Hassan Nasrallah delivered on November 11 2001:

> The Arab people cannot be terminated and isolated in deserts and mountains. Never! In this region there are living nations that will not consent to submitting to any invader! Therefore, I predict: The beginning of the extensive American-Israeli offensive in our region means the end of the American world takeover. This is because the United States will place itself in a new and unequal confrontational arena; in this arena the people are the commanders, they are the officers and the soldiers, not a state that can be threatened or a specific organization that can be crumbled and have its financing resources dried up...
>   This is a war of a despotic, condescending and tyrannical country against the peoples of the world, the peoples of the Arab, Islamic and Muslim world, against the Latin American peoples, the Christians, the Buddhists, the Hindu, and the pagans. This is the war of a tyrannical, despotic and condescending country against anyone who will not give in to it....The definition of the Imam Khomeini should be adopted; he said that this is the war of the arrogant against the Depressed of the world.[43]

In another speech delivered on January 26, 2003, Nasrallah said:

> If they insist on a war and a general confrontation...the Americans will find themselves in a battlefield where the balance cannot be swayed, because the airplanes, tanks, economic siege and drying out of funds will not help them.... Because in this nation we can talk about millions of young people, each one of whom, no matter what country and which organization he is from, with his strength and the sweat of his brow will buy a weapon, a knife or explosives in order to fight these invaders.[44]

Thus, the Hizballah fights an anti-American incitement and propaganda campaign in Lebanon, which is welcomed in the Arab and Muslim world with Iranian inspiration. Central tools used for the dissemination of the hatred messages and the propaganda are the Al-Manar television network, Radio Nur, and Internet sites operated by the organization. Other Arab television stations help to disseminate the messages of hatred by providing a communication medium for the organization's leader Nasrallah, who enjoys considerable popularity in the Arab world, and by quoting Al-Manar and other Hizballah media.[45]

Prior to the U.S. campaign in Iraq, the Hizballah exacerbated the tone of the anti-American rhetoric. A reflection of this development can be observed in a speech that Nasrallah delivered in Beirut:

The Americans intend to appoint a military governor in Iraq who will serve in this role for many years. They will act in Iraq to cause controversy, ethnic struggles and raise old conflicts among Iraqis.

The United States, which carries the banner of democracy, is the entity that established dictatorial regimes in the Middle East and it is the United States that led the region into all the disasters...

The United States and the West are the ones who provided mass destruction weapons to Iraq, including chemical weapons, so that the Arab and Muslim countries will kill each other and so that several regimes will take over these peoples.

The United States is a partner to the exploitation and oppression, the massacres and tyranny in dictatorial regimes, deaths by chemical warfare and melting a body in acid here and there.[46]

In summary, it appears that Iran and its sponsored organization, the Hizballah, are aware of the looming danger in the framework of the continued development of the campaign against terror headed by the United States, and they are therefore situated at a crossroads regarding the continuation of their involvement and activities in the area of terror.

In the aftermath of the American coalition's war against Iraq (2004), it was clear to the Iranian regime that their support of terror, and their continued development and acquisition of non-conventional weapons would propel them into a conflict with the United States, whose forces were located at its borders. With this background Iran opened negotiations with EU about the future of the Iranian "Nuclear Programs." On Nov 7, 2004, Iran reached an agreement with the EU to freeze the Uranium enrichment project.

According to the Iranian foreign ministry spokesman Hamid Reza Asefi, "it was the best decision under the current circumstances." *

France

When the Islamic republic first ascended, its leaders still remembered France's benevolence in hosting Khomeini and his followers during his exile when the Shah reigned. At the time, Iran ignored various principles of its policy and France's "past," which subsequently became central butting points against the latter, such as its imperialist past in the Middle East in general and in Algeria in particular, as well as the friendly ties that it maintained with the Shah's reign and with Israel.[47] The relations worsened gradually; the main focal points for tension and criticism were:[48]

1. France's strong ties with Iraq and the supply of French weapons to its army (particularly the "Super Attender" airplanes and "Exhaust" missiles, which were supplied to Iraq in 1983, thus presenting it with improved abilities to hit Iranian vessels and oil facilities in the Gulf);
2. France's willingness to "host" Iranian expatriates and entities opposed to the revolutionary regime in Iran, starting with Bakhtiar, former prime minster

---

* Islam Online, web site , November 8, 2004

during the Shah's days, through generals from the Shah's army, and ending with the Sader family (Iran's first president following the revolution) as well as leaders of the Mujahidin Khalq;

3. A demand that France return about a billion dollars which France had refused to return based on the argument that the money had been payment for a power station during the Shah's reign;
4. France's support of Israel during the war in Lebanon in 1982;
5. France's political and military involvement in Lebanon (in the framework of the multinational force) and its activities against the Iranian forces in the Bak'a in November 1983;
6. France's involvement in Chad against Libya (Iran's ally in the war against Iraq).

Conflicts of interest sharpened the animosity of the Iranian regime towards France and led to its addition to the group of countries defined as enemies of the revolution, as well as the coining of the title "Little Satan" alongside Britain and Israel, beside the Great Satan—the United States.

As on the political level Iran failed to induce France to change its positions in the above-mentioned issues, Iran quickly moved on to the use of the terror weapon in an attempt to force its will upon France. The Iranian activity against France focused on three diferent levels:

> In the Lebanese arena a planned terror campaign was initiated through Shiite entities in Lebanon (mainly the Hizballah), with the help of the Iranian Revolutionary Guards, in order to oust the French forces, reduce France's influence in this arena, and change its position vis-à-vis its allies in Lebanon.[49] On October 23, 1983, a car bomb detonated at the headquarters of the French forces in Beirut, killing fifty-eight officers and soldiers. This attack and others (albeit less impressive ones) generated public pressure in France, and in the end achieved their goal when the French evacuated Lebanon. Subsequently, due to the lack of a French miltary presence in Lebanon, the kidnapping of French citizens in Lebanon was initiated; the kidnapped French citizens were held as hostages in order to place pressure on the French government so that it would revise its policy, pay ransom money to the kidnappers, and release the Shiite terrorists arrested in France.[50]

Another level of terror activity against French targets was the hijacking of French airplanes throughout the world. Two hijackings during the years 1983-84 were particularly significant:

- *August 26 1983*—An Air France airplane was hijacked after taking off from Austria. The hijackers, apparently Hizballah members, demanded the release of Lebanese detainees in France and cessation of French military aid to Iraq, Lebanon, and Chad.
- *July 31 1984*—An Air France aircraft was hijacked en route from Frankfurt to France. The plane was forced to land in Iran, where it was detonated by the hijackers. "The Islamic Organization for the Liberation of Jerusalem" (apparently a cover name for an Iranian/Shiite organization), claimed responsiiblity for the incident.

Aside from the hijacking of airplanes, additional attacks were perpetrated against French targets, such as the detonation of a car bomb on December 12, 1983, near the French Embassy in Kuwait. The Shiite al Dawa organization, which acts under Iranian guidance, claimed responsibility for the attack.

The third level of operation was the perpetration of terror attacks on French territory against Iranian expatriates and opposition members who found refuge there. An example of an assassination attempt in 1980 was the attack against the former Iranian prime minister in exile, Shahfur Bakhtiar. The attempt failed and the assassin Anis Nakash, who was acting in Iran's name, was apprehended and sentenced to life imprisonment. As to attacks against French targets on French soil: The first attack of this sort was perpetrated on December 13, 1983, when two explosive devices detonated at a train station and in a railway car of the express train from Paris to Marseilles. The Islamic Jihad claimed responsibility for the attack. During the years 1984-85, several attacks were perpetrated by the Palestinian terror group FARL,[51] headed by the terrorist George Ibrahim Abdallah. It is impossible to unequivocally indicate a Shite/Iranian connection to the series of terror attacks perpetrated by this organization, but it appears that there was indeed such a link; this is evident from the repeated demands made by Iranian/Shiite perpetrators to release George Ibrahim Abdallah from the French prison.

A prominent example of the operational activation of Shiite organizations abroad is the episode of the organization, activity and exposure of a pro-Iranian terror network connected to the Hizballah, which acted in France during the years 1985-1987, and was involved in the perpetration of about a dozen attacks in this country.[52] This network was headed by Fuad Ali Salah, a Tunisian subject with French citizenship, who recruited and activated additional activists in order to create a logistical infrastructure for additional terror cells that were to arrive from Lebanon to perpetrate attacks. This method of organization was not unique to France; set-ups with comparable characteristics were exposed in Italy, Germany, Turkey, and Spain.

The network launched its activities in 1985, upon the arrival of the network's commander in Paris, and the first year was dedicated to the recruitment of the network's members and the preparation of infrastructures. In the beginning of 1986, the network was ready to perpetrate attacks; its targets were sites that attracted crowds with the aim of causing indiscrimate killings which would influence public opinion and the French government to meet the following demands:

1. Release of the terrorist George Ibrahim Abdallah (the leader of the FARL terror organization);
2. Release of Anis Nakash, commander of the assassination cell that attacked the former prime minister of Iran Shahfur Bakhtiar;
3. Release of the Armenian terrorist Rojian Garbidjan;

4. A change in France's policy, particularly cessation of aid to Iraq in the Iran-Iraq war.[53]

In February 1986, a terror campaign was launched that lasted for nine months, during which the network members perpetrated thirteen attacks in France. In this series of attacks thirteen people were killed and some 250 were injured. Fuad Ali Salah and the other network members were arrested in March 1987, at which time they were found to be in the final stages of preparations for a new wave of attacks.

January 30, 1990 marked the opening of the trial of Fuad Ali Salah, his wife, and another member of the the network (a Lebanese driver). The remaining eight members of the network were tried separately. After the reading of the verdict, Fuad Ali Salah burst out, saying: "I am the terrorist. The Koran said: 'Terrorize the enemies of God.'"[54]

The network's members were charged with conspiring to perpetrate terror attacks and illegally harboring explosives, as well as with additional specific charges regarding sabotage acitivities that they had conducted during which French citizens had been killed and wounded. According to the prosecution, the network was acting on behalf of the pro-Iranian Hizballah organization in order to force France to stop aiding the Iraqis during the the Iran-Iraq war, and to release prisoners who had been found guilty of terror attacks in France. The responsibility for the attacks was claimed by an organization calling itself "The Council for Solidarity with Arab and Political Prisoners in the Middle East." A French police source claimed that this was a cover name for the Hizballah, in whose name Fuad Ali Salah's network was active.[55]

During the Iranian/Shiite terror activity, several terrorists were arrested in France. The release of these prisoners became a goal in itself for other terrorists and the Iranian government. The issue of demanding the release of incarcerated terrorists constitutes interesting proof of the operational cooperation between the various terrorist groups. Prominent examples are the demands made by Fuad Ali Salah's network to release George Ibrahim Abdallah, Anis Nakash, and an additional terrorist from an Armenian terror organization—Rojian Garbidjan.

An analysis of Iranian/Shiite terror activity against France indicates at least two achievements for Iran: First, the terror campaign in 1983 against French targets achieved its main goal—the withdrawal of French forces from Lebanon and minimization of that country's influence in Lebanon; and second, the series of attacks perpetrated in 1986 by Fuad Ali Salah's network forced France to attempt to improve its ties with Iran (in exchange for putting a stop to the terror campaign). The "price" for this attempt was the deportation of several Iranian expatriates and opposition organizations from France, and mainly the transfer of Masoud Rajavi and the headquarters of the Mujahidin Khalq from Paris to Iraq in July 1986, as well as the return of part of the monies which France owed Iran as a "gesture of goodwill."

Table 4.4
**Examples of Iranian/Shiite Terror Attacks against French Targets and Central
Incidents Connected to Them**

Date	Place	Description of the event
27.1.1983	Spain	An explosive device was detonated at the French Consulate in Barcelona and another device was discovered and neutralized.
31.12.1983	France	Two explosive devices went off at a train station and in a railway car on the express train from Paris to Marseilles. The Islamic Jihad claimed responsibility for the incident.
3.2.1986	France	An explosive device detonated at a shopping center in the Calaridge Passage on the Champs Elysee.
3.2.1986	France	An explosive device was discovered on the third floor of the Eiffel Tower.
4.2.1986	France	An explosive device went off in the Les Jeune bookstore.
5.2.1986	France	An explosive device detonated at the Les Halles shopping center (also a Metro station).
17.3 1986	France	An explosive device detonated on the express train from Paris to Lyon (TGV) as it was leaving Paris.
20.3.1986	France	An explosive device detonated at the Point Show Passage on the Champs Elysee. One of the two victims was identified as an associate of the FARL organization.
20.3.1986	France	An explosive device was discovered on the Metro before it exploded.
4.9.1986	France	An explosive device exploded on the Metro in Paris.
8.9.1986	France	An explosive device detonated in the post office at the building of the Paris Municipality.
12.9.1986	France	An explosive device detonated at the cafeteria at the La Defense shopping center (also a Metro station).
14.9.1986	France	An explosive device detonated at the Renault Pub at the Champs Elysee.
15.9. 1986	France	An explosive device detonated at the waiting room of the Paris Police headquarters.
17.9.1986	France	An explosive device detonated at the Tati department store in Paris (Montfort Quarter).
13.1.1986	Lebanon	The French photographer Roger Auque was kidnapped by the Hizballah.
22.3.1987	France	Terrorists (six Tunisians, a Lebanese, and an Iranian of Armenian descent) connected to the Hizballah terror network in Europe were apprehended in Paris. Ten additional suspects were arrested in France during April and May 1987. The network in France was exposed following an investigation carried out after the arrest of network members in Italy and Germany in January

Table 4.4 (cont.)

		1987.The network dealt in the preparation of an infrastructure for terrorist activities and was in contact with the Iranian Embassy in Paris. The network members were planning a series of attacks in France. Some of the detainees had participated in the series of terror attacks that had been perpetrated in September 1986 by the FARL, whose members were Palestinians, Lebanese, and Armenians. The attacks were perpetrated on behalf of the "Council for Solidarity with the Arab and Political Prisoners in the Middle East." The organization demanded the release of incarcerated terrorists in France. In 1987, sixty people were arrested on suspicion of involvement or membership in this terror network.
20.10.1987	France	Three envelope bombs were sent to the Tunisian Consulate, the Moroccan news agency, and the Pakistani Embassy. Two were discovered before they exploded while the third exploded, injuring a Moroccan citizen.The "Islamic Resistance Front," a group identified with the Hizballah, claimed responsibility for the attacks and stated that they had been perpetrated in retaliation for the French government's anti-Islamic activities in North Africa.
29.10.1987	Lebanon	Two guards at the French Embassy in Beirut were killed and a third was injured in a shooting attack perpetrated by an organization that called itself "The Armed Units of Tantus Shahin" (apparently a cover name). The organization demanded release of the terrorist George Ibrahim Abdallah from the French prison and the end of French involvement in Lebanon and Chad.
8.11.1993	Iran	Two hand grenades were lobbed at the courtyard of the French Embassy in Teheran. No one was hurt and the damage was negligible. On the same day, a grenade was also thrown at the Air France offices in Teheran. In this attack a French citizen was hurt. An organization calling itself "The Council of the Hizballah" claimed responsibility for the attacks and stated they had been perpetrated in protest against the aid that the French government had been giving to the Mujahidin Khalq Organization.

Iran accepted this turnabout and, in fact, welcomed it, but just when it seemed that reconciliation was at hand, a new Iranian terror episode exploded (Spring 1987) when the terror activity of an Iranian terrorist named Wahid Gorgi was exposed—he escaped and found refuge at the Iranian Embassy in Paris. The exacerbation of the relations ultimately led to the severance of diplomatic ties in July 1987 and to the "embassy war."

Terror activities against French targets and the kidnapping of French hostages stopped in 1988, with the end of the Iran-Iraq war, due to the aspiration of the regime in Teheran to improve its ties with Western countries in order to hasten Iran's rehabilitation. Nevertheless, France continued to serve as an arena for the assassination of Iranian expatriates and opposition entities at the hands of Iranian agents. These terror attacks caused crises in the relations between the countries, which exchanged accusations; Iran accused France of offering refuge and aid to opposition entities, while France accused Iran of perpetrating terror attacks on its soil. From the middle of the 1990s, there was a significant improvement in the ties between the two countries, manly due to the French interest in strengthening economic ties between the two countries. Expressions of French gestures towards Iran and its protégé, the Hizballah, are reflected in the participation of the secretary-general of the Hizballah at a meeting of the Lebanese administration with the French president during his visit to Lebanon in 2002.

Britain

During Khomeini's regime in Iran, the latter took a hostile stand against Britain, due to its colonial policy in the past and its current policy, tagging it as one of the enemies of the Islamic revolution. The historical memory of Iran regarded Britain itself as a colonial and imperialist power that for decades had attempted to exploit and abuse Iran.

The British involvement in Iran began in the eighteenth century. In the framework of its efforts to strengthen its control in Southern Asia (particularly India), Britain expanded its influence to Iran as well, mainly in order to block the penetration and influence of tsarist Russia. The use of oil in British industry increased Iran's importance, and, in 1908, APOC—the Anglo-Persian Oil Company—was founded and began producing commercial oil in 1912. From 1912, the issue of the control of Iranian oil became an important component of British policy in Iran, and over the years the British forced Iran to sign several contracts in which they undertook to export oil to Britain under preferred conditions.[56]

During WWII, Iran's importance increased in the Allies' view because of the need for the supply of oil for the war machine and in view of its status as a land bridge to the Soviet Union for the purpose of transferring military equipment and supplies from Britain and the United States. The year 1941 constitutes an historical milestone, as this was the year that active American involvement began in Iran, which gradually supplanted the British presence there.

During the years 1941-1948, the supply of Iranian oil rose from 50.8 million barrels to 190.4 million barrels per annum, but its income only grew from four million to nine million and two hundred thousand pounds sterling. Over the years the unrest stemming from the British injustice to Iran increased, leading to strikes and demonstrations by AIOC employees,[57] which were suppressed when the army opened fire on them.

In 1951, upon his appointment as prime minister, Muhammad Musadek declared the nationalization of the oil company (and established NICO—National Iranian Oil Company). During the years 1951-1952, Britain placed heavy pressure on Iran to revoke the nationalization, and even turned to the United States, which used its influence to help the British (in this framework the U.S. ceased military and economic aid to Iran). Iran's shaky economic and social status and the fear of a Soviet invasion ultimately generated U.S. and British action to terminate Musadek's government—a mission that was given to the CIA.[58] Indeed, in August 1952, Musadek's government was ousted.

The change of government did indeed cause the nationalization to be terminated, but left harsh historical scars, and constituted a central milestone in the loss of British influence in Iran. Thus, Khomeini's regime viewed Britain as one of the potential enemies of the revolution, due both to the historical scars and also because of Britain's policy which had expressed its reservations vis-à-vis Khomeini when he was in the opposition and maintained close ties with the Shah. Britain's support for the United States regarding the issue of the hostages worsened Britain's image in Iran even more.[59] Khomeini included Britain in the category of the "the oppressive capitalist states," and granted it the demonic title of the "Small Satan" alongside France and Israel, and near the Great Satan of the United States.

During the initial months following the revolution in 1979, Mahadi Bazargan, the prime minster of Iran, attempted to formulate a pragmatic foreign policy towards the Western states, including Britain, but within a short period, the radical stream in Iran gained the upper hand, dictating a tough and hostile policy towards the West. This policy found expression in a campaign to eliminate Western and imperialist influences in Iran. One of the first targets of this campaign was the Anglican Church in Iran, which had put down roots in the seventeenth and eighteenth centuries in various areas of Iran, particularly Isfahan.[60] The Iranian persecution of the church activists and its facilities caused a rapid deterioration in the relations between the two countries.

Two additional incidents that occurred in Britain also contributed to this decline: In July 1980, Iranian expatriates occupied the Iranian Embassy in London. The British security forces took over the building and freed the Iranian diplomatic staff, but Iran accused Britain of collusion with the invasion and damaging Iranian interests. In August 1980, a demonstration of pro-Iranian entities was held opposite the U.S. Embassy in London (under Iranian guidance and direction). The demonstration became violent, and British authorities arrested eighty demonstrators. Some of the detainees started a hunger strike, and at the same time hunger strikes and mass demonstrations took place opposite the British Embassy in Teheran.

Due to the deterioration between the countries, Britain decided to recall all of its diplomatic staff from Iran, for fear that their fate would be the same as that of the U.S. Embassy employees who at that time had already been held as hostages for six months by Iranian "students." The British Embassy in Teheran was closed and Sweden was asked to represent British interests. However, the Iranian Embassy in London continued to function as usual. From the end of 1980 until December 1987, Britain was represented in Iran by a handful of British diplomats who acted from the Swedish Embassy.

In 1987, an employee of the Iranian Consulate in Manchester was accused of shoplifting. In retaliation, a British diplomat was attacked and beaten in Teheran. Following this incident, once again the British hastened to recall all British representatives in Iran. British representation in Iran was only renewed at the end of 1988, following an agreement pertaining to the renewal of British diplomatic representation in Iran, and an entity responsible for handling the matters of the British Embassy was dispatched to Teheran.

During the years 1985-1987, four British citizens were kidnapped by the Hizballah (the "Islamic Jihad"):[61]

- On March 14, 1985, Geoffrey Nash was kidnapped, and the next day Brian Lewick was kidnapped. Both were released within two weeks (between the March 27 and March 30, 1985). It is not clear what served as the motive for the kidnappings and what brought about their release.
- On May 27, 1985, an additional British citizen—Dennis Holtz—was kidnapped. He was murdered by his captors.
- On January 20, 1987, the British cleric Terry White, who was involved in efforts to free the Western hostages in Lebanon at the bidding of the Anglican Church, was kidnapped. (He was freed in 1991.)[62]

These kidnappings also constituted a stumbling block in the relations between the countries, and almost assuredly served as an Iranian bargaining card to promote Iranian political targets vis-à-vis Britain. However, during the entire period, Britain demonstrated an uncompromising policy and refused to cave in to the kidnappers' extortion, in contrast to most Western states that acquiesced to the demands of the kidnappers. This resolute stand was reflected in the words of the British Prime Minister Margaret Thatcher when she addressed the Parliament in May 1990:

We very much want to get our hostages out and every day we try to achieve that end, but Britain and the U.S. believe it would be quite wrong to make deals with those who take hostages and we shall not do that. Giving into blackmail would only encourage more hostage taking.[63]

The Salman Rushdie Incident

In early 1989, the Indian writer Salman Rushdie published his book, *The Satanic Verses*, which incurred the wrath of Muslims worldwide. Over the years Rushdie, who was a British citizen (since 1968), had published several texts that were conspicuously critical of Islam, but *The Satanic Verses* incited considerable rage and affronted Islamic believers.

Rushdie's book is a parody that portrays the Koran merely as a story and presents Islamic symbols in a contemptful and disparaging tone, while hurling demeaning insults at it leaders and holy figures, particularly the Prophet Muhammad, who is described as a false prophet and as a hallucinating man who found his wives in a brothel.

The book's publication outraged the Muslim world and on February 14, 1989, Khomeini issued a religious ruling (*fatwa*) in which he sentenced Rushdie to death and called upon all believers to prevent distribution of the book.

The Muslim world was united in its opposition to the book's publication, but was divided regarding the issue of Khomeini's fatwa. One group of religious clerics and radical Islamic figures supported Khomeini's ruling and demanded that Muslims worldwide defend Islam by carrying out Rushdie's sentence. This group mainly included religious clerics from within the Iranian regime and Hizballah leaders in Lebanon, who bluntly condemned the West and mainly Britain for allowing the publication of the book under the alleged pretense of protecting the freedom of expression. These circles' argument was that behind the episode there was a conspiracy against Islam, whose purpose was to blacken its name and distort its values. In an interview with an American television network, Sheikh Fadallah (the Hizballah's spiritual leader) stated:

> The non-Muslim world must understand that Islam regards the matter of human rights from a different aspect than the customary outlook in the West. The Shariya establishes punishments for deeds that Western laws do not address. The way to deal with Islamic thought is through counter-thought but not by insulting someone else's religion and holy figures. Therefore the problem which must be raised is not individual rights, but rather the right of a billion Muslims to protect the reputation of their religion.[64]

At a conference of Islamic scholars, held at the Muhammad Mosque in Beirut, Fadallah said:

> The ruling that Khomeiini issued has proved to the West for the first time that the Muslim world is unwilling to make do with words and threats against the outside world, and that its intentions to carry out the sentence against Rushdie are real and serious. The question under discussion is not whether Rushdie will or will not be put to death: The real problem is how to contend with the international conspiracy behind the attempt to publish

the book. Khomeini's ruling is not swayed by interests and it is not connected to politics, but rather it represents the entire Muslim world. Therefore, we call upon other Muslim states worldwide to join hands in the effort to persecute the writer, the publishing houses and anyone who has acted to disseminate this book in the world.[65]

An announcement published by the Hizballah on February 4, 1989 stated:

We regard the widespread propaganda campaign of Western imperialism against Khomeini's ruling in connection to the satanic writer Saliman Rushdie as a new indication of the criminal conspiracy against Muslims that the imperialist forces engender while hiding behind slogans of progress and freedom. The religious ruling issued by the commanding Imam and imperialism's response proved to the oppressed nations and the Muslims that liberty from the Western point of view is a slogan that the West uses to humiliate Islam and distort Islamic cultural concepts. The Muslims (according to the West) have no right to use their freedom in order to carry out their sentence. The Hizballah in Lebanon, as an entity connected to the execution of Khomeini's verdict, will invest all of its efforts in order to win this honor. The organization expresses its complete faithfulness to the Islamic path that Khomeini represents.[66]

The chairman of the Iranian Parliament Rafsanjani[67] announced that "Iran is not responsible for the assassination of Rushdie by a Muslim." He defended the death sentence against Rushdie and declared the beginning of an ongoing campaign. "The publication of the book is part of a Zionist plot, and Khomeini became involved because he understood that the issue is complex and it cannot be resolved in a regular Islamic court."

In contrast, a group of more moderate religious clerics proposed compromises when dealing with the problem. People such as Sheikh Alazhar and the Egyptian Mufti proposed publishing a book that would refute Rushdie's claims, and to put Rushdie on trial as a heretic vis-à-vis Islam in order to enable him to retract his positions. Saudi philsophers maintained that Islam should rid itself of responsibility for Rushdie and opposed the verdict by claiming that "Islam does not concur with murder and terror." Clerics from the Iranian opposition also expressed emphatic reservations, such as Alstar al Tawilla or Hamid Sliman, who wrote:

It seems that some of those who led the aggressive campaign against Salman Rushdie are "more Salman" than Rushdie himself, and it would appear that they inflicted more damage on Islam and Muslims than Rushdie. For example, Khomeini is the "Salman" of Iran, who inflicted damage upon Islam when he ruled his country in the name of Islam, and hurt the Muslims when he published a religious ruling regarding the waging of a holy war against Iraq.[68]

Khomeini's verdict against Rushdie constitutes a clear example of the dilemma that is characteristic of Iran's policy, which is torn between a tough ideology and political pragmatism. In this case, unequivocal preference was granted to the ideological line. It was clear to Iran's leadership, including Khomeini, that the Rushdie episode could seriously impair Iran's ties with the West, particularly Britain, at a time when Iran's need for economic and military rehabilitation at the end of many years of war necessitated improved relations with the West. As stated above, this case is an example of Iran's willingness to sacrifice political and economic interests in order to realize the regime's principles. By its very existence, the verdict constituted the issuing of an open challenge against Western countries in general and Britain in particular, because it was characterized by a complete disregard for international judiciary rules and customs.

Britain's refusal to hand over Rushdie and stop distribution of his book—an approach that was quickly adopted by additional Western countries—caused a deterioration in relations and the severing of diplomatic ties between Iran and Britain, as well as a wave of terror perpetrated by Shiites/Iranians or by their followers against British targets and commercial entities that dealt in the distribution of Rushdie's book worldwide. Salman Rushdie went into hiding, and he was granted security by British security entities due to the repeated threats against his life.

In this case, Iran again proved that when it does not achieve its goals through accepted political channels (turning Rushdie over and ceasing the distribution of his book), the terror weapon turns into a legitimate tool in the regime's eyes in order to achieve these goals. Eighteen attacks were perpetrated worldwide due to the Rushdie episode, and Britain was the main victim of these attacks:[69]

- Six attacks were perpetrated in London, mostly against shops that distributed *The Satanic Verses*.
- Three attacks were perpetrated in Pakistan against British cultural centers and libraries.
- In Turkey, an attack was perpetrated against a British target (the British consul's car was detonated), and an additional attack was perpetrated against the British language center in Kuala Lumpur, Malaysia.
- Attacks were perpetrated against stores in the United States, Italy, and Greece that dealt in the distribution of the book.
- Another target for attacks was Muslim religious leaders who did not concur with Khomeini's fatwa or expressed moderate opinions in this matter. On March 20, 1989, two Muslim clerics were murdered in Brussels, after one of them had expressed public opposition to Rushdie's death verdict. The "Organization of the True Soldiers" claimed responsibility for the attack in Beirut, and stated that "the two were traitors who dealt in anti-Muslim activity."

In contrast to most Western states, which condemned the verdict but at the same time acted to develop ties with Iran, the diplomatic relations between Iran and Britain were not renewed, and the Rushdie affair continued to constitute one of the main stumbling blocks to the relations between them (diplomatic ties between Britain and Iran were only renewed in August 1991).

Following Khomeini's death in 1989, hopes were aroused in the West that Iran's new leadership headed by Rafsanjani would rescind the verdict or at least refrain from encouraging Islamic believers to execute it. These hopes were dashed quickly. On February 14, 1990, assemblies celebrating the anniversary of the fatwa regarding Rushdie's death sentence were convened. Most of the speakers stressed that Khomeini's ruling could not be rescinded and that it was still valid. Khomeini's successor, Ayatollah Ali Khamenei claimed that Rushdie must pay with his life for his deeds. Ayatollah Muhdar al Din Anuri was quoted by Reuters as saying:

> There is no way back whatsoever, not even if he (Rushdie) repents or whether or not our relations with Britain improve. The fatwa of Muslim scholars in books of jurisprudence is that a Muslim who renounces Allah...or insults the Prophet or the infallible (Shii) Imams must be killed.[70]

By taking this stand, Khomeini's successors, who were interested in ties with the West and aid for their country, represented two central aspects of the Iranian policy: Primarily, loyalty to Khomeini's path constitutes a central basis for the legitimacy of the regime, mainly due to the existence of a radical opposition that consistently opposes any reconciliation with the West (headed by the former Minister of Interior Mukhtashemi Pur): And secondly, the ideological/religious aspect continues to play a central role even among the pragmatic leaders, thus perpetuating the polarization. So it is reasonable to summarize that even during the era of Khomeini's successors, his philosophy has continued to serve as a guideline for Iranian policy, including its willingness to confront the West over an ideological issue.

After the election of President Khatami (1996), renewed hopes were aroused regarding the resolution of the Salman Rushdie episode, but even in 2004, much like during his predecessor's (Rafsanjani) era, Iran has not reconsidered the implementation of Khomeini's fatwa, although, according to Khatami, "Iran will not eradicate the fatwa but will also not take actual steps to implement it."

In spite of Khatami's policy, the reformist newspaper *Shark* reported on the first Iranian convention to recruit volunteers for acts of self-sacrifice (*Shuhada*). The following is the newspaper's report (*Shark*, Teheran, June 1, 2004):

> There are three options on the forms, each volunteer may choose one: The assassination of Salman Rushdie, acts of self-sacrifice in the holy (Shiite) cities in Iraq against the Americans, and attacks against Israeli forces in Palestine.

The message was clear, even after 15 years, Salman Rushdie is still a high priority target for Iran.

Britain was a central ally of the United States in the Gulf War (1991) and during the recent war in Iraq (2003). Britain adopted the American approach regarding the war against terror organizations and states that support terror. Thus, Iran may assess that due to its definition as one of the "Axis of Evil" states it may find itself in a confrontation in the future opposite the American-British front much like the 2004 situation in Iraq.

At this time, it is to be noted that the Iranian rhetoric mainly attacks the United States and Israel, and generally avoids similarly attacking Britain. It is possible that this is the result of an Iranian desire to prevent or postpone any possible confrontation with Britain, and to place a wedge within the American-Anglo coalition.

Table 4.5
List of Iranian/Shiite Attacks Perpetrated against the Background of the Rushdie Incident and Central Events Connected to Them

Date	Place	Description of the incident
28.1.1989	New York	An anonymous person threw an explosive device from a moving vehicle into the offices of the *Riverdale Press* weekly, causing serious damage to the premises. It would appear that the attack was perpetrated due to an editorial that was published in support of Rushdie.
February 1989		An Iranian "charity" the "Fund of the 15 at Kordad" offered a $1 million prize to whoever kills Rushdie.[71]
27.2.1989	Karachi (Pakistan)	A large explosive device detonated at the library of the British Cultural Center causing damage to the building.
1.3.1989	California	Explosive devices detonated at two book shops in Berkeley. No one was hurt, and slight damage was caused to the premises.
5.3.1989	Padova (Italy)	A detonation at a book store that had *The Satanic Verses* on display. The following day an anonymous phone call was received and a demand was made in the name of the Islamic Jihad to remove the book from the shelves; the caller threatened to place "bombs like in Lebanon" if the books were not removed.
15.3.1989	Peshawar (Pakistan)	A library owned by the British Cultural Office was damaged from a bombing.
28.3.1989	Islamabad (Pakistan)	An explosive device detonated near the British Consulate's library. No one was hurt but nearby buildings were damaged.
29.3.1989	Brussels (Belgium)	Two Muslim religious leaders of Tunisian and Saudi descent were shot to death in a mosque in Brussels, after one of them criticized Rushdie's death sentence. The organization

Table 4.5 (cont.)

		"Soldiers of the Truth" claimed reponsibility for the event in Beirut, and stated that the two were "traitors who committed anti-Muslim deeds."
1.4.1989	London (Britain)	An explosive device went off near a shopping center in London. Advance warning was given over the phone, during which the Rushdie affair was named as the reason for the attack.
2.4.1989	Ankara (Turkey)	The car belonging to the Deputy-Consul of the British Embassy was totally demolished by a bomb. Another bomb caused damage to the garage of the British Council in Ankara.
10.4.1989	London (Britain)	Two book shops were demolished as a result of explosions.
11.4.1989	Kuala Lumpur (Malaysia)	A bomb went off near the language center affiliated with the British Embassy. Four Malaysian citizens were hurt.
13.5.1989	London (Britain)	A bomb was thrown at a book shop. No one was hurt.
5.6.1989	Athens (Greece)	Detonation of a book store belonging to a distributor of *The Satanic Verses*. No one was hurt but there was considerable damage.
3.8.1989	London (Britain)	A terrorist was killed in a hotel in London from the detonation of a bomb in his possession. An organization called "Mujahidin al Islam" took responsibility for planning the attack, and announced that its aim was to kill Rushdie (the organization is not known).
13.9.1989	London (Britain)	Four explosive devices were planted in London near stores belonging to the distributor of *The Satanic Verses*. Only one went off—the rest were discovered and neutralized.
July 1991		The Italian translator of the book was attacked and seriously injured, while the Japanese translator of the book was killed.
November 1992		The "Fund of the 15 in Kordad" doubled the prize money for Rushdie's head (putting it at $2 million), and promised the assassin coverage of additional expenses.
October 1993		The Norwegian publisher of the book was shot and seriously injured.
12.2.1997		The "Fund for the 15 in Kordad" upped the prize for Rushdie's head to $2 million five hundred thousand dollars.

Germany

Iran's ties with Germany began at the end of the eighteenth century, when Iran aspired to strengthen its ties with Germany as a counter-balance to tzarist Russia and Britain, which competed over influence in Iran. During the regime of Riza Shah in the years 1928-1933, several important contracts were signed that guaranteed German aid to Iran, including the establishment of the national Iranian bank in 1928, the concession awarded to the "Yonkers" company for all domestic flights in Iran, and the concession for establishing the trans-Iranian railway in 1933.

In contrast to other Western countries, such as Britain and France, Germany was not blemished by the stamp of colonialism or imperialism, but rather was perceived as a country with a tradition of aid and friendship for Iran.

The ties between revolutionary Iran and Germany were based mainly on mutual economic interests relating to both countries. On the one hand, Germany was a central oil consumer, while on the other, Iran needed industrial products and technologies that Germany was capable of supplying.[72] This need intensified due to the rift between Iran and the United States and West-European states such as Britain and France. But even with regard to the relations between these two countries there was no lack of friction points, related chiefly to Germany's fast ties with the United States.

In 1982, several riots were instigated by Iranian students who supported the revolution in the city of Meintz, as a result of which seventeen Iranians were arrested and deported from Germany. The Iranian response was to close the Iranian Embassy and Consulate in Germany. However, these incidents did not disrupt the continued prosperity vis-à-vis the economic ties between the countries. The visit of German Foreign Minister Genscher to Teheran in July 1984, and his declared support for the revolution and Iran's position in the Iran-Iraq war, contributed to the strengthening of the bond between the two countries. (During the years 1983-1984 Iranian imports from Germany were greater than the imports from any other country, constituting some 19 percent of all Iranian imports.)

Although there supposedly exists a clear Iranian interest to maintain good ties with Germany, during the past decade there have been several incidents where Germany served as a transit station or base for the Iranian terror infrastructure, perhaps based on the Iranian assessment that it can act with relative security within that country. The exposure of these activities by the German authorities aggravated the relations between the two countries and caused the perpetration of a wave of terror attacks against German targets, whose main goal was to liberate terrorists arrested in Germany. It is important to note that in all of these activities it was impossible to indicate direct Iranian involvement, only the activity of Hizballah activists. This situation enabled Iran to continue to preserve its ties with Germany alongside the terror activity, and

Table 4.6
Examples of Iranian/Shiite Attacks against German Targets and Central
Incidents Connected to Them

Date	Place	Description of the incident
January 13, 1987	Frankfurt, Germany	Muhammad Ali Hamadi, a member of the Hizballah, was arrested upon arrival on a flight from Beirut, in the possession of explosives. The terrorist was a member of the European network—another member of this network had been arrested in Milan, Italy, the previous day. Hamadi participated in the hijacking of a TWA flight to Beirut in 1985, and thus was wanted by the United States.
January 17 -21, 1987	Lebanon	Rudolph Kordas, a German citizen, was kidnapped on January 17 in Beirut. The organization "The Depressed on Earth" (a cover name for the Hizballah) claimed responsibility. On January 21, another German citizen, Alfred Schmidt, was kidnapped. Abd al Hadi Hamadi, a member of the Hizballah, was behind this kidnapping, aiming to free his brothers.
January 27, 1988	Lebanon	Rudolph Shray, a German citizen, was kidnapped in Beirut by the Hizballah. The kidnappers demanded the release of the Hamadi brothers, who had been arrested in January 1987.As a result of Syrian and Iranian pressure, Shray was released on March 3, 1988, perhaps as the result of a secret agreement with Germany.
February 12, 1988	Lebanon	Two Swedish journalists were kidnapped in Beirut by the Hizballah. They were released within a short period of time when it became clear to the kidnappers that they were not German. It appears that this kidnapping was also geared at taking German hostages, followed by a demand to release the Hamadi brothers.
May 1988	Germany	"Guards of Islam," apparently a cover name for pro-Iranian entities or Iranian agents, claimed responsibility for the murder of a German banker by detonating a bomb in his car. Iran accused the banker of being involved in the development of long-range missiles for Iraq.
March 1, 1989	Germany	Hizballah member Basam Machi was arrested in Germany; he had in his possession information about Israeli and American targets in Germany.

Table 4.6 (cont.)

| May 16, 1989 | Lebanon | Two German citizens, Heinrich Strubig and Tomas Kamptenner, employed by a humanitarian organization, were kidnapped by an unidentified Lebanese organization. The assumption was that the kidnappers were affiliated with the Hizballah and that the purpose of the kidnapping was to bring about the release of the Hamadi brothers. |
| September 18, 1992 | Berlin (Germany) | Four leaders of the Kurd opposition organization were assassinated at the Mikonos restaurant by Iranian agents. On April 9, 1997, the trial of the five individuals suspected of involvement in the murder took place, and they were sentenced to various prison terms. In his verdict, the German judge indicated that the leaders of the Iranian regime were responsible for dispatching the assassination unit to Germany, and issued a warrant for the arrest of the Iranian Intelligence Minister Ali Falahian. |

even present itself as the mediator who was supposedly able to help the Germans to solve their problems vis-à-vis the Hizballah.

Two Shiite terrorists (from the same family) were incarcerated in German prisons: Muhammad Ali Hamadi, who was arrested for the hijacking of a plane in 1985, during which one of the passengers was killed; and his younger brother, Abas Hamadi, who was arrested in Germany while trying to smuggle explosives into the country. A third brother, Abd al Hadi Hamadi, who played a central role in the Hizballah's security mechanism, applied heavy pressure with Iranian aid, in order to bring about the release of his brothers.[73] Following the arrest of the Hamadi brothers in Germany several German citizens in Lebanon were kidnapped in order to try and force the Germans to release them: Several days after the arrest, a German citizen named Rudolph Kordas was kidnapped in Lebanon, and a few days later another citizen was kidnapped (Alfred Schmidt). On May 16, 1989, after the release of the two previous hostages did not bring about the freedom of the Hamadi brothers, two additional Germans (Heinrich Strubig and Tomas Kamptenner), who worked for a German humanitarian organization in Lebanon, were kidnapped. Abd al Hadi Hamadi was apparently behind the kidnappings, due to his determination to free his brothers.[74]

In May 1988, the first attack against a German citizen on German soil took place when a German banker was killed by a bomb planted in his car. The organization "The Guards of Islam" (apparently a cover name for a pro-Iranian entity) claimed responsibility for the attack and accused the banker of involvement in the development of long-range missiles for Iraq. Another incident occurred in March 1989 when Hizballah member Basam Machi was arrested in Germany in possession of information regarding Israeli and American targets in Germany.

Also, although Iran perceived Germany as one of the "friendlier" nations, this does not prevent it from acting on German soil against Iranian expatriates and opposition entities. The exposure of the involvement of senior Iranian leaders in assassination actions against Iranian opposition entities in Germany (see the Mikonos episode) ultimately caused a grave crisis in the relations between the two countries.

Switzerland

Although Switzerland constitutes an example of a country of which there is supposedly no reason for mutual tension or hostility with Iran, nevertheless it was the arena for several terror attacks perpetrated by Shiite and Iranian entities. Over time, as a result of the arrest of Iranian/Shiite terrorists and their trials in Switzerland, this state also became a victim of terror attacks, with the main aim being the demanded release of incarcerated terrorists as well as providing ransom money to the terror organization.[75]

The main incident that turned Switzerland into a victim of Shiite terror was the hijacking of an Air Africa plane in Geneva. During the hijacking, one of the passengers was killed and the hijacker Ali Muhammad Hariri, who tuarned himself in to the Swiss authorities, was tried and sentenced to imprisonment. During the years 1987-1989, several attacks and kidnappings involving Swiss citizens were perpetrated in Lebanon in order to bring about the terrorist's release.[76]

Aside from this incident, Iranian entities made use of Switzerland as a transit station for terrorists in the framework of their activity in Europe, and also assassinated Iranian expatriates and opposition members who were living in Switzerland.

Table 4.7
List of Iranian/Shiite Attacks Perpetrated in Switzerland or against Swiss Targets Worldwide, and Central Incidents Connected to Them

Date	Place	Description of the incident
December 18, 1984	Switzerland	A Hizballah activist who arrived in Switzerland from Lebanon was arrested in possession of weapons. His arrest brought about the exposure of a Hizballah network in Rome that intended to perpetrate attacks against the U.S. Embassy in Rome (the Ladispoli incident).

Table 4.7 (cont.)

December 17, 1985	Cyprus	An armed terrorist was arrested attempting to board a Swissair flight that was about to take off for Jordan. It is possible that he intended to hijack the airplane.
July 24, 1987	Switzerland	An Air Africa plane en route from Congo to Paris was hijacked to Geneva by Hizballah member Ali Muhammad Harizi. The hijacker demanded the release of Muhammad Ali Hamadi from Germany, the release of Shiite terrorists incarcerated in France since 1986, including the leader of the FARL terror organization George Ibrahim Abdallah, as well as the release of all Arab detainees in Israel. An unknown organization claimed responsibility for the hijacking in Beirut, and threatened to attack Swiss targets if the hijacker was not released. Also, the organization threatened to execute French and American hostages if French authorities did not call off the siege of the Iranian Embassy in Paris (against the background of the exposure of Shiite terror cells and the escape of Gorgi—the Iranian terrorist—to his country's embassy in Paris). The demands of the organization and the hijacker attest to the Hizballah's involvement, and perhaps Iran's as well, in the hijacking.
End of July, 1987	Lebanon	An explosive device detonated near the Swiss Embassy in Beirut. No organization claimed responsibility for the attack, but it appears that it was also connected to the demand to free the hijacker of the Air Africa flight who had been arrested on July 24 in Switzerland.
August 1987	Switzerland	An explosive device went off in Geneva. No organization claimed responsibility for the attack, but it appears that it was also perpetrated against the background of the demand to release Ali Muhammad Hariri, hijacker of the Air Africa flight, who had been arrested on July 24 in Switzerland.
November 17, 1988	Lebanon	Peter Winkler, a Swiss citizen and a member of the Red Cross, was kidnapped, apparently by Abu Nidal's men, and was subsequently handed over to the Hizballah. The kidnapping was to be used as leverage against the Swiss government

Table 4.7 (cont.)

November 17, 1988 (cont.)	Lebanon	to cancel the trial of Ali Muhammad Hariri, hijacker of the Air Africa airplane. As a result of the kidnapping and due to the threat to other Red Cross workers, the Red Cross and Swiss government evacuated all their employees and citizens from Lebanon. Winkler was released in December 1988 with the help of the Swiss government. The Swiss government denied that it had negotiated with the kidnappers and Hariri remained in a Swiss prison.

Arab Targets

The Persian Gulf States

The policy of the revolutionary regime in Iran towards the Persian Gulf States constitutes a combination of pragmatic political considerations alongside radical ideological approaches. Khomeini regarded himself as an ally of the Gulf States, particularly in light of the existence of large Shiite minorities in these states, but he did not recognize the legitimacy of the Arab regimes and defined them as anti-Islamic reactionary servants of imperialism.[77]

Khomeini rejected these regimes due to their background and identity (as they are not based on religious clerics), because of their monarchial form of government (which contradicts Islamic principles), and as a result of their serving the imperialists that encourage the infiltration of Western influence, as well as the manipulation of oil resources in favor of a small minority while perpetuating social gaps. According to Khomeini's outlook, it was Iran's duty to help the Depressed "Umma" (community of believers) in the Gulf States, without taking boundaries and rulers into consideration. Therefore, these states quickly became a central target for the export of the Islamic revolution, thus turning Iran into the most severe threat to the stability of the regimes in the Gulf States.[78]

However, alongside the basic hostility towards "the reactionary regimes," several vital economic and political considerations stood at the foundations of the Iranian policy, which necessitated a pragmatic and tolerant policy. The Iran-Iraq war constituted an important component in this issue; Iran's basic objective was to try to preserve the status quo in the Gulf and to ensure that a neutral (if unenthusiastic) stand was adopted by the states in the area.[79] Thus, Iran made every effort to present the Iran-Iraq war not as another layer in the historical struggle between the Persians and the Arabs over control of that area, and not even as a battle between the Sunna and the Shia, but rather as a struggle of "the true Islam" against "the despicable anti-Islamic reign," which every Muslim, no matter whether he is Sunni or Shiite, has an interest in abolishing. Iran also made sure to emphasize that the true danger to the Gulf States lay in the expansion aspirations of Saddam Hussein, and that Iran was merely the first victim to these aspirations. The Iranians also claimed that if they did not succeed in halting Iraq, the Gulf States would be the next in line.

The Iranians endeavored to emphasize not only the dangers inherent to the region, but also the existence of a common enemy to all of Islam—Israel. Iraq's defeat, according to the Iranians, was a condition for Iran's mobilization in the true struggle—none other than the struggle against Israel—and this struggle was common to the entire Muslim world. During a visit to Saudi Arabia in 1985, Iranian Foreign Minister Valyati claimed that "the failures that the Arabs experienced in the past in their struggle against Israel stemmed from lack of Islamic fervor" and that "the road to Jerusalem passes through Carbala."[80]

As noted above, Iran's policy towards the Gulf States was ambivalent and underwent considerable fluctuation, starting with placatory and conciliatory messages, through threats and terror attacks, and culminating on the verge of a limited military confrontation, such as planting land mines in the Gulf's waters and the firing of "Silkworm" missiles at Kuwaiti oil targets in 1987.

In the long term, Iran aspired to bring about changes in the region and to establish "Islamic republics based on the Iranian format,"[81] but in the short term Iran needed "relative quiet" at the Gulf which would enable the free flow of Iranian oil and the import of weapons for the war against Iraq.

In any event, it appears that the Gulf States perceived "the Iranian threat" as immediate and extremely dangerous, even beyond the inter-Arab feeling of solidarity that they felt for Iraq. This worldview motivated them to adopt a policy of walking "a tightrope" between neutrality and offering Iraq active aid during the war.

Due to their fear of Iran, in 1981, the Gulf States founded the Gulf States Alliance, whose goal was to provide collective security to its members against aggression faced by any one of them. Iran, which viewed the allaince as a threat and evidence of the Gulf States' support for Iraq in the Gulf struggle, responded sharply to the establishment of the alliance. The issue of the alliance and the support of the Gulf States for Iraq became a central issue in their conflict with Iran, which accused them of providing financial, logistic, and even operational aid to Iraq (funding the transfer of weapons to Iraq via the Gulf States, the use of ports, assistance in exporting Iraqi oil, and enabling the landing of Iraqi combat planes).[82]

As through diplomatic channels, Iran failed to convince the Gulf States to adopt a more "balanced" (or rather—pro-Iranian) policy, the Iranians endeavored to force this upon them through terror attacks. The majority of the terror activities was directed at Saudi Arabia and Kuwait (see subsequent elaboration)—both against targets inside their territory, through the use of local Shiite entities, and against their targets worldwide. In most cases, it was impossible to prove direct Iranian invovement, thus enabling Iran to deny this activity and to maintain, at least officially, diplomatic relations with the Gulf States, despite the former's covert activities.[83]

During the years 1982-1989, about half of Iran's terror activities were directed at targets in the Gulf States. It is possible to point out three main goals vis-à-vis those activities:

1.   To modify the Gulf States' policy towards Iran in the matter of the war with Iraq, and put an end to the provision of aid to Iraq;
2.   To free terrorists incarcerated in the Gulf States or avenge their execution;
3.   To undermine and topple these regimes in order to establish Islamic regimes.

The Persian Gulf is of primary strategic importance from Iran's point of view, due to the fact that it is the main channel for the export of Iranian oil and the import of merchandise required for the Iranian economy. Thus, Iran has an essential interest in preserving its status in the region. Therefore, since the mid-1990s Iran has been involved in efforts to improve its relations with the Gulf States and has significantly reduced its involvement in terror in this arena.

Saudi Arabia

From the very first, the relationship between revolutionary Iran and the monarchial regime in Saudi Arabia was characterized by suspicion and basic hostility. The first and most essential point of controversy lies in the ambition of both regimes to be the bearer of the banner of Islam. This struggle is rooted in the rivalry between Muhammad's heirs and was perpetuated in the enmity between the Shia and the Sunna. Saudi Arabia regarded itself as the cradle of Islam and as the "protector of the holy sites," and claimed the crown of "leader of Islam," while in the Iranian view the Saudi regime was perceived as "reactionary" and anti-Islam.

The Iranians regard Saudi Arabia as a U.S. ally, and therefore refer to it as "the loyal pig" of the United States and its adjutant in the region. In Iran's view, Saudi Arabia serves the interests of Western imperialism and enables its infitration and influence within the Muslim nation. As the Iranians see it, despite Saudi Arabia's strength and wealth it has not contributed enough to the struggle against Israel and has even obstructed it at the command of its master, the United States.

To this, one must add various steps related to the Saudi policy that were as thorns in the flesh of Iran, such as the Saudi aid offered to Iraq during its war with Iran, its conciliatory stand towards Israel (the Fahed Plan), its decision to refrain from offering the Palestinians aid during the war in Lebanon, the massive acquisition of weaponry that was perceived by Iran as mainly directed against itself, the competition in the oil market, and Saudi Arabia's ties with the Iranian opposition (mainly its links with Gutbzada's coup attempt).[84]

The reciprocal tension in the relations increased annually near the time of the Haj. The mutual criticism that accompanied the pilgrimage reflected the ideological and politicial chasm that yawned between these two regimes. Iran regarded the Haj as "a large religious-political congress," that constituted a golden opportunity to promote Iran's revolutionary concepts among Muslim believers. In October 1981, some 75,000 Iranian pilgrims arrived in Mecca, some of whom were unruly; they distributed inflammatory leaflets and called out slogans against imperialism and the Saudi regime. The Saudi authorities took immediate and tough action in the form of arrests and deportation. Following these incidents, Khomeini sent a letter to King Khaled (on October 10, 1981), in which he expressed his doubts regarding "the measure of understanding of Islam" of the Saudi "Ulama" and the extent to which the King was aware of what was happening in his country. He also complained that the Haj was run according to the dictates of "the United States, Israel and the other enemies of Islam." He emphasized that Iran would act during the Haj according to the commandments of Islam. The meaning of Khomeini's declaration was that he was reserving the right to continue using the Haj as a political stage for the promotion of the concept of the Islamic revolution and to denounce the Saudi regime.[85]

Arabic newspapers printed in Teheran (mainly *Al-Shahid, Al-Umma,* and the periodical published by the Islamic Republican Party) turned Saudi Arabia into a regular target of criticism. They portrayed Khomeini as "the Imam of all the Muslims," while highlghting the treacherous nature of King Khaled.

In 1982, the violent struggle surrounding the Haj continued, when radical Iranian pilgrims instigated violent riots in Mecca and Medina. The Iranian activities at that time were not spontaneous, but rather were prepared and orchestrated by the official Iranian representative (in charge of his country's pilgrims). These riots were exploited by Iran to point out Saudi Arabia's inability to supervise the pilgrimage effectively and neutrally. In 1983, and during subsequent years, the Haj was turned into an arena for Iranian demonstrations and political activity.

The steps taken by Saudi Arabia in order to restrict the number of pilgrims (by raising difficulties in matters related to flights, limiting hotel accommodations, etc.) as well as the Iranian propaganda caused violent confrontations, which sometimes culminated in arrests or even in the death of some of the demonstrators, thus increasing the tension. Iran claimed that Saudi Arabia should be divested of the right to manage the holy sites. Hujat al Islam Khaniya, who was Khomeini's personal representative at the Haj up until 1985, claimed that the Saudi leaders were "the emissaries of Satan" and that the Ulma are "representatives of the secret police." He called on the Muslims "to put an end to the government of manipulators controlling God's house." The Minister of the Revolutionary Guards also protested the fact that "heathens" control the holy places, and called on the Muslims to cast them off.[86]

It is to be noted that despite the ongoing religious-ideological conflict, beginning in 1984 several attempts were made to decrease the level of tension between them. Iran acted via diplomatic channels to persuade Saudi Arabia to reduce its support of Iraq, and responded with restraint to an incident in which Saudi airplanes downed an Iranian airplane over the Persian Gulf in June 1984.

But 1987 constituted a new high in the tension between the two countries, against the background of the escalation of the war in the Gulf and growing U.S. involvement through the sponsoring of Kuwaiti ships under the U.S. flag and American navy escort. The tension stemming from the incidents in the Gulf also expressed itself during the Haj that year. Iran again initiated extensive riots among the pilgrims against the Saudi authorities in which 400 to 600 people were killed, most of them Iranians. Iran's response was harsh condemnation and a terror campaign against Saudi Arabia and Saudi targets worldwide (see subsequent elaboration).

The struggle between the two countries regarding the Haj continued in 1989, and in September the trial of sixteen Kuwaiti citizens of Shiite descent opened. The Saudi authorities charged them with involvement in explosions that occurred during the Haj in July 1989. Some of the accused confessed that they were affiliated with a radical Shiite organization and had received aid from entities at the Iranian Embassy in Kuwait in order to perpatrate attacks. The Shiite terrorists were sentenced to death and executed. Iran denied any connection to the attacks but sharply condemned the executions. Following the executions, a series of retaliatory attacks was initiated, in which six Saudi diplomats were killed in various places worldwide (one in Lebanon in November 1989, two in Turkey in October 1989 and January 1990, and three in Thailand in February 1990).[87]

Another point of controversy between the two countries was the question of the scope of oil export and its price. Iran urgently needed to increase its oil production and to raise its prices in order to finance the war needs in Iraq, while Saudi Arabia was interested in stablizing the price market and opposed the creation of an artifical shortage in order to raise prices. This conflict of interests was peceived by the Iranians as part of a policy of Saudi steps aimed at weakening Iran's strength, or as Iran called it, "the oil conspiracy." Khamenei stated in this regard that the war over oil prices was no less important to Iran than the war at the front.

Saudi Arabia's resolute decision not to capitulate to Iranian terror, the trial of the Shiite terrorists and their execution, and that country's unwillingness to submit to the Iranian demands regarding the Haj—all of these factors led to an ongoing series of terror attacks in an Iranian attempt to change these policies and avenge the deaths of the Shiite terrorists who had been executed in Saudi Arabia.

After the conclusion of the Iran-Iraq war, and in light of Iran's desire to improve its ties with the West and the Arab states, there was also some improvement in the relations between the two countries. Although the suspicions had not disappeared, and Iran continued to support Islamic terror organizations in Saudi Arabia and in other Gulf states, the Iranian rhetoric became more moderate, terror against Saudi targets lessened, and Iran ceased to use the Haj in order to censure the administration in Riyadh. Iraq's invasion of Kuwait and the Gulf War that followed in its wake (1990-1991) posed both ideological and political dilemmas for the Iranian administration. Iraq's invasion of Kuwait and the Iraqi threat to achieve hegemony in the Gulf once again endangered Iran's status, only two years after concluding an eight-year war with Iraq. The American involvement, the concentration of a large international force in Saudi Arabia, and the fact that the majority of the Arab world chose to side with the Western-Saudi coalition were all thorns in Iran's flesh, but they created a strategic balance vis-à-vis Iraq's strength and its aspirations for expansion.

Therefore, Iran took a neutral stand: It criticized the Iraqi aggression on the one hand, and the coalition forces and the involvement of the West, on the other. The overwhelming triumph of the United States and her allies in the Gulf War weakened Iraq, strengthened Iran's position and brought about Iraqi concessions regarding several issues that were still in dispute between the two countries.

During the years 1995-1996 two attacks were perpetrated against U.S. targets on Saudi Arabian territory:

- On November 13, 1995, a car bomb exploded near the consultancy headquarters of the Saudi National Guard in Riyadh.
- On June 25, 1996, a car bomb exploded near an American military base at al Khobar Daharan.

The investigation of these attacks indicated that radical Saudi organizations were responsible for the attacks, but Iranian involvement in aiding these organizations was also evident. These attacks exacerbated the tension in the Saudi-Iranian relations. The controversy between Iran and Saudi Arabia also intensified as a result of Saudi aid that was provided to the Taliban regime in Afghanistan and also due to Saudi support for the peace process in the Middle East.

The election of Khatami as Iran's president in 1997 led to improved relations between the two countries, and, in 1998, the first historical visit of an Iranian president to Saudi Arabia since the Islamic revolution in Iran took place. However, Saudi Arabia's decision to join the U.S. coalition in the war against Iraq in 2003 caused the tension to escalate again and renewed Iranian suspicion towards Saudi Arabia, due to Iran's fear that after the campaign against Iraq it would find itself in a face-to-face confrontation with the United States and the other members of the coalition.

Table 4.8
Examples of Iranian/Shiite Attacks Perpetrated against Saudi Targets

Date	Place	Description of the incident
1987	Morocco	Bendar Ibn-Sultan, the Saudi Ambassador to Morocco, was injured in the explosion of a device planted in his car. Iranian agents took responsibility for the incident, which was performed against the background of the opening of the Islamic conference in Kuwait.
January 12, 1987	Lebanon	A Saudi citizen, Baher al Damenhuri, was kidnapped by the Hizballah, and was released in March 1987 after the Saudi government paid ransom with Syrian mediation.
January 26, 1987	Lebanon	A Saudi citizen, Khaled Dia, was kidnapped by the Hizballah in Beirut, and was released in March 1987 after the Saudi government paid ransom with Syrian mediation.
August 2, 1987	Lebanon	Explosive devices detonated near the Saudi Arabian Embassy, the Saudi Cultural Center, and the offices of the Saudi national carrier. The attacks were perpetrated by Shiite entities in retaliation for the death of Iranian demonstrators who were killed in the riots in Mecca, during the pilgrimage in July 1987.
August 15, 1987	Saudi Arabia	An explosion at a gas facility of the ARAMCO company injured several employees. Pro-Iranian entities were suspected of perpetrating the attack.
September 8-10, 1987	France	On September 8, an explosion occurred near the Saudi bank in Paris, and on September 10 another device exploded near the Kuwaiti-French bank. No one was hurt in either of the attacks. It appears that the attacks were perpetrated to avenge the deaths of the Iranian pilgrims during the riots that were initiated in the Haj to Mecca.
March-April 1988	Far East	Against the background of the escalating tension between Saudi Arabia and Iran, a series of attacks was perpetrated against the offices of the Saudi national carrier in several countries in the Far East—Singapore, Japan, and Pakistan. The attacks were carried out by Pro-Iranian entities.Also, some time in March (the exact date is unknown) a Saudi diplomat was shot and injured in Lagos, Nigeria. It would appear that this attack was also perpetrated by pro-Iranian entities.

Table 4.8 (cont.)

April 18, 1988	Germany	A bomb was thrown from a moving vehicle at the offices of the Saudi national carrier in Frankfurt. A few minutes earlier a similar bomb had been thrown at the Jewish community center in the city.
April 27, 1988	Kuwait	A bomb went off near the Saudi national carrier's offices in Kuwait, causing extensive damage and injuring one person. The Hizballah claimed responsibility for the incident, which was perpetrated as a resultl of the worsening relationship between Saudi Arabia and Iran.
October 1988	Turkey	Abdallah Badawi, second secretary at the Saudi Embassy in Ankara, was shot dead by a gunman. "The Islamic Jihad of the Hajaz" claimed responsibility for the assassination in Beirut, and claimed that it was meant to avenge the execution of four organization members that were sentenced to death in Saudi Arabia (there are no data regarding the attacks in which they participated).
December 29, 1988	Pakistan	The Saudi Deputy Consul Hassan al Amiri fell victim to an assassination perpetrated by the "Soldiers of Justice." Radical Shiite entities were behind the attack, which was meant to avenge the execution of four Shiite terrorists in Saudi Arabia (on October 1, 1988), as well as to torpedo the improved relations between Saudi Arabia and Iran.
January 4, 1989	Thailand	Saudi diplomat Salah Almalkhi was shot by an assassin with Middle Eastern features. Two organizations claimed responsibility for the attack: • The "Soldiers of Justice" announced in Beirut (on January 5) that it was responsible for the murder, and issued a warning to all those who served the Wahabian Saudi family. • The "Hajaz Islamic Jihad" claimed responsibility for the attack, and stated that its aim was to avenge the death of four of its members who were executed by Saudi authorities.
June 20, 1989	Belgium	An Egyptian employee at the Saudi Embassy in Brussels was shot to death near his residence in the city.

Table 4.8 (cont.)

October 16, 1989	Turkey	The Saudi military attache Abd al Rahman Shrawi was seriously injured when a bomb that had been planted in his car went off. The Islamic Jihad claimed responsibility for the incident and stated that it had been perpetrated to avenge the execution of the sixteen Kuwaiti organization members in Saudi Arabia.
November 1, 1989	Lebanon	Saudi diplomat Ali al Marzuki was shot dead, and his driver was injured by gunshots fired from a moving vehicle. The Islamic Jihad claimed responsibility and stated that the attack had been perpetrated to avenge the execution of the sixteen Kuwaiti organization members in Saudi Arabia.

Kuwait

The basis for the dispute between Iran and Kuwait was essentially no different from the controversy with Saudi Arabia (with the exception of the issue of the Islamic holy places). Kuwait was more afraid of the results of the war in the Gulf (the Iran-Iraq war) and the Iranian influence, mainly among the Iranian and Shiite population in its territory.

Iran, for its own part, was particularly enraged about the placing of transportation routes in Kuwait at the disposal of the Iraqis, complained about the suppression of Shiites and Iranians in Kuwait, and protested the hostile attitude of many Kuwaiti newspapers towards the revolution. Khomeini also never forgave Kuwait for turning him away when he was deported from Iraq (October 1978).[88]

From the time of the establishment of the revolutionary regime in Iran, Kuwait constitued a central target for Shiite terror (more than a third of the Iranian/Shiite attacks were perpetrated against Kuwaiti targets).There were several reasons that motivated the Iranians to concentrate on the perpetration of attacks against Kuwait:

1. Kuwait's proximity to Iran and the existence of a relatively large Shiite population (which constitutes some 24 percent of the overall population in Kuwait) turned that country into a preferred target for "exporting the revolution," and enabled the construction of an extensive Iranian terror infrastructure on its soil.
2. Kuwait's military and political weakness, on the one hand, and its solidarity with an anti-Iranian line, on the other, turned it into an easy target for attacks (during the Iran-Iraq war).

3. Kuwait's resolute stand and its refusal to capitulate to terror activities exposed it to repeated attempts to free arrested terrorists or bring about mitigated sentences.

The Iranian threats posed against Kuwait were particularly overt and obvious. In 1982, after a successful Iranian Spring campaign, the Iranian newspaper *Kihan* stated: "Up until now we quietly gnashed our teeth knowing that Kuwat acted out of fear of Iraq and Saudi Arabia, but now Kuwait must know that tomorrow may be too late."[89] In 1983, Iran accused Kuwait of placing three ports at the disposal of Iraq and thus warned Kuwait that in its view it was an accomplice to "Iraq's crimes." In December of that year, a wave of terror attacks occurred in Kuwait. In response, the local authorities arrested a large number of Shiites and Iranians, and deported many others beyond Kuwait's boundaries.

Tension peaked again between the two countries in 1987, against the background of the escort of Kuwaiti oil tankers under a foreign flag and the presence of the U.S. Navy as well as European fleets, which protected the movement of shipping vessels in the Gulf. The "oil tanker war" brought the countries to the brink of a confrontation, when the Iranians sought to plant mines in the Gulf, attacked Kuwaiti oil tankers, and even fired Chinese-made "Silkworm" missiles at Kuwaiti ports and oil facilities.

A central bone of contention between Iran and the Hizballah on the one hand, and the Kuwaiti authorities on the other, was the arrest of a terror network from the ranks of the Iraqi al Dawa organization (an extremist Shiite organization that had fast ties with the Hizballah and Iran) and the death sentences awaiting some of the members. Kuwaiti authorities exposed the network in December 1983 and arrested twenty-five suspects.[90] Two of the detainees were related to Hussein Musawi (Hussein al Sayyid and Yosef al Musawi) and to Imad Muraniya (Elias Fuad Cha'am), both of whom were leaders of the Hizballah.[91] From the moment they were arrested, the issue of their release became a central goal of the Hizballah, and the Kuwaiti government's resolute stand caused ongoing terror attacks against Kuwait and the United States in order to induce the latter to use its influence on the Kuwaiti authorities.[92]

On February 11, 1984, twenty-one of the suspects went on trial. During the trial, which ended on March 27, 1984, the Hizballah perpetrated a series of kidnappings in order to apply pressure on the Kuwaiti authorities to cancel the trial or at least to influence their sentence (among others, three American citizens and one French citizen were kidnapped in Lebanon). On March 27, 1984, the Kuwaiti court sentenced five network members to death, including Elais Fuad Cha'am, and the rest of the network members were sentenced to life imprisonment.[93] From this stage onward, the Iranian/Shiite terror campaign against Kuwait persevered in order to prevent the executions and bring about

Table 4.9
Examples of Iranian/Shiite Attacks Perpetrated against Kuwaiti Targets

Date	Place	Description of the incident
December 12, 1983	Kuwait	Two car bombs exploded near the French and U.S. Embassies and four explosive devices detonated at public Kuwaiti facilities. Another bomb was found and dismantled. The al Dawa organization claimed responsibility for this series of attacks.
August 5, 1984	Spain	An attack was perpetrated at a Kuwaiti guesthouse in Marabella; one Kuwaiti businessman was injured.
December 4, 1984	Kuwait	A Kuwaiti airplane was hijacked en route from Dubai to Pakistan and was forced to land in Teheran.
May 25, 1985	Kuwait	An assassination attempt was made against the Emir of Kuwait via a car bomb driven by a suicide terrorist (the Emir was not hurt).
June 12, 1986	Kuwait	Several sabotage/arson attempts were carried out at oil facilities. Damage was caused to the facilities but no one was hurt.
January 8, 1987	Cyprus	An explosive device detonated in the center of Nicosia, near the offices of the Saudi national carrier, the Kuwaiti national carrier, and Pan Am. No one was hurt.
March 20, 1987	Turkey	A bomb went off at the front of the Emirates travel agency. No one hurt, but the explosion caused serious damage.
January 19-26, 1987	Kuwait	Attacks using explosive devices were perpetrated by Iranian agents, under various cover names several days prior to the convening of the Islamic conference in Kuwait: 19.1.1987—Detonation at oil facilities; 24.1.1987—Detonation at a police station; 24.1.1987—A car bomb near a hotel 26.1.1987—Two bombs went off. The targets are not clear. Eleven Shiite Kuwaitis of Iranian descent were arrested and charged with responsibility for these attacks and for the series of attacks against oil facilities carried out in June 1986. In June 1987, some of them were sentenced to death, and others received various prison sentences.

Table 4.9 (cont.)

April 5-20, 1987	Kuwait	A Boeing airplane belonging to the Kuwaiti national carrier with 112 passengers on board was hijacked during a flight from Thailand to Kuwait and was forced to land in Mashad, Iran. The hijackers, Hizballah members, demanded the release of the organization's members arrested in Kuwait in 1983. Imad Muraniya, who had also been involved in the kidnapping of many hostages in Beirut, was behind the hijacking. The incident was apparently perpetrated by radical Iranian elements that aspired to polarize the relations with Kuwait and the West due to the imminent elections for the Iranian Parliament.
April 21, 1987	Kuwait	Eight explosive devices detonated almost simultaneously at oil facilities in Kuwait, causing damage to the facilities.
July 15, 1987	Kuwait	Two people were killed in the detonation of an explosive device at a shopping center. The attack was perpetrated by pro-Iranian entities.
October 24, 1987	Kuwait	An explosive device detonated near a travel agency representing Pan Am. The attack came in retaliation for an attack against two Iranian oil rigs by U.S. forces in the Persian Gulf on October 19, and was apparently perpetrated by Shiite/Iranian entities.
May 7, 1988	Kuwait	An explosive device detonated near the offices of the Saudi national carrier in Kuwait.
1990	Kuwait	During the Iraqi invasion of Kuwait, the Iraqis released Shiite terrorists incarcerated in that country. As stated earlier, many attacks were perpetrated by Shiite terror organizations in order to bring about the group's release.

the members' release. These prisoners were released when Iraq invaded Kuwait in 1990.

During the Gulf War, Iran condemned the Iraqi invasion of Kuwait but also denounced the campaign of the U.S.-headed coalition, which brought about the liberation of Kuwait. Relations between Iran and Kuwait became "correct." On the one hand, Iran disparaged the Kuwaiti regime, which it perceived as an accomplice and lackey of the United States, but on the other hand, it refrained from generating tension in the gulf, which, in 2004, would not serve its economic and political interests.

Bahrain

During the years 1994-1998, radical Shiite circles in Bahrain, which acted with Iranian aid and at its inspiration, launched extensive subversive activities.[94] Iran has historical claims vis-à-vis the ownership of Bahrain, and since this state was granted independence, its relations with Iran have been characterized by fluctuating tension. During the Iran-Iraq war, the tension between the two countries rose against the background of the "oil tanker war" and Bahrain's support of the pro-Iraqi and pro-American camp. The tension abated at the end of the war in 1988, due to Iran's desire to improve relations with its Arab neighbors and the West.

Bahrain has a large Shiite minority that is hostile to the regime and aspires to change the character of the state and reach a more just distribution of its resources (based mainly on huge income from oil). In November 1994, extremist Shiite entities organized widespread demonstrations and riots throughout Bahrain. The authorities took a tough stand, killed twenty people, and arrested several thousands. Bahrain publicly accused Iran of causing the riots, severed diplomatic ties with it, ceased air traffic between the two countries, and prohibited economic ties with Iran.

At the same time, neighboring Kuwait was making arrests among the Kuwaiti Hizballah organization (a radical Shiite Kuwaiti organization). An interrogation of the organization's detainees revealed that the Kuwaiti Hizballah had helped Shiite opposition organizations in Bahrain to smuggle weapons into the country. During 1986, the wave of terror and violence was renewed in Bahrain and was directed mainly at foreign residents and workers (mainly Asians). Here follows a list of several prominent incidents that took place that year:

- February 11, 1996—a bomb went off in front of the Diplomat Hotel in Manama, causing injuries to one British citizen and two local workers. It also damaged the front of the hotel. The Islamic "Front for the Liberation of Bahrain" claimed responsibility for the attack.
- March 14, 1996—Molotov Cocktails were thrown into a restaurant. Seven workers from Bangladesh perished in the fire.
- August 25, 1996—A Pakistani guard was shot and injured at the Russian Consulate building.
- September 14, 1996—A spare parts store for cars was torched. An Indian worker was killed in the fire.
- November 12, 1996—An explosive device detonated near the Hyundai car agency and injured a guard.
- December 31, 1996—Eight attackers threw Molotov Cocktails at a building housing foreign workers. One foreign worker was killed in the fire and two were wounded.

In the month of June 1997, eight members of the Bahraini Hizballah were apprehended. They confessed to perpetrating the attack on March 14, 1996. Their interrogation revealed that they had undergone training in Iran and were equipped with money and weapons in order to oust the government of the Khalifa family. On July 1 1997, three members of the organization were sentenced to death, while the others were sentenced to prolonged prison sentences.

It would appear that Iran continues to stir up the "Bahrain cauldron" to this very day, but is careful to avoid exposure regarding direct involvement in the events in that country due to its awareness of the close ties between Bahrain and the United States, and Iran's desire to avoid a confrontation with the latter.

Iranian Expatriates and Opposition Organizations

Iranian Expatriates

The key characteristic of the expatriate Iranian population is its internal division and the rivalry between its various members. Therefore, this is not actually "an opposition" but rather "oppositions" that are antagonistic to each other no less than to Khomeini and his successors. It is for this reason that these movements have been unable to find a leader over the years who will be acceptable to everyone and unite the ranks of the opposers of the Islamic regime in Iran.

The expatriate movements (most of which have representation in Paris and Iraq) are divided into three main groups:[95]

- Former supporters of the Shah (including members of the royal family, army officers, and administrators);
- Entities that opposed the Shah during his regime but also opposed Khomeini (such as the National Kurd Party);
- Entities that supported Khomeini or were even members of his camp that split away from him later, such as the Mujahidin Khalq or former followers such as Bani Sader. (These circles expanded gradually following the growing disappointment among Khomeini's former supporters.)

In ideological terms, it is possible to place most of the expatriate movements at the center of the political map. Some of them, such as the Tuda, were affiliated with the left, while others, including monarchists and military figures, were right wing. Ideological differences and personal rivalries existed within each of these groups. The expatriates even disagreed about the tactical question regarding the need to organize a broad coalition in order to fight Khomeini's regime. It appears that personal rivalry was the main reason for the splits, and that each leader of the various groups tended to regard himself, and only himself, as the homeland's savior.

At the beginning of 1982, former Iranian Prime Minister Ali Amini, who resided in Paris, established "The Front for the Salvation of Iran," which raised its banner for the liberation of Iran from Khomeini's regime. His initiative to unite the expatriate factions met with only partial success. Bakhtiar, who was also a former Iranian prime minister, refrained from publicly spurning Amini's initiative, but was unenthusiastic about it because he regarded himself as the sole leader capable of standing at the head of a movement to "save Iran."

Koresh Reza Pahlavi (the Shah's son) crowned himself king on October 31, 1980 (his twentieth birthday), in a modest ceremony that took place at the Kubeh Palace in Cairo, after his father's demise (the Shah died in Egypt on October 29). Koresh Reza swore to take action to oust Khomeini and his successors and to regain the monarchy. Although none of the countries worldwide recognized his monarchy, Reza began to assemble Iranian expatriates around him, mainly military figures, in order to solicit their aid in effecting an uprising. He endeavored to stay uninvolved in the rivalry separating the various movements, as "the role of the king," so he said, "is to remain above the various streams. I regard myself as the king of all Iranians, including those who oppose the monarchy."[96] He also made sure to remove two women from the public eye who had retained a major influence in his father's court—his mother and aunt—as he assessed that they were identified with the negative aspects of his father's reign.

Initially, Reza acted from Cairo, and President Sadat placed one of the broadcasting studios in the city at his disposal in order to enable him to call on his people to overthrow Khomeini's regime, but several months later he transferred his activities to Rabat in Morocco. Various reports from inside Iran indicate that at the time a certain dimension of change was indeed noted within several circles in Iran vis-à-vis the monarchy, but this change was far from constituting a threat to Khomeini's status.

Reza was surrounded by generals and many advisors, including the former chief-of-staff General Jaam and Colonel Obeisi, the former Iranian military attaché in Paris and son of General Gulam Ali Obeisi who had served as the commander of the ground forces. The activity of the military figures focused on an attempt to organize a military infrastructure in order to execute a coup d'état. Some tried to make contact and acquire aid from Washington; others, including Gulam Ali Obeisi, contacted Iraq regarding this matter.

In his book, *The Iranian Connection,*[97] Shmuel Segev claims that the expatriate Iranians planned to acquire weapons from Israel, and perhaps even request assistance in the form of instructors, and then transfer the weapons via Sudan with the consent of former President Numeiri, who even agreed to place at the disposal of the "conspirators" a training base where individuals who planned to participate in the coup would undergo training. Saudi entities headed by the businessman Adnan Khashoggi (and even King Fahed was apparently in on the secret) were involved in the coordination and funding of the coup. However, ultimately, the plan was never executed.

In this connection, it is important to note that in July 1980 preparations were made by several Iranian air force officers to carry out a coup. They had planned to bomb Khomeini's house in Qum, but the conspiracy was exposed; the conspirators were caught and executed.[98]

In 1981, Bani Sader and Masoud Rajavi, the leader of the Mujahidin Khalq, established the "Council for National Resistance," which was subsequently joined by the Ayatollah Matin Daftari (leader of the National Democratic Front) and Abd al Rahman Kasmelo (leader of the Democratic Kurd Party). This alliance, however, did not endure either and it disintegrated in 1984, after it experienced no success in battling Khomeini. It is noteworthy that the direct cause for the rift in this front was Bani Sader's opposition to the ties that Rajavi and the Mujahidin Khalq maintained with Iraq.[99]

In 1986, after France's capitulation to the Iranian terror campaign, Rajavi was forced to leave France with most of his followers and move to Iraq. Nevertheless, the Mujahidin Khalq organization endeavored to stay in contact with the other opposition movements and even increased its activities against Iran.

After the dismantling of the Council for National Resistance, its various components persevered in their own independent struggles against Khomeini's regime, and Bani Sader continued to view himself as Iran's legitimate president, while noting the alleged mass support for him in the Iranian public and army—a claim that had no basis in reality. The most senior religious leader who acted against Khomeini outside of the Iranian borders was Mahdi Rukhani, but he lacked an elevated religious status and had no real support inside the country.

The opposition's difficulties escalated following the strengthening and stabilization of Khomeini's regime, due to the subjugation measures enacted against opposition entities in Iran and their persecution outside of the country's boundaries, and also because of the loss of trust and support on the part of foreign governments for the opposition organizations, which appeared to be both splintered and ineffective. These organizations constituted a militant opposition to the revolutionary regime in Iran, but they did not succeed in becoming an alternative or a real threat to the regime, as they themselves became a central target of the Iranian authorities, which took ruthless steps to restrict their activities and eradicate them. During that period, the leaders of the expatriates became central targets for eradication by Iranian and Shiite terror cells in their places of exile. Following is a list of the main incidents related to this aspect (see a more comprehensive list in Table 3.2 chapter three):

- In 1979, Shariar Shafik—the son of Princess Ashraf, the Shah's twin sister, was murdered, apparently by Iranian agents.
- In 1981, an assassination attempt was made against former Iranian Prime Minister Shahfur Bakhtiar. The assassin, Anis Nakash, who was

acting for the Hizballah (with Iranian inspiration) was caught and imprisoned in France.

- In 1984, General Gulam Ali Obeisi, commander of the Iranian ground forces during the Shah's reign, was murdered.
- In 1989, Abd al Rahman Kasmelo was murdered in Vienna, apparently by Iranian agents.
- In 1990, Kazem Rajavi, brother of the leader of Mujahidin Khalq, Masud Rajavi, was murdered in Switzerland, apparently by Iranian agents.
- On August 8, 1991, Shahfur Bakhtiar, the last prime minister during the Shah's reign, was murdered in his Parisian apartment by Iranian agents. (It is to be recalled that a previous assassination attempt failed in 1981.)
- In 1993, Muhammad Hussein Nahdi, a geologist and former employee of the Iranian national oil company and of the Iranian nuclear agency, was shot to death in is car. He had moved to Rome in 1981 and was active in Iranian opposition circles.
- In 1993, Muhammad Hassan Arbab was shot in the neck in Karachi, Pakistan. He was also active in the Iranian opposition.
- A single shot killed Hashem Abdulhi on September 17, 1995, in his home in Paris. He was the son of a key witness in the trial of the assassins of Shahfur Bakhtiar.
- In 1996, Zahra Rajavi and Ali Murdi, two Iranian opposition activists, were killed in their homes in Istanbul.
- In 1996, two Sunni Iranian clerics (*Baluchis*) were killed in Karachi, Pakistan. They, too, were opposers of the Iranian regime.
- In 1996, Reza Mezluman, a criminology professor and a deputy minister during the Shah's era, was killed in his home in Paris.

Opposition Organizations—The Mujahidin Khalq

The Mujahidin Khalq was established in 1965 by a group of Teheran University alumni. The organization's theorists, Muhammad Khanifezada and Ahmed Razi, claimed that the monotheistic order in the Prophet's words was directed against capitalist feudals and merchants as a means to establish a society without classes, and that every Muslim must persevere with Hussein's struggle and fight exploitation, imperialism, capitalism, tyranny, and the conservative Ulma.[100]

The Mujahidin recognized the central role of the Shia in preparing the spirit of the people for the struggle, both due to the revolutionary message in Hussein's philosophy and also because of the central place that the Shia claims in the hearts of the Iranian people. Nevertheless, they did not conceal their enthusiasm for Marxism "as a progressive method for social analysis." The Mujahidin claimed that it is impossible to be a good Muslim without being a rebel. They also argued that Islam and Marxism share a common enemy—the Shah—who brought about "organic unity" between Islam and Marxism. They argued that "Islam and Marxism share the same message, that of providing inspiration for struggle and sacrifice. The unity between Islam and Marxism stems from the joint struggle against reactionary imperialism."[101] The double component of Communism and Islam was also reflected in the movement's emblem: It was composed of the map of Iran against the background of the sickle and the scythe, as well as a machine gun alongside a verse from the Koran.

The actual activities of the Mujahidin were initiated in 1971, against the background of the "Koresh festivities" held by the Shah. The Iranian intelligence service during the Shah's reign—the SAVAK—succeeded in eradicating a large part of the organization's infrastructure and operators, but it continued in its violent struggle, which included bank robberies, the assassination of American officers (in 1973 and 1975), and American citizens (in 1976) who were connected to military projects in Iran, as well as attacks against police stations and Reza Shah's mausoleums, in addition to the offices of El Al, Shell, and British Petroleum.

In 1975, the Mujahidin's leanings towards Marxism intensified, and some of the organization's leaders came to the conclusion that Marxism was the true revolutionary philosophy rather than Islam. This turnabout caused a rift in the organization in May 1975: One faction, the Fadayn Khalq, distanced itself from Islam in favor of a Marxist-Leninist direction, which aspired to establish a popular republic in which religion would be defined as the personal business of every individual in society; the other faction, the Mujahidin Khalq headed by Masud Rajavi, continued to adhere to religion and an armed struggle, and aspired to establish an Islamic, socialist republic.

With the outbreak of overt opposition to the Shah's reign, the two organizations began perpetrating terror attacks against the regime.[102] The release of Mujahidin prisoners in the framework of the Shah's liberalization measures, during the years 1977 and 1978, only served to strengthen it and the organization played an important role in the process of the government takeover by revolutionary forces (mainly in the fateful days of February 1979). During the entire period of the struggle against the Shah's regime, the organization demonstrated impressive operational capabilities, and it even succeeded in bolstering its status in the view of the Iranian public and expanding its ranks. The organization's increased strength turned it into an important ally in the fight against the Shah, but also into a potential threat against the status of the Islamic movement led by Khomeini after the victorious revolution. Thus, if the period of the struggle against the Shah's reign was characterized by cooperation between the Mujahidin and Khomeini's revolutionary Islamic movement, with the ascent of the new regime the profound differences between the two organizations escalated and led to a rift and struggle between them.

In the beginning, the Mujahidin, like other political movements, attempted to take part in the new regime via the political processes involving the establishment of government institutions and by participating in the election process. The movement's failure in the elections (mainly due to the revised "game rules" in favor of Khomeini's party), and the suppressive measures employed by the regime against the Mujahidin supporters directed the organization's activity to the only channel still available to it—terror.

After 1981, the violent struggle between the regime and the opposition parties turned into a focus on the fight for the regime's stability, and the Mujahidin quickly set the tone for terror activity against the regime, while demonstrating impressive organizational capabilities and considerable daring. The most significant attack of the Mujahidin was the detonation of the headquarters of the "Islamic Republican Party" on June 28, 1981, during a conference attended by many of the new political leaders. Over seventy people were killed, including four government ministers and twenty-seven members of the Majlis (the Iranian Parliament). The prime minister was slightly wounded and Rafsanjani, who had left the premises only minutes earlier, was saved. A day earlier, an explosive device had detonated during public prayer services led by Ali Khamenei, and he was one of the injured.

The authorities vented their wrath on the opposition in general and the Mujahidin in particular. They declared it "a war to the bitter end...either they will survive or we will." Khomeini called on his loyal followers "not to be irresolute or merciful in the battle against the sharp-teethed wolves."[103]

From 1981 to date, an uncompromising struggle has been raging between the Mujahidin and the Iranian revolutionary regime. This struggle is being waged by the Mujahidin inside Iran, from its borders (mainly the Iraqi border) and throughout the world. Following a wave of terror attacks in the summer of 1981, the revolutionary regime initiated a campaign to eradicate the Mujahidin, in the course of which many of the movement's leaders were killed, others were arrested or went underground; the organization's leader Masoud Rajavi fled to Paris, and the center of activity moved to Kurdistan in Iraq. Despite the mortal blow inflicted on the organization, the Iranian regime continued to regard the Mujahidin as a real threat, and therefore continued to persecute its followers and damage their public image. The organization's ties with Iraq (mainly Rajavi's meeting with Tariq Aziz in January 1983) were exploited to demonstrate the organization's betrayal due to its willingness to join forces with Iran's enemies on the outside. The organization's arrested members were brought in front of television cameras where they gave long "confessions" in which they revealed their organization's alleged crimes against the Iranian people, as well as the anti-Islamic character of their organization and the violent methods that they used against "innocent people," culminating in expressing their support for Khomeini.[104]

In 1981, Bani Sader, the former Iranian president, and Masoud Rajavi, together with other leaders of the Mujahidin, founded the "National Resistance Front for the Liberation of Iran." The Mujahidin claimed responsibility for a string of terror attacks inside Iran, including some large-scale attacks against the "National Opposition Army of Iran" at the end of the Iran-Iraq war (June 1988).[105]

As stated earlier, over the years Khomeini's regime fought an all out war against the leaders of the Mujahidin. The struggle included placing pressure on various countries, particularly France, to expel the organization's activists from their soil, a demand that emerged in the framework of terror attacks perpetrated by pro-Iranian entities, but also in diplomatic talks and contacts. In addition to the pressure that the Iranian government put on foreign governments to deport organization members, the Iranian authorities also took direct action in attempts to wipe out the organization's leaders through assassinations in various European countries. Here are listed several examples of assassinations of organization members (in Iraq, Turkey, and Switzerland):

- In 1989, four assassinations of senior Mujahidin members took place in Turkey, where there is a large population of Iranian expatriates, including organization activists.
- On March 14, 1990, assassins shot organization activist Abandini near the Istanbul Airport, wounding him gravely. The Mujahidin accused Iran of perpetrating the assassination attempt, and pointed to the involvement of Iranian "diplomats" in the shooting. The Iranians claimed that the assassination had been perpetrated by a rival faction of the Mujahidin, but Iranian Radio broadcasting from Nicosia quoted the assassins and claimed that "the victim of the attack was one on the leaders of the organization, Muhammad Almudasin (head of the political arm and the entity responsible for the organization's ties with Iraq), who "got what was coming to him due to acts of espionage and treason which he committed in the service of the organization."[106] The leaders of the Mujahidin dismissed the Iranian denial and claimed that the Iranian agents had erred in identifying their victim and that the attack victim was actually a junior activist, Hussein Abandini, and not Almudasin as the Iranians had thought.
- On April 24, 1990, there was an assassination attempt against Kazem Rajavi (the brother of Masoud Rajavi, leader of the Mujahidin). Kazem Rajavi had lived for over ten years in Switzerland and worked as a Sociology lecturer in the University of Geneva. He had served as representative of the Mujahidin at the European headquarters of the UN. He was injured in the assassination attempt, and from his headquarters in Iraq, his brother Masoud Rajavi accused Iran of perpetrating the attack. Subsequently, the spokesperson for the Lausanne police announced that two suspects had been arrested. Both were Iranian citizens who were staying in Geneva and had rented the car from which the assassination attempt against Rajavi had been conducted.[107]

- On May 15, 1995, at a press conference in Baghdad, the spokesperson of the Mujahidin Khalq exposed an attempted attack against the Mujahidin headquarters in Iraq and its leader Masoud Rajavi,[108] that had been perpetrated by the Iranian intelligence (VEVAK). An Iranian terror cell had smuggled a 320-mm. mortar over the border, which had been developed specifically for this attack. The mortar was smuggled in three parts under the camouflage of piping, and was reassembled close to the time of the attack. The ammunition for the mortar was composed of special shells, each containing some twenty-five kilograms of explosives. The cell members underwent some six months of training in Iran and fired live ammunition with the mortar that was to serve in the attack. The cell members rented a house near the Mujahidin headquarters, from which they planned to fire mortar shells at the headquarters, but the Iraqi security authorities arrested the cell and confiscated the equipment.

  This attempted attack constitutes an example of the *direct* involvement of Iran in terror activities: The Iranian military industry especially developed the mortar and ammunition for the attack according to the operational specifications of the Iranian intelligence, and the cell members were trained under the patronage of the Iranian intelligence at various training areas and facilities in the country. It appears that Iran does everything it can to strike out at Mujahidin Khalq factors and will not let anything get in its way of achieving this goal.

- In the framework of its struggle against the organization and due to its desire to deter Iraq from abetting and supporting its activities, Iran has fired surface-to-surface (SSM) missiles at least twice against Mujahidin facilities and camps on Iraqi soil. The launching of the missiles was a harsh and blunt step, which could have caused escalated tension between the two countries, but despite this fact, Iran did indeed take this step at least twice, in May 1999 and April 2001.[109] In this framework, the Iranian Revolutionary Guards fired several dozen Scuds that hit the following camps: The Ashraf Camp north of Baghdad, the Anzali Camp near Jallalla, the Faiza Camp near Qut, the Habib Camp near Basra, the Humiyun Camp near al Abra, and another camp near Mantsuria. The missiles caused injuries to several Mujahidin Khalq members and some Iraqi citizens.

A senior member of the Iranian Revolutionary Guards stated that the firing of the missiles constituted a warning for the Mujahidin Khalq and Iraq to cease their attacks against Iran. Iran dispatched a letter to the Security Council stating that it had attacked several headquarters, training camps, and logistic infrastructures of the Mujahidin Khalq in Iraq in self-defense, in order to stop the organization's attacks inside Iran. The letter also appealed to Iraq to uphold acceptable and friendly neighborly relations.[110] Iraq's response was sharp protest against the Iranian attack, and an Iraqi spokesperson stressed that his country was maintaining the right to retaliate.

Ethnic Minorities—The Kurd Underground

A prominent example of the stand that the revolutionary regime in Iran adopts vis-à-vis ethnic and religious minorities can be discerned in its relationship with the Kurd minority. The Kurds in Iran, much like their brethren in Iraq, have been waging a prolonged historical battle to achieve autonomy in the areas that they inhabit. The change of regimes in Iran instilled hope among the Kurd minority for the realization of their national aspirations, but these were dashed within a short time.

In the first two years of the Islamic republic, the relations between the regime and the Kurds fluctuated between periods of negotiations and times of violence. The Kurds demanded autonomy while the regime was willing to offer only cultural autonomy, under the precondition of disarmament of the Kurds, which the Kurds rejected. The Kurds' counter demand was for the withdrawal of all Revolutionary Guards' forces from the Kurd areas as a precondition to arriving at an arrangement with the administration.[111]

The Iranian regime regarded its opposition among ethnic and religious minorities as "the enemies of Allah." This approach was reflected in the outlawing of the "Kurd Democratic Party" in August 1979, and in the various terms that Khomeini coined for them—"Satan's party" and "the enemy of Islam."

Any Kurd hopes to reach an understanding and arrangement with the regime died completely in 1981, due to the Iranian regime's decision to postpone the handling of autonomy problems until the end of the war against Iraq. At the end of 1981, Abd al Rahman Kasmelo, leader of the Kurd Democratic Party, declared that the Kurds had no illusions regarding Khomeini; as a result, the party began to accelerate its terror activities against the Iranian regime and strengthened its ties with other opposition organizations, particularly the Fadayn Khalq and the Mujahidin Khalq, in order to form a united coalition. Kasmelo refused the Iranian administration's appeal to join in "the war of national liberation" against Iraq, and on October 1, 1981, presented an ultimatum to the government, demanding "recognition of the principle of granting autonomy to Kurdistan and withdrawal of government forces from the area prior to requesting that Kurd guerrilla fighters turn their weapons against the Iraqi invader."[112]

The Iranian regime attempted to use the "carrot and the stick" policy vis-à-vis the Kurds: On the one hand, the government called on Kurd groups fighting the regime to put down their weapons, and attempted to recruit the help of the traditional leadership for "the side of the "revolution"; but on the other hand, the government spokespersons stressed that anyone who did not lay down his weapons would be destroyed.[113]

During all of the years of the Iranian revolutionary regime's existence, the Kurds have waged an ongoing battle to achieve "self government," while the regime has concentrated on suppressing this national awakening, with the additional aim of taking the wind out of the sails of other minorities, which regarded the Kurd struggle as a model for emulation.[114]

In July 1989, Kasmelo was killed together with two other leaders of the Kurd Democratic Party in an apartment in Vienna. The Austrian authorities conducted a manhunt for the two Iranians with whom the Kurd leaders had met and who apparently were the assassins. The two Iranians had fled to the Iranian Embassy in Vienna, and for several weeks Austrian policemen laid "siege" on the embassy building in order to try to catch them if they made an attempt to leave the building.[115]

This incident led to increased tension in the relations between the two countries and to the exchange of accusations on both sides: The Iranians claimed that the Kurds had been murdered by Iraqi agents, and accused the Austrians of impinging upon the freedom of movement of Iranian diplomats, thus contravening accepted diplomatic norms between countries; in contrast, a spokesperson of the Austrian police claimed that the police were acting according to the law in order to arrest suspects hiding in the Iranian Embassy.[116] The tension between the two countries continued for several weeks, at the end of which the parties apparently reached some kind of arrangement, which was never publicized, after which diplomatic relations returned to normal.

Another incident involving the termination of Kurd opposition entities by Iran hit the headlines after the apprehension of the perpetrators in the Mikonos episode and their trial in Germany.

The Mikonos Epsiode

On September 18, 1992, near midnight, two armed men entered the Mikonos restaurant in Berlin and opened fire on four Kurd expatriates who were seated at a table in the restaurant. The four were killed in the fire and the assassins fled. The four victims were: Dr. Sadek Sharafkandi, secretary-general of the Kurd Democratic Party (successor to Abd al Rahman Kasmelo, who had been murdered by Iranian agents in 1989 in Vienna); Fathkhul Abduli, the organization's representative in Europe; Humiyun Ardalan, the organization's representative in Germany; and Nuri Dekurdi, a translator by profession. Three of the victims had arrived in Berlin to attend the Socialist Internacionale Convention, and on that night they were supposed to meet Iranian expatriates at the restaurant.[117] German security authorities, in cooperation with other Western countries, conducted a comprehensive investigation and a widespread manhunt to apprehend the suspected assassins.

On April 9, 1997, a German court in Berlin, headed by Judge Feritiuph Kovash, ruled that instructions to carry out the assassination of the four Kurd leaders (who had opposed the Iranian regime) in the Mikonos restaurant in Berlin in 1992 had been issued by Iran's leaders. The judge stated in his verdict that the murder of the four Kurds had been ordered by a covert operations committee—"the committee for special activities"—whose members included the Iranian president, its spiritual leader, the intelligence minister, and the individual responsible for foreign policy. Although the judge did not specifically mention the names of President Ali Akbar Hashemi Rafsanjani or of Spiritual Leader Ali Khamenei, whom the state prosecutor had accused during the trial, he did mention the name of Intelligence Minister Falahian. He stated that this covert committee had empowered Falahian to implement the plan, and that his agents had recruited an assassination unit in Berlin led by the accused Kazem Darabi, a former member of the Iranian Revolutionary Guards. As proof, the judge stated that the gun used for the assassination had formerly been stored in the Shah's weapon depot, and that a state of alert had been declared among the Iranian forces in the Kurd region two days before the murders.[118]

The judge sentenced the Iranian Darabi and the Lebanese Abas Kial, who were found guilty of the murders, to life imprisonment. Two additional Lebanese citizens were accused of being accomplices to the crime—one was sentenced to eleven years of imprisonment and the other to fifteen years of imprisonment. A fifth individual was acquitted.[119]

This was the first time that a European court attributed the responsibility for terror activity and the murder of Iranian expatriates to the political echelons in Iran. In his verdict, the German judge stated that "the political leadership in Iran is the entity that instructed that this crime be perpetrated; this is an official step of execution without a verdict."[120]

Many times Iran has been behind terror activities and assassinations that were perpetrated worldwide by its emissaries, but even though the "Iranian fingerprint" was clear, there was never solid proof of the direct involvement of the Iranian leadership in the planning and plotting of these actions.

Following the verdict in the Berlin court, the German government announced that it was ceasing its "critical dialogue" with Iran, gave instructions to deport four Iranian diplomats from its territory, recalled its ambassador from Iran for consultation, all in the framework of which Germany accused Iran of "shameful violation of international law." The European Union nations announced that the members of the organization had also decided to recall their ambassadors and to stop the critical dialogue with Iran. The United States called on Germany and the European states to sever their economic ties with Iran, but the EU states did not sever diplomatic relations with Iran and did not announce the cessation of commercial ties with it.[121]

In response to the verdict passed by the German court, a huge demonstration with over 100,000 participants took place in Iran; the demonstrators marched from the University of Teheran towards the German Embassy in the city. Hundreds of Iranian policemen separated the demonstrators from the embassy compound. The demonstrators called out the slogans, "death to America" and "death to Israel," and the Israeli flag was set on fire. However, no anti-German slogans were heard, and the organizers prevented the burning of the German flag as well as the picture of the German judge. The official Iranian news agency stated that demonstrations were also held in the city of Khomeini's birth, Qum, and Radio Teheran reported that in these demonstrations, calls were heard such as "this malicious conspiracy has turned Germany into a target for everyone's hatred," and "Germany has become an American toy."[122]

At that same time, the Iranian Majlis (Parliament) was holding a discussion behind closed doors regarding the country's relations with Germany. Hassan Rukhani, deputy-chairman of the Parliament, called for "a general revision of relations with Germany." He called on the government to halt all its investments in Germany and to forbid the acquisition of German equipment. "Iran no longer needs to participate in the critical dialogue with the EU because we feel that this dialogue has become ineffective and we do not want to continue with it any longer." Iranian Foreign Minister Ali Akbar Valyati stated at the end of the parliamentary session that "the recalling of the EU ambassadors in an indication of solidarity with Germany is a temporary and symbolic step." He also added that "we have no problem with our ties with European countries, but we will respond to any unilateral diplomatic resolution."[123]

The expatriate parties opposed to the Iranian regime warmly welcomed the German court's verdict. The National Resistance Council (an umbrella organization of Iranian opposition movements) called on all European countries to cease the critical dialogue and to impose economic sanctions on Iran. The chairman of the council, Masoud Rajavi, released the following statement in Paris:

> Over the years there have been few doubts regarding the involvement of the regime's Mullah leaders in acts of terror. Now for the first time a European court has identified the Spiritual Leader Ayatollah Ali Khamenei and Iranian President Ali Akbar Hashemi Rafsanjani as the entities behind the attack in Berlin and behind the governmental terror in Teheran.[124]

Despite the Iranian failure in connection to the Mikonos affair, Iran continued in its war against Iranian expatriates and against opposition organizations, but directed its assassination efforts to more convenient and relatively safe arenas such as Iraqi Kurdistan, Pakistan, and Turkey. For example, according to reports by opposition entities, in the year 1996, eleven people were assassinated in various places all over the world due to suspicions of the Iranian regime that they were hostile to the Islamic regime in Teheran.

Notes

1.   *Ma'ariv*, February 18, 2003.
2.   *Al-Manar*, Lebanon, April 9 2002.
3.   *Al-Manar*, Lebanon, September 28, 2001.
4.   *Al-Manar*, Lebanon, May 7, 1998.
5.   *Al-Manar*, Lebanon, February 7, 2003.
6.   Shlomo Brom, *Israel and South Lebanon Prior to a Peace Agreement with Syria*, Jaffe Center, TelAviv University, 1999, pp. 18-19.
7.   *Hizballah*, A Special Collection of Information, the Center for Intelligence Heritage, The Information Center for Intelligence and Terror, March 2003, p. 44.
8.   Ibid., p. 46.
9.   Ibid., p. 47.
10. Ibid., p. 48.
11. *Al Liva'a*, October 9, 2002.
12. Mustafa Dirani and Abd al Karim Obeid—Two senior members of Shiite terror organizations being held in Israeli prisons. They were released in the POW exchange deal in summer 2004.
13. Sheikh Kauk in an interview in *Al Liva'a*, October 9, 2002.
14. *Hizballah*, pp. 83-86.
15. Ibid., pp. 61-62.
16. Based on Intelligence Department document ref. no. 688/0050, September 2002.
17. *Hizballah*, pp. 87-88.
18. Based on Intelligence Department document ref. no. 688/0050, September 2002.
19. This sections is based on the following sources: The announcements of the IDF Spokesperson on January 4-5, 2002; Intelligence Department document ref. no. 688/0050, September 2002; *Hizballah*, pp. 92-93.
20. This section is based on the following sources:
     The announcements of the IDF Spokesperson on January 4-5, 2002;
     Intelligence Department document ref. no. 688/0050, September 2002;
     Hizballah, pp. 90-91.
21. This section is based on the following sources:
     Ma'ariv, May 23, 2003; *Yediot Aharonot*, May 23, 2003; *Ha'aretz*, May 23, 2003.
22. Intelligence Department document ref. no. 688/0050, September 2002.
23. Ibid.
24. Among the member of these circles were the Foreign Minister Sanjabi and Prime Minister Bazargan. David Menashri, *Iran in Revolution*, Hakibbutz Hameuhad, Tel Aviv, 1988, p. 206.
25. Ibid.
26. R. K. Ramzani, "Iran's Foreign Policy Contending Orientations," *The Middle East Journal* 34, 2 (Spring 1989), pp. 208-209.
27. Douglas Stanglin, *US News & World Report*, March 6, 1989, pp. 26-27.
28. Ethier Rosamund, *The Iranian Hostage Crisis–American President Decision Making*, Leigh University, Michigan, 1988, pp. 20-21.
29. David Menashri, *Iran in Revolution*, p. 207.
30. Kate Gillespie, "US Corporation and Iran at The Hague," *The Middle East Journal* 44 (1988).
31. Anat Kurz, Maskit Burgin, David Tal, *Islamic Terror and Israel*, Papyrus Publishing, Tel Aviv University, 1993, pp. 52-53.
32. R. K. Ramazani, "Iran's Foreign Policy Contending Orientations," pp. 202-203.
33. *Kihan*, October 15, 1983.

34. David Menashri, *Iran in Revolution*, p. 243.
35. Reuben Miller, "International Terrorism," *Conflict Quarterly* 1, 4 (Fall 1989).
36. Shmuel Segev, *The Iranian Connection*, Domino Publications, Jerusalem, 1988, pp. 124-125.
37. Ilan Kfir, *The Iranian Affair—The Tower Committee Report*, Modan Publishing, Tel Aviv, 1988, pp. 21-23.
38. *Hizballah*, pp. 46-51.
39. Ibid.
40. Ibid.
41. Ibid.
42. Ibid.
43. Ibid.
44. Ibid.
45. Ibid.
46. David Menashri, *Iran in Revolution*, pp. 209-210.
47. Anthony Parsons, "Iran and Western Europe," *The Middle East Journal* 43, 2 (Spring 1989), pp. 224-225.
48. Anat Kurz, Maskit Burgin, David Tal, *Islamic Terror and Israel*, pp. 52-53.
49. Edgar O'Ballance, *Islamic Fundamentalist Terrorism, 1979-95*, New York University Press, 1997, pp. 101-105.
50. FARL—Initials in French for the terror organization "the Armed Lebanese Revolutionary Factions," a faction that broke away from the Vadiah Hadad.
51. *US News and World Report*, March 6, 1989, pp. 20-25.
52. Hiro Dilip, *Iran Under the Ayatollahs*, Routledge & Kegan Paul, London, 1987, p. 30.
53. Reuters, January 30 1990.
54. Ibid.
55. The first contract was signed in 1919, in which British control of 40 percent of the APOC shares was ensured, as well as the supply of oil until 1961. In 1930, after friction between Iran and Britain, the issue was discussed in the League of Nations, and in 1933 a new contract was signed which decreased the area of British concessions, increased the payment for oil, ensured a minimum annual income for the oil to the scope of seven hundred and fifty thousand pounds sterling, and extended the concession's validity to 1993.
56. Due to the adoption of the name "Iran" by the Persians, the name was changed from APOC to AIOC—Anglo Iranian Oil Company.
57. The CIA planned an operation called Ajax. The CIA organized a military coup by Iranian officers who ousted Musadek's government. R. K. Ramazani, *Iran's Foreign Policy 1941-1973—A Study of Foreign Policy in Modernising Nations*, University of Virginia Press, Charlotte, 1975, p. 35.
58. Anthony Parsons, "Iran and Western Europe," *The Middle East Journal* 43, 2 (Spring 1989), pp. 168-185.
59. R. K. Ramazani, "Iran's Foreign Policy Contending Orientations," *The Middle East Journal* 34, 2 (Spring 1989), pp. 168-185.
60. Maskit Burgin, Ariel Merari, Anat Kurz, "Foreign Hostages in Lebanon," (Memorandum No. 25), JCSS, Tel Aviv University, August 1988.
61. Magnus Ranstorp, *Hizballah in Lebanon—The Politics of the Western Hostage Crisis*, St. Martin's Press, New York, 1997, pp. 99-100.
62. *Observer*, May 3, 1990 (quoting Reuters).
63. An interview with Sheikh Fadallah—CNN, February 22 1989.
64. *Aljihad*, Lebanon, February 24, 1989.

65. *Aljihad*, Lebanon, March 3, 1989.
66. *Aljihad*, Lebanon, February 24, 1989
67. *A'ahar*, Egypt, March 8, 1989.
68. Edgar O'Ballance, *Islamic Fundamental Terrorism, 1979-95*pp. 153-155.
69. *Times*, February 14, 1990 (quoting Reuters, Nicosia).
70. "The Fund of the 15 in Kordad" is a private fund headed by Ayatollah Hassan Sanai.
71. Anthony Parsons, "Iran and Western Europe," *The Middle East Journal* 43, 2 (Spring 1989).
72. Magnus Ranstorp, *Hizballah in Lebanon—The Politics of the Western Hostage Crisis*, pp. 99-100.
73. According to *Stern*, Germany, July 4, 1990, Hussein Musawi, one of the leaders of the Hizballah, demanded the release of the Hamadi brothers in exchange for the release of the German hostages Strubig and Kamptenner.
74. *The Jerusalem Post*, December 13, 1985.
75. According to *Al Muharar*, Lebanon, May 13, 1990, the Hizballah was holding secret talks at that time with Switzerland, under the mediation of a Lebanese businessman, in order to release two Swiss citizens who were Red Cross workers in Lebanon (Emmanuel Kristian and Eleen Arknaz). In exchange for their release, the Hizballah demanded the release of Ali Muhammad Hariri, who was being held in Switzerland for hijacking an Air Africa plane.
76. David Menashri, *Iran in Revolution*, pp. 221-222.
77. Joseph Kostiner, "Shi'i Unrest in the Gulf" in Martin Kramer (ed.), *Shi'ism, Resistance and Revolution*, Westview Press, Boulder, CO, 1987, pp. 88-90.
78. Rafsanjani, *Teheran Times*, March 5, 1984.
79. David Menshari, *Iran in Revolution*, p. 211.
80. Khomeini and his associates aspired to establish a united revolutionary Islamic force that would include "a billion Muslims," *Islamic Jamhuri*, September 29, 1984.
81. Shahram Chubin "Iran and Its Neighbors: The Impact of the Gulf War," *Conflict Studies* 204 (1986).
82. Amir Taheri, *The Holy Terror—The Inside Story of Islamic Terrorism*, Sphere Books, London, 1987, pp. 85-86.
83. David Menshari, *Iran in Revolution*, pp. 224-225.
84. *Kihan*, October 10, 1981.
85. *Kihan*, August 17, 1985.
86. *Al-Yom*, June 11, 1990. In the editorial, the Saudi newspaper, which reflects the administration's views, claimed that a foreign country stood behind the murder of the Saudi diplomats in Thailand, whose involvement in the murders would be exposed at the end of the investigation carried out by the Thai authorities.
87. David Menashri, *Iran in Revolution*, pp. 225-226.
88. *Kihan*, February 14, 1982.
89. The arrested individuals included three Lebanese citizens, seventeen Iraqi citizens (members of al Dawa), three Kuwaiti citizens, and two detainees without citizenship.
90. *Ha'aretz*, February 27, 1986; April 14, 1988.
91. *Kuwait Times*, January 25, 1984.
92. *Kuwait Times*, March 28, 1984
93. Office of the Secretary of State, Office of the Coordinator for Counter Terrorism, *Patterns of Global Terrorism*, U.S. Department of State Publications, 1997.
94. David Menshari, *Iran in Revolution*, pp. 144-145.
95. *Al-Majla*, November 21-27, 1982.
96. Shmuel Segev, *The Iranian Connection*, pp. 9-14.
97. Edgar O'Ballance, *Islamic Fundamentalist Terrorism, 1979-95*, pp. 53-56.

98. *Kihan*, October 18, 1985.

99. David Menashri, *Iran in Revolution*, p. 79.

100. Ibid.

101. *Majhad* (No. 6), July 1976, pp. 131-144.

102. *Kihan*, June 29, 1981.

103. *Kihan*, September 4, 5, 14, 21, 1983.

104. Anthony Kurdsman, Abraham Wagner, *The Iran Iraq War*, Ma'archot Publishing, Tel Aviv, 1998, pp. 417-419.

105. Anwar Faruqs, AP, Nicosia, March 22, 1990.

106. The Swiss authorities announced that the assassination suspects were two Iranian citizens: Yadullah Samadi and Muhammad Razbani (according to Reuters, May 3, 1990).

107. Eric Avebury, Robert Wilkinson, *Iran: State of Terror*, Parliamentary Human Rights Group, London, June 1996, pp. 60-62.

108. Globalsecurity.org/wmd/world.

109. *AEROTECHNES* and Review, April 20, 2001.

110. Edgar O'Ballance, *Islamic Fundamentalist Terrorism, 1979-95*, pp. 132-133.

111. David Menashri, *Iran in Revolution*, p. 191.

112. On July 11, 1983, the *Atla'at* newspaper published an interview with Ziad Shirazi, commander of the land forces, who threatened anyone who refused to turn in his weapons.

113. Anthony Kurdsman, Abraham Wagner, *The Iran Iraq War*, p. 44.

114. Edgar O'Ballance, *Islamic Fundamentalist Terrorism, 1979-95*, pp. 155-156.

115. AP Report from Vienna, July 15, 1989.

116. Edgar O'Ballance, *Islamic Fundamentalist Terrorism, 1979-95*, pp. 155-156.

117. *Der Spiegel*, April 9, 1997.

118. Ibid.

119. Ibid.

120. Ely Karmon, *Iran's Policy on Terrorism in the 1990's*, ICT (The International Policy Institute for Counter Terrorism), September 8, 1998.

121. *Berliner Morgan Post*, April 11, 1997.

122. Ibid.

123. Ibid.

5

Iran and Terror—Financing and Policy

Financing Shiite Terror via Criminal Activity[1]

The Hizballah's budget is estimated by intelligence sources at about $100 million per annum, most of which is provided by Iran. This sum is used for financing the organization's military-terrorist activity (acquisition of weaponry, payroll for fighters, training, and more), funding social and economic activities (including schools, hospitals, welfare institutions, and more), and also to cover various organizational expenses (rental fees for offices, acquisition of office equipment, payment for non-combat activists, and more).

As stated above, more than half of the Hizballah's budget is covered by Iran, which finances Hizbalah activities via two main channels:

- Government entities—A budget transferred via the Revolutionary Guards and the Foreign Ministry (via its embassies in Lebanon and Syria).
- Semi-governmental entities—After the 1979 revolution, charitable foundations were established in Iran that are under the supervision of the Iranian leader. These foundations have branches in Lebanon, which as part of the "export of the revolution" provide extensive social and financial aid to the Hizballah and to the Shiite population that identifies with it.

Alongside the Iranian established aid, over the years the Hizballah has endeavored to acquire secondary financing sources that are deployed throughout the world. We believe that this step was taken in order to reduce its dependence upon Iranian aid, albeit the scope of the secondary financing is still low in comparison to Iranian financial allocations. These secondary funding sources are mainly based on criminal activity as detailed below.

Cultivation, Production, and Drug Trafficking

Lebanon is considered a country that produces drugs on a large scale. It grows poppies (opium) and cannabis, and even imports "raw materials" from outside of the country from which it manufactures heroin and cocaine. The raw materials for the drugs production in Lebanon arrive from three sources:

- The poppy and cannabis that grow in the Lebanon Valley serve as a basis for the production of heroin (poppy), hashish, and marijuana (cannabis).
- Raw materials for the production of (morphine-based) heroin are imported from the Far East, as well as Pakistan, Afghanistan, and Turkey.
- Cocaine is imported to Lebanon directly from Latin American countries (Colombia, Venezuela, Brazil) or via Europe.

The processing of these raw materials and their adaptation into drugs are performed in scores of home laboratories spread all over the villages in the Lebanon Valley, mainly in the area of Ba'al Bek. From Lebanon, the drugs are sent out to Middle Eastern countries (including Israel), to Western countries (the United States and Europe), and to other destinations throughout the world. The profits from this flourishing "industry" are assessed at over a billion dollars a year, and the Hizballah gets a piece of these funds.

The cultivation of the poppies and cannabis, much like the activities of the drug production laboratories, are performed in areas inhabited by the Shiite population in which the Hizballah is the main source of power and the Lebanese government's control is very weak. Moreover, most of the families in the Lebanon Valley that deal in the cultivation and marketing of drugs are Shiite clans whose sons play senior roles in the Hizballah. In addition, the Hizballah also controls the smuggling routes from Lebanon—by land and by sea—to Middle East countries (Egypt is an important customer for hashish), and to the West, a fact that increases the organization's importance vis-à-vis the drug industry.

The scope of the cultivation and production of drugs in the Baka'a valley has experienced ups and downs. Between the years 1992 and 1996 there was a decline in the range of drug cultivation in the Lebanon Valley due to the Syrian and Lebanese aspiration to create the impression (mainly for the United States) that they had joined the battle against "drug affliction." However, since 1997, there has been an increase in the extent of cannabis cultivation due to the economic crisis in Lebanon and the economic difficulties of the local population, for which the cultivation of drugs constitutes an important source of income.

It is also to be noted that during those years when the cultivation of poppies and cannabis in the Lebanon Valley waned, the production of "hard" drugs in the laboratories of the Bakaa villages, particularly the production of heroin from raw materials, increased. Hashish is the most important "export branch" in Lebanon, while the production of heroin and cocaine is secondary. The Israeli Police estimate that the amount of hashish brought into Israel in 2002 was about ten tons. The Hizballah takes advantage of its control of the Israeli-Lebanese border area and of the routes leading to it in order to spread its protection over drug smuggling, while incorporating missions meant to facilitate operational-terrorist activity in Israel (as specified above). The Hizballah regards the distribution of drugs in Israel as an additional tool serving its struggle to undermine and weaken Israeli society.

Money Counterfeiting

Iran constitutes an important focal point in the global money counterfeiting industry. During the 1990s, Iranian attempts to spread high quality counterfeit American dollars in the world markets were identified, although this was attempted on a scale that could not cause significant damage to the U.S. economy.

Iran's relative advantage lies in its access to advanced technologies that enable the high quality counterfeiting of a one hundred dollar note ("Super Dollar" or "Super Note"). Photogravure, sophisticated printing plates, special paper and ink, specialization in separating colors, and the technical ability to fake protection means (such as "the safety line" that appears in bills) are necessary for the production of the "Super Dollar." These are capabilities and technologies that only a country can develop, and not criminal organizations, let alone individuals. These advanced technological capabilities were transferred in the past to the Shah's regime in Iran, and the Khomeini regime made use of them to produce counterfeit dollars.

In order to distance themselves and to avoid confrontation with the United States, the Iranians preferred to use the Hizballah (and possibly other Lebanese entities) as leverage for the production and distribution of counterfeit bills. For this purpose, they transferred counterfeit notes and their advanced technologies to Lebanon. In the beginning of the 1990s, Super Dollar bills were found in the Lebanon Valley. It appears that the bills were initially printed in Teheran, and Lebanon served only as a distribution point, but at some point in the early 1990s the printing machines were transferred from Iran to Lebanon, and the Lebanon Valley (the Ba'al Bek area), which is under Syrian control, became a center for the production and marketing of the Super Dollar notes.

The village of Britel, south of Ba'al Bek (with about 7,000 Shiite inhabitants), is the money-counterfeiting center. In the second half of the 1990s it was reported that there were ten to fifteen print shops, located in homes and workshops, which specialize in various aspects of counterfeiting high-quality American hundred-dollar bills. In the past, they also produced counterfeit twenty- and fifty-dollar bills, as well as counterfeit notes from other Western countries and Arab countries, of various qualities.

The Hizballah plays an important role in the industry of counterfeiting money due to its powerful position at the counterfeiting locations in the Lebanon Valley, particularly in the village of Britel, and thanks to its ties with Iran and Syria. Its involvement in this industry enables it to enjoy its profits, while also gaining operational advantages in its activities abroad. The technical expertise necessary for counterfeiting money was also used for the development of an extensive industry of documentation forgery, including the forgery of passports used by the Hizballah. The output of this industry is transferred all over the world, with emphasis on Russia, the Ukraine, Cyprus, the Americas, and Arab countries.

Due to American pressure placed on Syria at the highest levels (including during the Clinton-Assad meeting in 1994), the printing machines of the Super Dollar were moved from Lebanon to another country, but the counterfeiting industry did not cease. In the second half of the 1990s, the money counterfeiting industry continued to thrive in the Lebanon Valley, although the counterfeit bills (which were of good quality) could not compete with the top quality of the Super Dollar.

In the past, counterfeit dollars from Lebanon were discovered in Israel, but to date there has been no significant attempt to export large numbers of counterfeit bills to Israel. However, it is important to note that Iran and the Hizballah have technological abilities enabling them to "flood" the Israeli market with high quality counterfeit bills, if and when a decision is made to this effect.

In Latin America, Shiite crime and terror entities connected to the Hizballah also act according to same familiar criminal patterns (smuggling, drug trafficking, extortion, and fraud). They generally transfer part of the sums as a contribution to the funding of the organization's activities in Lebanon and abroad. The most prominent focal point of activity is the "Tri Border" area (Brazil, Paraguay, and Argentina), where law enforcement by police and security forces is weak.

Iranian Policy in the Era of Khomeini's Successors

During his reign, Khomeini served as both a religious and a political authority. After his death in June 1989 no successor of his caliber was found who could serve as a Spiritual Leader (*Valiat Fakia*), and therefore his inherited government was divided between a political successor and a religious successor.

In contrast to the assessments of various experts, a violent war among successors did not develop, and Khomeini's political successor was chosen on the basis of a political and parliamentary struggle between two main camps, the moderate camp led by Rafsanjani and the radical camp headed by Mukhtashemi

Pur. The victory of the moderate camp resulted in the appointment of Rafsanjani as leader of the Iranian regime, a man who was considered moderate and pragmatic (in Iranian terms), and the appointment of Ali Khamenei as the religious leader. Nonetheless, the conservative and radical camp within the Iranian leadership remained strong and enjoyed broad public support, a fact that required Rafsanjani to be extremely cautious if he wanted to preserve his regime.[2]

Khomeini's philosophy, including its religious rules and political lines, effectively defined what was "permissible and forbidden" for his successors' eras as well, and the new regime emphasized its loyalty to these lines. Some basic givens changed at the end of Khomeini's regime and during the beginning of his successors' regime:

- The end of the Iran-Iraq war (1980-1988);
- The collapse of the Eastern Bloc and the Soviet Union;
- The Gulf War (1991);
- The peace process between Israel and the Arabs (Madrid, Oslo, the peace agreement with Jordan).

The Era of Rafsanjani's Presidency

At the end of the Iran-Iraq war, Iran's economic and military rehabilitation was given high priority. This process necessitated significant financing and technological aid that could only be acquired in the West. The collapse of the Soviet Union, and America and the West's growing dominance diminished Iran's former maneuvering space, which it had possessed in the inter-bloc power system, and fortified the understanding among government circles in Iran that they must strengthen their ties with the United States and the West. Thus, one of the central components of Iranian foreign policy was the experiment to gradually bolster relations in order to acquire the technological and economic aid necessary for Iran's rehabilitation, while making sure not to "incense" the radical circles that negated this approach.

Several steps were taken by the Iranian regime already in 1989 that signaled its willingness to improve relations with the West:

- In July 1989, in response to the Israeli kidnapping of Sheike Obeid, the Hizballah threatened to retaliate against Israeli and Western targets. In this framework, the organization called "the Depressed on Earth" announced that it had executed American hostage Colonel William Higgins, and threatened to execute other hostages.[3]
  The Iranians applied the full weight of their influence to prevent the execution of additional hostages and the threats did indeed stop.

- Additional testimony to the Iranian attempt to moderate the conflicts vis-à-vis the West can be observed in the fact that from 1989 there were no further abductions of Western hostages.[4]

A public expression of Rafsanjani's approach to the terror issue was provided at a press conference held on October 24, 1989, in the presence of over 100 Western reporters. Rafsanjani addressed most of the issues in which Iran was accused of involvement in terror.[5] As to the Western hostages in Lebanon, Rafsanjani claimed that Iran did not possess information about their fate, and that he was not at all interested in dealing with that problem as long as the West chose to ignore its demands. He claimed that the people holding the hostages in Lebanon were unknown to Iran, and that contact with them was only through a few intermediaries. Rafsanjani described these groups as "militant, radical and willing to commit self-sacrifice," and stated that they are "completely controlled by their leaders and therefore act independently, using radical methods."

As to the British hostage Terry White, Rafsanjani claimed that in 1987 he had indeed informed the Archbishop of Canterbury that White was alive, but since then he knew nothing of his fate. In turn, Rafsanjani demanded that the West disclose information about four Iranians who had been abducted in Lebanon in 1982 and whom he believed were being held by the Christians. He denied any Iranian involvement in the detonation of the Pan Am flight over Lockerbie, and claimed that Iran opposed the very concept of downing a passenger plane as a retaliatory measure. He also stated that no Western entity had proven that Jibril's organization was responsible for the explosion, and certainly no link to Iran had been detected.

In the matter of the assassinations of Iranian expatriates, Rafsanjani denied any Iranian involvement, and claimed that Abd al Rahman Kasmelo, and other Kurd expatriates who were killed on July 13, 1989, in Vienna, were terminated by the Iraqis or by rival Kurd entities. As to the British citizen, Roger Cooper, who had been imprisoned in Iran since 1986 under the charge of "espionage," Rafsanjani stated: "Roger Cooper is charged with espionage, and the Iranian people hates spies." Regarding Salman Rushdie, author of "*The Satanic Verses*," whom Khomeini had sentenced to death and called upon Islamic believers to carry out this verdict, Rafsanjani stated that the verdict was still valid and no one could change it.

An analysis of this important and comprehensive interview, which touched on most of the issues vis-à-vis Iranian involvement in terror, indicates that Rafsanjani was continuing with the political line that characterized the Iranian approach during Khomeini's era, that is, on the one hand, denial of Iranian involvement in terror and flinging counter-accusations at the West; while on the other hand, leaving the door open for Iranian involvement in resolving problems should circumstances arise that would motivate Iran to mediate between the organizations that hold hostages and Western countries.[6]

To a great extent this interview accurately reflects the problematic aspects related to understanding the Iranian involvement in the terror issue, in light of the yawning gap between public Iranian policy and the evidence testifying to Iran's active involvement in terror (mainly via sponsored Shiite organizations). In this connection, it is important to stress that even during 1989, following Khomeini's death, terror activities perpetrated by Iran or its sponsored organizations continued against Saudi targets and expatriates, as well as opposition entities.[7]

Two different approaches were to be discerned among Western researchers regarding Iranian policy vis-à-vis the issue of terror in the era of Khomeini's successors: One approach asserted that nothing had changed regarding this issue in Iranian policy, and that the regime was taking a diplomatic approach to promote Iranian interests while still employing terror in order to strike out at opponents or as a threat and bargaining card when facing entities with which it was negotiating; the other view claimed that Rafsanjani refrained from initiating terror attacks, and that the attacks were perpetrated under the influence of radical entities inside the Iranian leadership and their loyal followers within the sponsored Shiite and Palestinian organizations.

In a report prepared in December 1989 by the Counter-terror Office in the U.S. State Department, Iran's involvement in terror activities was emphasized, and the experts specified that the only way to block Iranian use of terror was to impose political and economic pressures that would influence the Iranian leadership. "The use of terror is part of the official Iranian policy—its initiators may be among the more radical entities in the regime, but it is also acceptable to Iranian President Rafsanjani and other senior leaders. This is a national policy under governmental supervision, and not the actions of uninhibited radicals who make use of violence."[8]

In any event, it is evident that during 1989 and in the early 1990s the struggle between Rafsanjani and Mukhtashemi Pur regarding the planning of Iran's course continued both on the domestic level and in connection to foreign policy. Arenas for the contention were the Iranian Parliament, the media, and the reciprocal relations with Iranian power centers as well as with Shiite sponsored organizations and communities outside of Iran, particularly in Lebanon. In this framework, Mukhtashemi Pur visited Lebanon at the end of 1989 in order to boost his status and influence in the Hizballah, which he had helped to found.

During the early 1990s, several incidents can be identified that indicate the strengthening of the pro-West pragmatic approach in Iran:

- On January 8, 1990, the Majlis approved a five-year plan, which included taking large-scale loans from foreign entities. This can be viewed as a victory for Rafsanjani in light of the opposition of radical circles.[9]
- In the month of May 1990, the Shiite terror organizations in Lebanon released two American hostages (Reed and Fullhill) with Iranian-Syr-

ian arbitration. Their release was presented as a gesture of goodwill by the organization and its patron, Iran. The rest of the hostages were released by the beginning of 1992.

- In the framework of contacts between Iran and Western countries and with the aim of improving reciprocal relations, the terrorist Anis Nakash was released from a French jail. (It will be recalled that Nakash was imprisoned after an assassination attempt against former Iranian Prime Minister Shahfur Bakhtiar in France.)
- In 1990, diplomatic relations between Iran and Britain were renewed, thanks mainly to Iran's stand regarding the crisis in Kuwait, despite the fact that the Iranians refused to meet the British demand to rescind Salman Rushdie's verdict.

However, despite signs that testified to Iran's desire to improve its relations with the West (the cessation of abductions of foreign nationals in Lebanon, the termination of aircraft hijackings, and Iranian abstention from perpetrating terror attacks against Western targets), Iran continued to perpetrate assassinations of Iranian expatriates and members of the opposition parties, as well as to support radical Islamic organizations. Moreover, the number of attacks in which Iran was involved, particularly against opposition targets, was even larger than their number during Khomeini's term of office.[10]

During the Gulf War, Iran adopted a "neutral" policy and was one of the chief beneficiaries of the war's results. The defeat of the Iraqi army at the hands of the Coalition, the neutralization of part of the weapons for mass destruction which Iraq had developed, and the imposition of a regime of sanctions and supervision significantly weakened Iraq—Iran's rival—and contributed to the boosting of Iran's status in the region.

After the Gulf War and at the beginning of the Arab-Israeli peace process (the Madrid Conference), Iran positioned itself at the head of the opposition camp to the peace negotiations. Iran under Rafsanjani's leadership continued to support the Hizballah in Lebanon and as noted earlier also bestowed its patronage upon Palestinian terror organizations that opposed the peace talks, such as the Palestinian Islamic Jihad, the Hamas, and Jibril's Front, which were inspired by Iran to torpedo the peace process through terror attacks against Israel.

As to Saudi Arabia and the Gulf States, despite Iran's neutral stand during the Gulf war and its ostensible desire to maintain normal relations with these countries, Iran continued to support Islamic organizations that acted in those countries in an attempt to oust the regimes and banish the American (foreign) presence. Iranian "fingerprints" were evident at various attacks perpetrated against American targets in Saudi Arabia (in Riyadh and al-Khobar).

The Bahrain government accused Iran of involvement in riots and terror activities perpetrated by Shiite entities in Bahrain. Also, during Rafsanjani's term of office, Iran intensified its ties with the Islamic regime in Sudan, which became a "front base" in Africa for the dissemination of radical Islam, particularly in Egypt and Algeria. Egypt and Algeria accused Sudan several times of providing aid and a safe haven to Islamic terrorists acting against them.

In summary, during the 1990s Iran did indeed decrease its involvement in international terror but nevertheless, its fingerprints were found at the sites of at least four grave attacks: the attack against the Israeli Embassy in Argentina in 1992, the attack against the Jewish Community of Buenos Aires in 1994, and the attacks against American targets in Riyadh and al-Khobar in Saudi Arabia (1995 and 1996). In addition, the Iranian activity against expatriates and Iranian opposition entities continued worldwide, as did Iran's support for Shiite and Palestinian terror in the confrontation against Israel. For this reason, during the entire period of Rafsanjani's term of office (1989-1996) Iran continued to appear on U.S. State Department documents as a leading state in the area of terror and as a supporter of foreign terror organizations.

The Period of Khatami's Presidency

The appointment of Khatami as the president of Iran in 1997 awakened considerable hope in the West (much like the hopes that arose in 1989 upon Rafsanjani's election) that this would bring about a real change in Iran's approach to the issue of utilizing and supporting terror.

President Khatami did indeed represent an approach that strove to achieve liberalization of the regime in Iran and to improve Iranian ties with the Western and Arab worlds, but it would appear that he came up against the rigid opposition of the more conservative circles in his country, headed by the spiritual leader Khamenei. The internal power struggles in Iran affected its foreign policy, which on the one hand broadcast placating messages conveyed by President Khatami regarding the desire for cooperation, while on the other hand radical and conservative messages were relayed by his opposers.

In the course of Khatami's presidency, Iran underwent a series of incidents related to the struggle between the radical camp led by Khamenei and the liberal camp headed by President Khatami. In the framework of this struggle several leading intellectuals, writers, and politicians who supported the liberal line were murdered and the tracks led to the Iranian intelligence, which reports directly to Khamenei's associates.

One of the prominent examples of this process is the case of Ahmad Khomeini, son of the supreme leader of the Islamic revolution. In the mid-1980s, Khomeini junior led the camp that called for a dialogue between Iran, and the United States and Israel. He served as head of his father's office and did not conceal his wish to inherit him. After the demise of Ayatollah Khomeini in June 1989, his son adopted a more aggressive approach and took a radical stand, but even then did not conceal his ambition to be his father's successor. When his hopes were dashed, he called for the government to be dismissed and for the appointment of an advisory assembly (*shura*) according to Islamic spirit. His call was ignored and Khomeini junior was shoved aside. Six years later, in March 1995, he died of a heart attack at the age of fifty.[11]

In an interview, which he granted several weeks before his death, Ahmad Khomeini claimed that the Imam's successors had caused the war against Iraq to be needlessly prolonged. The interview was shelved and published only after his death. According to the son, his father had wanted to bring an end to the war about two years after its outbreak, following the recapture of the city of Khoramshar in 1983 when 30,000 officers and Iraqi soldiers were taken captive, after it had previously fallen into Iraqi hands. He claimed that Khomeini regarded this as an opportunity to interrupt the bloody cycle, but senior entities at the War Office, led by Hashemi Rafsanjani, persuaded the Imam to continue the war until the capture of Basra. According to the son's claims, the consequences were grave: the lengthening of the war for another six superfluous years.[12]

In an exposé, which leaked out five years after the event, it became clear that Ahmad Khomeini had been murdered by his father's associates, apparently due to their fear of his ambition to succeed his father. Ahmad Khomeini was buried near his father in the cemetery at Hajet a-Zahra, south of Teheran. "You have taken heavy secrets to the grave," his son Hassan stated in his eulogy. Today the latter is custodian of the burial plots of his grandfather and father. Only in 2002 did the meaning of the eulogy become clear. In an open letter, which was published in Iranian newspapers, Hassan Khomeini wrote that his father had been poisoned to death. The son maintained that the execution had been perpetrated by Iranian intelligence agents through the infusion of poison into the pills that his father had received at the hospital after suffering a heart attack.[13]

It is possible that this affair would not have hit the headlines if there had not been a rash of murders of intellectuals in Iran. As noted above, the tracks led to Iranian intelligence agents, who were interrogated and confessed that the execution command had come from the higher echelons of the Iranian leadership, and had been perpetrated by them and their colleagues. As a result, the agents were put on trial. The conservatives, to whom the murders had been attributed, launched a campaign to protect their reputations. Their representative, the president of the military court Muhammad Niaz, who served as the prosecutor in the trial of the agents, claimed that the story of the poisoning of Ahmad Khomeini lacked any factual basis, and that the agents had confessed to the deed in order to alter the course of the trial.

The murder of Khomeini junior apparently had been supervised by Ali Falahian, the former intelligence minister, and his right-hand man and deputy Sayyid Imami. The latter's days were numbered: After he was arrested and stood trial for a series of political murders, he was found dead in his cell. The official reason was suicide by ingesting poison.[14]

Another incident connected to an "institutionalized" execution is the case of Professor Hashem Arajari, a history lecturer at Teheran University, who was tried and sentenced to death for violations that included disparaging religion, incitement, and impairing governmental systems.[15] The popular forty-five-year-old lecturer had a long history. He had participated in the Khomeini revolution as a member of the Revolutionary Guards and fought in the Iran-Iraq war, where he lost his leg. In recent years, he had "crossed the lines," an occurrence common to many intellectuals in Iran, turned into one of the champions of state reform, and joined an Iranian organization, which, according to the Iranian regime, had ties with the opposition based in Iraq. After the trial, demonstrations broke out in Teheran and other cities throughout the country. The news agency of the students' association, an organization controlled by radicals, attempted to cover up the issue and to present it as a protest against the food served on the campuses; however, the intensity of the demonstrations clarified the true issue at stake to the public, but only to the public. The spiritual leader Khamenei understood that the demonstrations might be contagious and endanger the fragile monopoly of the conservatives' strength, and in an exceptional move, which was interpreted in Iran as a victory for the students, instructed the court of appeals to "reconsider" the sentence imposed on Arajari.[16]

I have chosen to elaborate on these incidents in order to illustrate the characteristics of the ruthless power struggles in Iran during the 2000s, between those who are in favor of reforms and the radical circles, and even among the various conservative powerbrokers themselves. But among the reformists in Iran there is also no consensus regarding the steps to be taken in order to alter the regime. For example, Mahdi Kharuvi, chairman of the reformist parliament, is a religious man who believes that the principles upon which the regime is founded are just, and he does not aspire to change them, only to improve them. Karuvi believes that there is a need to purge the government bodies of corruption, cease the nepotism plaguing government appointments, improve the economy, and even hold a dialogue with the West. But when there is talk of democratization and of the rule of the people, as is prevalent in the West, he also believes that this system is not suitable for Iran. This example illustrates the gap between the way Western entities view the reformists and the way that they themselves perceive the required reforms in Iran. It is to be noted that Khatami is himself a religious cleric, and he has never said that the type of regime should be replaced, but only modified.[17]

The overall and simplistic conception according to which Iran consists of one bloc or two—reformists and conservatives—caused many people to be caught by surprise when in February 2002 reformist students took to the streets in protest against the West and particularly the United States, which had added Iran to the "Axis of Evil." For a moment it seemed that the differences between the reformists and the conservatives had disappeared and everyone had become anti-American. The complex picture is illustrated in a survey conducted by the Iranian Survey Institute (which was subsequently closed down by the government), according to which 75 percent of all Iranians are interested in a dialogue with the United States, but are also critical of the United States. The explanation for this phenomenon is that Iranians are first and foremost patriotic. Thus, Bush's declaration contained a double slap in the fact that he both insulted the state and accused it of terror, and also lumped the reformists and conservatives together. Apparently, this type of affront could not be sustained by even the most ardent reformist.[18]

Iran has not yet reached a turning point or a shift in the power balance, and the demonstrations that have taken place in the past few years have failed to inspire the general public. The supporters of reforms believe that at this stage the United States should have offered a political and economic horizon that would help the reformists to provide the public with an alternative, and that this issue is particularly important in anticipation of the next elections. However, it is doubtful whether this gesture will be made in the near future.

In any case, as of 1997, following Khatami's election as president, changes have been introduced in Iran's policies. It has not ceased to utilize terror but has begun to make more restricted and selective use of this tool. Although from the aspect of timing it is possible to link this change in Iran's approach to Khatami's appointment, there may be several other causes that resulted in this revision:

- Some of the Iranian decision makers and part of the general public have come to believe that a radical policy that supports terrorism has damaged Iranian interests and has resulted in its regional and global isolation. Thus the approach of Khatami, who declared that he intends to promote Iranian ties and status in the world, has won broad public support.
- The Mikonos affair, which was exposed in a German court in the beginning of 1997, and which indicated that senior members of the Iranian regime were responsible for the murder of Kurd expatriates in the restaurant in Berlin, in addition to the investigation of the attack at al-Khobar in Saudi Arabia, which also indicated Iranian involvement, led to the conclusion that this policy endangers Iran.
- The series of political assassinations in Iran that began in 1998, in the framework of which individuals who advocated reforms and liberalism were murdered, showed the inherent dangers of terror to the Iranian public, in this case domestic terrorism. Objections raised in the Iranian media against internal terror exposed the use of terror outside of Iran's boundaries to criticism as well.
- Iran presented itself as a victim of terror activated by the Mujahidin Khalq organization, which acted against it from Iraq, and threatened to

take retaliatory action against Iraq, as it actually did several times (the firing of Scud missiles and counter-terror).
- The Taliban regime in Afghanistan advocated a radical Sunni Islamic line, in comparison to which Iran seemed to be a pragmatic and moderate state. The Taliban hostility towards the Shiite minority and the killing of Iranian diplomats in Mazar a-Sharif in 1998 enabled Iran to position itself as a moderate state taking action against radical Islam and cooperating with the international coalition acting against the Taliban regime (this coalition included Russia, and Muslim republics such as Uzbekistan and Tajekistan).

One of Khatami's successes was the development of ties between Iran and the European Union. During the entire period since the Islamic regime rose to power, Iran has succeeded in preventing the creation of an American-European front. The European states preferred the "critical dialogue" approach vis-à-vis Iran, a means that enabled elucidation of controversy and conflicts of interest while maintaining open communication channels between the two sides. However, the continued Iranian involvement in terror and the fatwa issued against Salman Rushdie (see further elaboration on the Salmam Rushdie affair in chapter 4) made implementation of this policy problematic for European countries.

To make matters even worse, on April 10, 1997, a German court indicated that the Iranian political level was directly responsible for the planning and perpetration of the assassination of Kurd expatriates opposed to the regime at the Mikonos restaurant in Berlin (see the Mikonos Episode in chapter 4). The Germans even issued warrants of arrest against several Iranian citizens, including Intelligence Minister Ali Fallahian.

Khatami was elected president of Iran a short time after ambassadors of the Western states had been recalled to their countries for consultation regarding the Mikonos affair. Khatami, who advocated improved relations with the West and enjoyed broad grassroots support, came up against the opposition of the conservative circles led by spiritual leader Ali Khamenei, which supported a tougher line towards the West and believed that sooner or later the Western countries would renew their political and economic ties with Iran due to their economic interests.[19] Khatami initiated a placatory policy towards the West; this was reflected in his speech at a conference of Muslim countries in November 1997, and in an interview that he granted to CNN in January 1998. Within a year, Khatami's policy had brought about a significant improvement in Iranian relations with European states, which believed that the moderate stream represented by Khatami needed outside help in order to triumph in the internal power struggles in Iran.[20]

A central obstacle to the improvement of relations continued to be Khomeini's religious ruling against the writer Salman Rushdie. In this matter,

Khatami claimed that from the religious point of view, only the person who issued the religious ruling (meaning Khomeini, who had died in the meantime) could rescind it, but that Iran was not interested in acting upon it. This argument of Khatami's satisfied Britain and the other European states. The British ambassador returned to Teheran in May 1999, and other European states also reassigned their ambassadors to their embassies in Teheran. In the years 1999-2000, Khatami carried out a series of successful visits in Europe (a visit to Italy in October 1999, and a visit to Germany in July 2000), and brought about significant improvement in Iran's foreign relations as well as the renewal of the critical dialogue.

The conservative circles in Iran did not make life easy for Khatami. The Fund of the 15 in Kordad (a semi-official fund) increased the reward for Rushdie's head (see above), and the Revolutionary Guards published an announcement in February 2001, according to which the fatwa against Rushdie was valid and they intended to execute it.[21] In his election campaign for his second term of office as the president of Iran, Khatami reiterated that from Iran's point of view "the affair of Salam Rushdie is closed" and that Iran opposes any form of terror, [22] but any declaration of this kind or visit to Europe was accompanied by a campaign of criticism enacted by the radical circles in Iran. Despite the domestic opposition, it would be accurate to say that Khatami succeeded in promoting Iran's ties with Western Europe and with its neighbors in the Persian Gulf, and in extricating it from the political and economic isolation in which it had sunk before Khatami was elected president.

However, despite the improved relations between Iran and its neighbors and the West, there remained several sensitive and controversial issues, such as Iran's continued efforts to develop long-range missiles and weapons of mass destruction, particularly nuclear weapons.

One of the central questions on the agenda is whether the improved relations with Europe constitute a preliminary step leading to the improvement of ties with the United States (according to the reformists' aspirations) or if the ties with Europe are to serve as a substitute for the links with the United States (according to the conservatives' aspirations). In any case, in 2004, the European Market (EU) is Iran's largest business partner. Ongoing meetings related to a wide range of issues—business meetings, issues relating to regional security, the war against drug trafficking, etc.—reflect the tightening ties between Iran and Western Europe.

But in contrast to the approach of most of the European states, the United States continues to regard Iran as one of the members of the "Axis of Evil," that is, a state that sponsors terror and deals in the development of non-conventional weapons, which poses a threat to the well-being and security of the free world. Therefore, it is reasonable to assert that Khatami's policy was effective in extricating Iran from its isolation and in driving a wedge between the United States and European countries. This crucial disparity between the United States and some of the NATO members became apparent against the background of the 2003-2004 war in Iraq, and a serious difference of opinion may arise in the event of intensification of the confrontation between the United States and Iran.

Iran, September 11 Attacks, and the U.S. War against Terror

The U.S. declaration of war against global terror also forced it to examine its position towards Iran, which traditionally has been considered a state that supports terror. On the one hand, as a neighbor of Afghanistan that was hostile towards the Taliban regime, Iran could serve as a significant ally in the war against terror, which began with a military campaign against the Taliban regime and Al Qaida in Afghanistan. But, on the other hand, Iran constituted a bitter and constant adversary vis-à-vis the United States, and appeared at the head of the State Department's list of states that support terror.

As for Iran, it had reservations vis-à-vis the campaign between the Coalition headed by the United States and the Taliban regime in Afghanistan:

- A fear of international legitimization for the United States to use force against regimes that support terror, which may in the future be directed against Iran, too;
- A war in Afghanistan and then in Iraq, too, could well lead to a prolonged American military presence along Iran's borders (as did indeed occur), and pose a potential American threat to Iran;
- A fear that waves of Afghan refugees will pour into Iran as a result of the war and join the 2 million Afghan refugees who already live in Iran and constitute an economic burden.

However, Iran's greatest fear was undoubtedly the unprecedented international legitimization of the war against terror, which the United States had declared, while the definition of terror organizations and states that support terror remained in U.S. hands, with all the inherent repercussions.

Moreover, already in October 2000, when the United States published its list of wanted terrorists, some Hizballah activists "starred" on it, with Imad Muraniya (who is closely associated with the Iranians) in the lead. The United States also imposed sanctions on the Hizballah, the Palestinian Islamic Jihad, and the Hamas, and froze all of their assets in the United States.[23]

In order to restrict the U.S. freedom of movement, Iran initiated a conference of the Islamic Conference Association (ICO). The participants condemned the September 11 attacks but also expressed their opposition to the American military campaign in Afghanistan, and demanded that the United States concentrate on resolving the problem of the Israeli conquest in Palestine.[24]

However, alongside Iran's reservations following the U.S. offensive in Afghanistan, there were entities in Iran who assessed that Iran might benefit from this action in the following ways:

- The American desire to establish as broad a coalition as possible prior to the war in Afghanistan created a "window of opportunity" for Iran to join the coalition, thus winning international legitimization and repulsing American pressures related to their involvement in terror.
- An American offensive that would topple the Taliban regime, which was at loggerheads with Iran and the Shiite population in Afghanistan, would serve the interests of Iran.
- The American offensive in Afghanistan, which won international consensus, enabled Iran to adopt an active line (and not a neutral one as it had in the Gulf War in 1991) within the international consensus without paying a political and ideological price, as the Taliban regime was perceived as non-legitimate among most Arab states as well, and even in conservative circles in Iran.

There were disputes within the leading echelon in Iran between the reformists and the conservatives regarding the issue of Iran's policy vis-à-vis the war waged by the United States and the Coalition in Afghanistan. A European Union delegation that arrived in Iran for consultations met with an ambivalent response in this matter. Iran condemned terror in general and the attacks of September 11 in particular, but demanded that any action against Afghanistan be undertaken with the UN's permission and expressed its reservations regarding the fact that the United States was the entity to define terror.

Iran refused to allow coalition planes to fly through its airspace, and expressed its reservations regarding President Bush's statement that there were only two choices that countries could make—either to side with the coalition or side with the terrorists. Ali Khamenei, the Supreme Leader, declared that he opposed both of the possibilities; "Not only does the retention of ties with the United States conflict with Iranian national interests, but even negotiating with it constitutes a conflict of interest."[25] These blunt words of Khamenei's were meant to put an end to the reformists' attempts to take advantage of the "window of opportunity" by forming an international coalition against the Taliban in order to emerge from political isolation and launch talks with the United States.

Thus, the policy that Iran adopted in practice was a compromise between these two contradictory approaches. With European arbitration, Iran consented to a secret arrangement whereby the United States could conduct rescue and extrication measures of American airmen if they were hit in Afghanistan and had to bail out over Iran.

Iran played an active role in the Afghan arena prior to and during the war on two main levels:

- It increased its military aid to its allies in the Northern alliance. (Iran mainly supported the Shiite and Tajiki communities, which were part of the Northern Alliance and fought the Taliban regime.)

- It participated in talks with Pakistan, as well as discussions in the framework of "the forum of states bordering on Afghanistan," coined the "6 + 2,"[26] which held discussions sponsored by the UN regarding the establishment of a future regime in Afghanistan after the collapse of the Taliban regime.

From time to time, Iran has arrested and deported Al Qaida activists who took refuge on its soil, but as a rule it refrains from extraditing activists to their lands of origin, and sometimes they are even allowed to choose the destination to which they will be deported. At the same time, Iran grants a haven, sponsorship, and aid to Al Qaida activists on its soil.[27] In this framework, several hundred Al Qaida activists live in Iran, including senior members like Sayyaf al-Adel (of Egyptian origin), Abu-Khaf (a Mauritanian), and Abu-Mutsab al Zarkawi (a Jordanian); it is possible that one of Osama Bin-Laden's sons is also in Iran. The Al Qaida activists deal in the preparation of attacks against targets outside of Iran. For example, an organization cell was caught while crossing the border between Iran and Turkey, with the intention of reaching Israel and perpetrating attacks there. Also, Iran has aided members of the "Antsar al Islam," a radical Islamic organization affiliated with Al Qaida. Until recently, this organization was active in the Kurd regions of Iraq, on the Iranian border, and its bases were attacked by the Americans during its campaign in Iraq. It would appear that in consequence at least some of the organization's members escaped to Iran.

It is our opinion that the support offered to Al Qaida by the Revolutionary Guards, the most important military body in the state, would be impossible without the approval of the Iranian leader Khamenei. Even if there are entities in the Iranian regime, such as the foreign ministry and the president, who oppose supporting Al Qaida due to the damage that this causes to Iran in the international arena, it is our understanding that they do not possess the strength to prevent it and some of them are even unaware of its existence.

We believe the Iranian aid provided to Al Qaida activists and the willingness to turn a blind eye to their activity in Iran stem from a combination of several motives: *An ideological motive*—A feeling of the Islamic "common goal" vis-à-vis joint opponents, namely the United States, Israel, and the West in general, despite the disparity between the beliefs and outlooks of the Sunni radical Islam and their Shiite counterparts; *A practical motive*—Use of Al Qaida members as "bargaining cards" for extradition (mainly vis-à-vis the Gulf States) on the one hand, and as an operational potential for violent action during times of trouble against the United States and its allies in the area (particularly if the counter-terror campaign is directed against Iran), on the other.

This policy of the "two-way game" and "walking on the brink" poses a certain risk for Iran, which as a member of the Axis of Evil is already in the

"U.S. sights." However, the Iranian regime believes that the risk is still limited due to the U.S. focus on the Iraqi issue.

As mentioned earlier, Iran's policy regarding the September 11 issue and the war in Afghanistan reflects the duality and internal tension between the diametrically opposed camps within the top Iranian leadership. It appears that both sides have similarly gauged the risks and dangers inherent to the process generated by the September 11 attacks but disagree as to the policy that Iran must adopt in the face of new challenges.

Generally, the Iranian response was pragmatic and levelheaded, and it can be concisely stated[28] in one sentence: "Iran's attitude to the United States was: 'Do the job quickly and then leave the region.'" It appears that from Iran's point of view, the optimal solution would indeed have been a quick American operation which would oust the Taliban regime, followed by the United States exiting the area; however, reality proved the Iranians wrong. The United States overcame the Taliban regime rapidly, but its forces still remain in that country in order to establish a new regime and a new regional reality.

Moreover, in the famous speech delivered by President Bush in February 2002, he described Iran as a member of the Axis of Evil, thus mixing up the Iranians' deck of cards. The latter had anticipated an improved status for Iran due to its alleged partnership in the coalition against terror. The American campaign in Iraq only served to exacerbate the Iranian dilemma even further regarding the policy that it must advocate in light of the fact that the "Great Satan" was parked along its eastern and western borders.

Iran and the War in Iraq (2003) (Iraqi Freedom)

During the crisis prior to the American offensive in Iraq, Iran took a neutral stand, similar to the policy that it had adopted during the Gulf War in 1991. On the one hand, Iran regarded Saddam Hussein's regime as an adversary and as a strategic threat to Iranian interests and thus took a favorable view of the ousting of his regime, based on the hope that he would be replaced by a government in which Shiites—who constitute a majority in Iraq—would have a decisive vote. An Iraqi government supportive of and amiably inclined towards Iran would enable the creation of a Shiite regional power center that would promote Iran's strategic interests.[29] On the other hand, Iran regarded the United States as one of its main opponents, and an American offensive leading to the ousting of Saddam's regime and the establishment of a pro-American government with a U.S. military presence on Iran's borders was perceived as a graver threat than the continued survival of Saddam Hussein's regime.

Therefore, Iran chose to take a neutral stand during the crisis, which meant abstaining from issuing supportive statements of solidarity siding with Saddam Hussein's regime while energetically striving to recruit international entities in order to prevent a military campaign in Iraq[30] (an approach adopted by France, Germany, additional European countries, Russia, China, and most of the Muslim and Arab countries). Thus, during the crisis, Iran adopted a policy that was within the international consensus.

After the outbreak of the American-British offensive in Iraq, Iran condemned the U.S. aggression but declared that it would maintain its neutral position in the conflict. The quick victory that the U.S. and British forces achieved in the war in Iraq created a new reality that forced Iran to reevaluate its policies.[31]

Iran's view of the war in Iraq can be gleaned from a speech delivered by the Iranian supreme leader Ali Khamenei on April 11, 2003, in which he emphasized the following points:[32]

- Iran never "supported" Saddam Hussein's regime and adopted a neutral stand in the confrontation between the latter and the United States, just as the Iraqi people remained neutral in this conflict.
- The killing of Iraqi civilians by U.S. and British forces is to be severely condemned.
- The American intentions to establish a military regime in Iraq are to be condemned, as the enforcement of an external regime violates the most basic rights of the Iraqi people.
- The occupation of Iraq is a new expression of colonialism stemming from an American and British desire to control the Iraqi oil resources.
- The UN did not fulfill its obligations during the crisis in Iraq.
- Britain made a serious error when it joined the United States in the war in Iraq, thus revealing its "ugly face" once again.
- Iran reiterates its opposition to the non-legitimate step of the U.S.-British campaign in Iraq.
- The Zionists played a major role in the Iraqi crisis, and it is they who motivated Britain and the United States to conquer Iraq. The Zionists are the main beneficiaries of the war, and the "Road Map" initiated by U.S. President Bush is meant to help them expand their control in the Middle East.
- Iran calls on the Iraqis not to cooperate with the United States and to cause chaos, which will force them to leave the country.

Iran is currently facing several serious challenges that the United States has posed:

- The United States, which has labeled Iran one of the countries in the Axis of Evil, demands that it cease its support of terror and its projects for acquiring weapons of mass destruction.
- The United States accuses Iran of providing a haven for Al Qaida members. Among the senior Al Qaida members located in Iran according to U.S. sources are Bin-Laden's son, Sayyaf al Adel (head of the organization's military branch), Abu-Mutsab al Zarkawi (a senior operational member of the organization and leading force against the Americans in Iraq) and Suliman Abu-Reit, the organization's spokesman.

- Since the beginning of the campaign in Iraq and mainly after its completion, the United States has been exerting heavy pressure on Syria, Iran's strategic ally, to end its support of terror, banish the headquarters of terror organizations from its territory, and put a stop to the aid it grants to the Hizballah.
- U.S. Secretary of State Colin Powell, who visited Syria and Lebanon in April 2003, demanded to banish the Hizballah from the Lebanese-Israeli border and to deploy forces of the Lebanese army in the south.
- The pressure placed on Iran's strategic allies—Syria, the Hizballah, and the Palestinian terror organizations—also constitutes a clear message for the Iranians as to the seriousness of U.S. intentions in the fight against terror.
- Moreover, the United States is currently acting to renew the Israeli-Palestinian peace talks based on President Bush's Road Map. Iran, which is a member of the camp that opposes the peace talks and encourages continued violence (the Al Aksa Intifada), is thus at loggerheads with the United States on this front as well.

Iran is obligated to contend with these challenges at a time when its geostrategic environment has shifted:

- U.S. forces are deployed in Afghanistan on Iran's eastern border, and in Afghanistan a pro-American regime is gaining power under the leadership of Hamid Karzai.
- U.S. forces are aligned along Iran's western border.
- U.S. influence is steadily increasing in the Muslim republics north of Iran (Azerbaijan, Kazakhstan, Turkmenistan, and more).

Thus Iran is surrounded on all sides by the American army, and its geostrategic environment is open to the influence of the American hegemony. At the same time, Iran is in the throes of an internal crisis due to power struggles between entities that aspire to achieve reforms and a change in the character of the Islamic regime, and the religious circles headed by the spiritual leader Khamenei. The American moves to replace the regimes in two of Iran's neighboring countries (Afghanistan and Iraq) constitute a clear signal to the regime in Teheran.

The United States also signed an agreement with the Iranian opposition organization Mujahidin Khalq, which in the past acted against the Iranian regime in Teheran under the patronage of Saddam Hussein's regime. According to this agreement the organization will hand its arms over to the U.S. army but the organization members will be allowed to continue wearing uniforms and act in Iraq, and this undoubtedly transmits another signal to Teheran.[33]

Iran has accused the United States of encouraging students and other opposition entities to hold riots and disturbances. During the month of June 2003, serious riots took place in Teheran and other Iranian cities, which were ruthlessly suppressed by the security forces.

In contrast to Iran's increasing strategic distress one can point out an almost single "ray of light" from the Iranian point of view: The ousting of Saddam Hussein's regime has opened "a window of opportunity" to establish a Shiite (pro-Iranian) regime in Iraq, which may help in the long term to establish a Shiite "bloc" with significant strategic power. Therefore, Iran has been "stirring" the Iraqi cauldron in order to attempt to promote its interests in the establishment of the regime in Iraq.

The Iraqi political system is currently in a state of chaos. The United States is attempting to resolve the situation, but to date only with limited success. The Shiite political power brokers are not united either, and the power struggles between them have reached the point of political assassinations in one of the holiest sites to the Shiites (see below).

The Shiites in Iraq in the Aftermath of the War[34]

Following the U.S. invasion, and against the background of the lack of a central government in Iraq, the Shiites in Iraq began to develop an independent administration, which is the first of its kind. In the cities of Carbala, Najef, as well as certain sections of Baghdad, Shiite religious clerics have been running the municipalities. Among other aspects, they handle water supply and some even succeed in paying the salaries of the clerks. In Carbala and Najef, armed militias guard the newly appointed administrators. American soldiers continue to move on the outskirts of the cities, but they do not interfere in the process.

The Americans, led by the head of the civil administration, do not as yet know how to handle these new leaders. There is a fear that the longer it takes to set up a new local government the harder it will be to remove them. "A theocratic state like Iran will not rise in Iraq," declared the U.S. Secretary of Defense Donald Rumsfeld at the end of the war, and hastened to warn Iran not to interfere in Iraq's internal affairs. But Rumsfeld is not the only one who has reason to worry. The Iranian regime also has a problem with the establishment of a Shiite state in Iraq, and among the Shiite leaders themselves in Iraq there is a theological dispute regarding the concept itself.

The Shiites constitute over 60 percent of the Iraqi population. It is customary to categorize three "generations" of Shiites in Iraq:[35]

- Those who lived there during the Iran-Iraq war and were deported by Saddam Hussein—mostly to Iran, and some to Europe and the United States;
- Shiites who left Iraq during the first Gulf War and after the brutal suppression of the Shiite rebellion in 1991;

- Shiites that stayed in the homeland and survived under Saddam Hussein's regime.

There is also a differentiation between secular Shiites, like Ahmad Shalabi, chairman of the Iraqi National Congress, and religious Shiites, and even among the religious ones themselves there are disputes related to conceptual-theological issues. Some maintain that it is possible to separate religion and state and that Shiite religious leaders must not deal in politics, while others seek to revive the concept of the Islamic state and are looking into possibilities related to political positions.

A violent controversy awakened in the city of Najef against this background, and on April 10, 2003, the Shiite religious leader al Majid al Khoei was murdered by Shiite radicals. Al Khoei was the son of the Supreme Ayatollah (the highest title in the Shiite religious hierarchy) Abu al Kasem al Khoei, and he was affiliated with a Shiite stream of thought that advocated that religious clerics should not take part in the political administration of the state. Al Khoei returned to Iraq from his place of exile in London after the Americans had conquered Carbala and Najef, but a short time thereafter was murdered inside the Imam Ali Mosque in Najef, one of the Shiites' holiest sites, by several assassins who stabbed him to death and fled. Al Khoei was considered pro-American, and according to some commentators his return to Iraq was part of an American attempt to establish an echelon of Iraqi leadership that would support the United States. The reason for the assassination is still unclear, but it is possible that al Khoei was murdered by Shiite entities that opposed his opinions and regarded him as a traitor. The United States and Britain both expressed their shock and sorrow following the murder. The spokesperson of the State Department Ari Fleischer said: "The very regrettable assassination of a Sheikh from An-Najaf, which the United States strongly condemns...we express our sympathies to the people of An-Najaf over this assassination...is another reminder of how dangerous the situation is inside Iraq."[36]

The British Foreign Minister Jack Straw said, "I knew Sheikh al Khoei. He was a resident in this country. He had huge expectations about the future of the Shia people post-Saddam.... It is an appalling tragedy that he has been killed before he could take part in that process."[37]

The spokesman of the Iranian Foreign Ministry also condemned al Khoei's murder in Najef and said: "From the Islamic Republic of Iran's standpoint, resorting to violence in order to achieve political ends is condemned.... The brave Iraqi people in the current sensitive juncture, while (maintaining) their unity, solidarity and vigilance, must not allow outside forces to impose their views on them by exploiting their disunity and conflicts."[38]

As stated above, Abd al Majid was the son of the Shiite leader Abu al Kasem al Khoei, who died in unclear circumstances following the Shiite uprising in

1991. After the suppression of the uprising Abd al Majid fled to London and established an Islamic group that dealt in raising funds.

"Religious clerics should instruct, guide and advise, but not govern," stated al Majid al Khoei in a newspaper interview just prior to his death. Supreme Ayatollah Ali Sistani, source of the religious authority in the Shiite seminary in Najef, concurs with this opinion. The seventy-two-year-old Sistani was al Khoei's student and today he is one of the liberal interpreters of the Shia in Iraq. Sistani was considered a scholarly genius. When he was young, before the age of thirty, he was already certified as an interpreter and a religious adjudicator. The list of his teachers and the writings that he authored have turned him into one of the most important and authoritative Shiite scholars in his generation. But even his illustrious theological sway cannot contend with the political aspirations of Muktada a-Sader, a young man in his twenties who has been dubbed "the learned (*Sayyid*) boy" by his critics; the latter seeks to turn the religious center in Najef into a political focal point and establish a state in Iraq along the lines of the Iranian model.

Muktada a-Sader is not a religious cleric despite the title of Sayyid that he carries. He certainly cannot stand up to those who are more veteran and educated than he, but he is of a highly distinguished lineage. His father was the Supreme Ayatollah Muhammad Sadek a-Sader, the spiritual leader of the Shiites in Iraq, who was murdered together with both of Muktada's brothers by Saddam Hussein's agents in 1999.

According to the Americans, a-Sader has connections with Iran and aspires to emulate in Iraq the Iranian method whereby religious clerics run the country. A-Sader's men led the anti-American demonstrators in Najef and Carbala, and there is reason to suspect that his men planned the murder of Abd al Majid al Khoei and perhaps even perpetrated it. The learned (Sayyid) boy organized armed shifts in Najef, established local committees for civil administration, and within several days took control of the city. His associates claim that he does not intend to relinquish it. He has at his disposal some 5,000 armed aides who serve, as it were, as a private army (The Army of Mahdi), and he has already succeeded in establishing representations in other cities in Iraq. In order to administer the city, a-Sader and his people need a steady source of income. This source may be located in the Iranian treasury, and the United States fears that Iran will indeed take advantage of the opportunity that has fallen into its hands to navigate Iraq's future.

Iran—so the Americans believe—does not only help a-Sader's men, but also aids the former opposition organization the "Supreme Council for the Islamic Revolution in Iraq." The organization is led by Muhammad Baker al Hakim, who was recently granted the title of Supreme Ayatollah, which enables him to compete as a religious authority with Ali Sistani. Al Hakim's Supreme Council, which until recently had opposed any cooperation with the Americans and refused an invitation to attend the first conference of the opposition representatives in Nasaria, changed its approach. Its representative attended a conference held on April 28, 2003, in which the head of the civil administration tried to promote the appointment of a temporary Iraqi government, although to date with little success.

Muhammad Baker al Hakim returned to Iraq on May 10, 2003, after a twenty-three-year exile, and was welcomed by tens of thousands of Shiite supporters. He came to the city of Basra from Teheran, where he had resided after fleeing Saddam Hussein's regime in 1980, and from there continued on to the Shiite holy city of Najef.[39]

Upon his return, al Hakim expressed his opposition to the prolonged stay of American and British troops in Iraq, and stressed that the Iraqi people themselves must determine its government and that the government must incorporate all Iraqi populations, including minorities. Nevertheless, al Hakim, who to date has used moderate terms in his comments about the United States, reiterated that the top Iraqi priority must be the eradication of the remnants of the Baath rule, which continue to perpetrate military campaigns and impair security. He defined the presence of the coalition forces in Iraq as the second problem.[40] In an interview with the satellite television station Al-Arabia, al Hakim emphasized that his organization is willing to help ensure security in Iraq, if the U.S. and British forces allow him to do so. Al Hakim placed the issue of establishing a new government in Iraq according to the people's will in fourth place in order of importance.[41]

Al Hakim's organization is considered the most prominent and important Shiite group. The organization has military power, the "Bader Brigades," which include thousands of fighters. The organization's uniqueness lies in the fact that in the last two decades it has been granted sponsorship and aid by the Iranian regime, but at the same time it continues to maintain ties with the American administration. The American administration regards al Hakim's organization with some suspicion, mostly because of the fear that it is too close to Iran. After the beginning of the war, Secretary of Defense Donald Rumsfeld warned al Hakim not to bring his soldiers into Iraq. Al Hakim, who was asked about the link between Iran and a future government in Iraq, noted that he opposed the "cloning" of regimes.[42] At a speech in Basra, al Hakim said, "We must now know our way to rehabilitate Iraq and forget the past. We Muslims must live together. We must build security for our new society. We must help each other to stand as one against imperialism." The Al-Jazeera network reported that al Hakim was addressing about 100,000 supporters. He also said, "We want a democratic government that represents the Iraqi nation, the Iraqi people, the Muslims, the Christians and all of the minorities." But according to him, "We refuse a government that will be forced upon us."[43]

If the convergence of Shiite religious clerics in Iraq is perceived by the Americans as signaling a possible danger that Iraq will turn into another "Iran," the Iranians regard the issue differently. The question of the Shiite religious leadership concerns Iran's spiritual leader Ali Khamenei, who aspires to be the source of spiritual authority of all Shiites worldwide. As long as the city of Qum in Iran was the alternative center to Najef he could at least have presented himself as such. The Shiite religious scholars in Iran could not publicly oppose this out of fear that it would be to their detriment, and the Iraqi Shiite scholars, who opposed his status as the global Shiite leader, were perceived as though they were under Saddam Hussein's pressure and therefore could not express an independent stand.[44]

The spiritual leader of the Hizballah, Muhammad Hussein Fadallah, was actually one of Khamenei's prominent opposers, as he claimed that the latter "is not sufficiently qualified from a religious aspect," to lead the Shia. Fadallah is not the only one to cast doubts upon Khamenei's status as a religious leader. Ayatollah Sistani and al Hakim, head of the Shiite opposition organization, regard themselves as worthy of the title "a source of emulation" (*Marja Talkid*), that is, the source of religious authority. Now that the gates have been reopened for the return of thousands of religious seminary students from Iran to Iraq, and hundreds of esteemed religious teachers are on the way to Najef, the greatness of the city of Qum in Iran may decline, together with the entire religious center in that country.[45]

In an interview with *Newsweek*, which was held when the war broke out in Iraq, Fadallah, an alumnus of the religious seminary in Najef, stated that he believes "that Najef is still the authoritative center of the Shia. Perhaps Qum took in many of its students because they were banned from coming to Najef and due to the lack of freedom there. But now that Najef has been liberated, it will attract students from all over the world. Najef was the leading Shiite center for more than a thousand years."[46]

The freedom that Fadallah refers to is the liberty to express an uninhibited opinion regarding religious matters and to hold an open debate—and this does not exist in Iran. Here lies the true danger to Khamenei's authority. He may discover that the idea of exporting the Islamic revolution to Iraq may just cost him his status. In order to ensure an Iranian foothold in Iraq, Khamenei granted assistance to Muhammad Baker al Hakim's Supreme Council. The Revolutionary Guards trained al Hakim's men, particularly the military branch called the Bader Brigades, and as of 2004 Iran is also granting support to Muktada a-Sader against Ali Sistani.[47] At this point, the United States does know who sides with it and who opposes it. There is also no certainty that Iran's current supporters will maintain this stand after matters stabilize in Iraq. At this time, it appears that the United States is acting to prevent "Shiitization" of the Iraqi government, but there is no doubt that Shiite politics will determine what Iraq will look like in the future.

At present, the American attempt to create an alternative government in Iraq has come up against obstacles, and they are being forced to fill the governmental void created in Iraq. Absurdly enough, the Americans want to establish a democratic government but also fear democracy in Iraq, because it is composed of a 60 percent Shiite population that may turn the country into something that will awaken longings for Saddam Hussein in the Americans' hearts.[48]

Syria and Its Involvement in Terror in the Aftermath of the War in Iraq[49]

In May 2003, U.S. Secretary of State Colin Powell visited Syria and Lebanon. Powell demanded that Syria adjust itself to the American plans regarding the Middle East after the war in Iraq: "The rules of the game have changed," he declared to President Assad. In a press conference held in Beirut, Powell revealed that Syria had informed him that it had closed the offices of several terror organizations, but he did not disclose their identity. According to Powell, the Syrian president had not done everything in his power in this matter, and the United States expected Syria to take additional steps regarding the activities of terror organizations on its soil. Powell demanded that Syria use its influence and facilitate the deployment of the Lebanese army in South Lebanon along the border with Israel, in place of the positions currently manned by the Hizballah. He expressed concern regarding the ongoing terror activities that the Hizballah had been perpetrating in the region and throughout the world, and called for an end to the armed presence of the Hizballah militias in Lebanon and for their disarmament.

Powell's meet with Syrian president Bahir al Assad, which lasted for two hours, focused on Syria's support of terror organizations, its plans for the development of chemical weapons of mass destruction, and its opposition to the Road Map, geared at putting an end to hostilities between Israel and the Palestinians. Powell clarified that the change in Iraq and the possibility of renewing the peace talks between Israel and the Palestinians would create "new strategic dynamics in the region." He made it clear that a new reality had been created in the Middle East, and that the United States was interested in a comprehensive solution that would include a Palestinian state and the resolution of all of the controversial issues between Syria and Israel, and between Lebanon and Israel.

Powell told Assad that the United States understood the importance of the Golan Heights to Syria, and stressed that the administration in Washington was interested in opening two parallel channels for discussions: between Israel and the Palestinians and between Israel and Syria. "It is possible that the Israeli-Syrian track will not move at the same tempo as the Israeli-Palestinian one, but this track must exist," Powell said. He added that in the future the United States would be willing to discuss the Syrian proposal to disarm the Middle East (including Israel) of weapons of mass destruction, but stressed that this was not the time to discuss the issue.

In a press conference that he held prior to his meeting with Assad, Powell announced that the United States had no intention of initiating a military offensive against Syria, and stated that President Bush possessed other means if Syria did not meet the U.S. demands, alluding to the possibility of imposing economic sanctions.

Powell was on his third visit to Damascus since February 2001, and it took place following a period of tension between the two countries, after the United States had accused Syria of providing a safe haven to senior Iraqis. Prior to his arrival in Damascus, Powell told reporters on the plane that he would never forget how Assad had lied to him two years earlier, when he promised that oil would not flow from Iraq to Syria. "I will always save that on my computer software," Powell noted.

At the end of his meeting with President Assad, Powell set out for Lebanon where he met with President Emil Lahoud and the chairman of the Parliament Nabia Beri. Powell described his talks in Lebanon as "constructive," but Lebanon's Foreign Minister, Jean Obeid, did not directly address the U.S. demands. It would appear that in 2003-2004 Bashar al Assad was implementing a policy of pinpointed handling of the crisis, and was not attempting to introduce significant changes into his policy: The Syrian response to the American demand to extradite senior Iraqis who had found refuge in Syria was to deny their presence on Syrian soil, but amazingly the next day several of them were caught near the Syrian border after they had apparently been banished from that country. The Syrian reaction to American accusations that it had enabled the passage of volunteers and weapons to Iraq during the war was to close the border terminal between Syria and Iraq; Syria responded to the American demand to cease activity of terror organizations on Syrian soil by "cosmetically" closing the organizations' offices. Thus, the action taken was partial and symbolic, aimed at placating the Americans without actually giving in to their demands.

The American activity poses a significant threat to the strategic axis of Iran and Syria, and to the status of the Iranian-sponsored organizations—first and foremost the Hizballah in Lebanon, but also Palestinian terror organizations such as the Palestinian Islamic Jihad, the Jibril Front, the Hamas, and others. The American steps drive a wedge between Iran and Syria, which is being made to choose whether to give in to the American demands regarding the issue of the activities of terror organizations on its soil and under its sponsorship, or to pay the price for refusal while risking economic and other sanctions and perhaps even an American military attack in the future. A Syrian capitulation to the American demands will deal a serious blow to the scope of presence and activity of the Palestinian terror organizations in Syria, as well as in Lebanon, and it is possible that it will impinge upon the continued freedom of activity and deployment of the Hizballah in Lebanon.

Against the background of the American activity, Iranian President Khatami paid visits to Lebanon, Syria, Yemen, and Bahrain. His visit to Lebanon on

May 12, 2003, was the first visit of an Iranian president to this state since the Islamic revolution in Iran, which took place in 1979. During the visit, Khatami met with top-level leaders in Lebanon and with the leader of the Hizballah, Hassan Nasrallah.[50]

Summary and Conclusions

Until 2004, Iran was one of the most prominent countries to support and utilize terror as a tool to promote its interests in the international arena. From a comprehensive analysis of the terror activities perpetrated from the time of the establishment of the Islamic republic in Iran (since 1979) up to 2003—an analysis based on data provided by research institutions and publications in the media—it is possible to indicate hundreds of attacks perpetrated by Iranian entities or by sponsored Shiite or Palestinian organizations.

The Iranian terror activity was implemented in a rational manner, with Iran endeavoring not to leave fingerprints that would identify it as the entity behind the terror activity. Moreover, in public statements the Iranian leadership expressed its reservations regarding terror attacks and condemned them, and this also applied to its sponsored organizations, for example, the Hizballah.

Iran's attempt to conceal the terror activity that it perpetrated enabled it to derive the maximum benefit from this activity—on the one hand, it barred the terror victim from retaliating for its activity, and on the other, it sometimes presented itself as a go-between striving to reach a compromise between the victim and the terror organizations. This way it was able to achieve its goals on both ends.

Most of the information that exposed Iran's involvement in terror activity surfaced due to the apprehension of the terror perpetrators and in their subsequent trials, following intensive investigations of attacks by law enforcement and intelligence agencies in various places worldwide, and also as the result of terror activity in which the entities' claiming of responsibility included declarations and/or demands that clearly reflected Iranian interests. The most prominent milestones in this connection are the investigation of the attacks in Argentina during the years 1992 and 1994, the attack at al-Khobar in Saudi Arabia, the Mikonos affair, and the capture of the *Karin A*.

It is possible to trace a strong connection between terror activity and Iran's foreign policy. The consistent and systematic use of terror in order to force Iranian wishes on other countries after a goal had not been achieved through acceptable diplomatic means is conspicuous. Typical examples are Kuwait and France, which during the 1980s were the main targets for Iranian/Shiite terror activity, mainly due to their positions regarding the Iran-Iraq war and the aid they offered to Iraq.

In most cases the terror weapon was activated in order to achieve a wide range of Iranian objectives vis-à-vis the victim. For example, Iran's demands of France during the 1980s included the removal of its forces from Lebanon, cessation of French military aid for Iraq, a change in its stand vis-à-vis the Arab-Israeli conflict, return of the Iranian funds frozen in France, deportation of expatriates and Iranian opposition organizations from French soil, and the release of Shiite terrorists arrested in France. These objectives were achieved one after the other through a series of various kinds of terror attacks (car bombs, abduction of hostages, sabotage, and more), which ultimately led to repeated French capitulations to most of the Iranian demands.

The timing of most of the terror attacks was planned very carefully, and was meant to serve political processes by negotiating with the victim or sometimes as a catalyst to launching the negotiations.

Although one might purportedly gauge the Iranian terror policy as a rational and pragmatic policy aimed at achieving Iran's goals, it is important to point out additional phenomena that also play an important role in the formulation of Iranian policy:

- The use of terror in the international arena constitutes a central point of dispute in the higher echelons of the Iranian regime between the circles that are called "moderate" and the "radical" circles that support a ruthless struggle against the enemies of the revolution. Thus, to a large extent the scope of the utilization of terror and its targets also reflect the internal power struggles in Iran.
- Iran has often advocated an ambivalent foreign policy, according to which the "moderates" aspire to negotiate and reach compromises, while the "radicals" continue with the terror activity (sometimes in order to "torpedo" the steps taken by the moderates.)
- Iran's ambivalent policy has generally provided it with flexibility vis-à-vis its political steps and has made it difficult for its adversaries to advocate a tough policy which will provide a response to Iranian terror, mostly due to the assumption that the moderate entities within the Iranian regime must be encouraged in their struggle against the radical entities, from the aspect of the "lesser of two evils."

There are several examples where Iranian willingness to sacrifice political interests on the ideological altar is evident—the most prominent example illustrating this issue is the Salman Rushdie affair. By sentencing the British writer to death, Khomeini instigated a confrontation with the Western democracies, as this issue placed the Islamic values and principles opposite the values of the democratic Western civilization.

This affair gives us insight into the nature of the Islamic leadership: First and foremost, this is one issue about which there was a total consensus between the radicals and the moderates, that is, that Rushdie must die. Secondly, even after Khomeini's demise, and under Rafsanjani and Khatami's leadership, it was made unequivocally clear that the verdict would remain valid (although Iran would not act to execute it). Thus, it is clear that there are basic religious and ideological values about which there exists a consensus in the Iranian regime, while in matters that are less fundamental, the Iranian policy is pragmatic and is primarily motivated by cost/benefit considerations.

The dilemma regarding the nature of the Iranian leadership (moderates or reformists opposite radicals) stems mainly from the angle of observation and judgment according to Western norms and values. A close investigation of the deeds and statements of the Iranian leaders, both moderate and radical, leads us to the conclusion that a more accurate differentiation should be made between radical and more radical leadership. As long as Khomeini's philosophy is maintained as the source of legitimization and as a guide for Iranian leadership, the differences between the radical and moderate elements will be expressed in different approaches to achieve goals, but not in their very essence.

In the matter of Iran's control over sponsored Shiite and Palestinian organizations, it is important to note that throughout the entire reviewed period Iran demonstrated control and influence over the sponsored organizations. But this statement must also be qualified because the control and influence over sponsored organizations are sometimes in the hands of entities that are not necessarily at the head of Iran's official leadership. Thus, it would be fair to say that the internal power struggles in Iran have a significant influence on the sponsored organizations that follow the orders of various factors in the Iranian regime. One must also stress that the extent of Iranian control over its sponsored organizations is also influenced by its cooperation with its strategic ally, Syria.

Let us also keep in mind that the sponsored organizations have their own goals and needs, which sometimes do not completely match the interests of the "patron." In this connection it is possible to observe that in most terror attacks the Shiite and Palestinian terror organizations raised demands that included the release of terrorists incarcerated in various countries as well as ransoms (demands that first and foremost serve the organizations themselves). The arrest of Shiite terrorists in various countries over the world turned the latter into victims of attacks although sometimes they were not initially planned to be the target of terror activity (for example, Switzerland and Germany). Attacks against these countries did not generally serve Iranian interests, and were directed at bringing about the release of the imprisoned terrorists.

Many books and articles have been written about how to contend with terror, and most argue that the capitulation to terror invites additional acts of terror. The conclusions that I must draw from this study do not fully validate this assumption. As stated earlier, among the most prominent states that fell victim to Iranian terror were France and Kuwait; France's policy was indeed characterized by repeated capitulation to the demands of the Shiite and Iranian terror organizations, and therefore the example of France verifies the theory that submission to terror invites additional terrorist acts. But on the other hand, Kuwait stood out due to its consistent policy not to give in to terror extortion under any circumstances, but despite this stand, or perhaps because of it, Kuwait suffered a particularly high number of attacks.

Therefore, capitulation or non-capitulation to terror is just one component out of a wide range of components that ultimately determine if the terror will continue or cease, and it is impossible to regard uncompromising refusal to give in to terror as a "wonder-formula" to prevent terror. Moreover, in certain situations this brought on even graver consequences.

It appears that Iranian terror is basically motivated by rational considerations (in addition to ideological and other motives, which should not be dismissed offhandedly). Thus, in most cases the use of terror is weighed according to cost/benefit calculations, and the decision is an offshoot of this reckoning. The main reason for this phenomenon stems from rational calculations on the part of the entities behind the terror regarding risks and the ability to obtain achievements vis-à-vis the terror victim.

In the overall balance Iran could (justifiably) have reached the conclusion that terror pays off. The Iranian balance in this issue testifies to a fairly impressive success rate in achieving political targets in comparison to a relatively low price that it has been made to pay, at least to date. But this picture has changed in the aftermath of September 11, 2001, and the U.S. declaration of war against global terror, events that constitute milestones and historical turnabouts in the way that the world contends with terror. The United States defines Iran as one of the Axis of Evil countries and has made it a central target in its struggle against terror. In light of the determination that the United States has demonstrated in its fight against terror in two campaigns that it has successfully fought to date—in Afghanistan and in Iraq—and which ended with the toppling of the pro-terror regimes and in the creation of a new regional and global reality, Iran now faces an unprecedented challenge vis-à-vis the terror strategy that it has employed to date with great success. Iran, which is experiencing internal disputes between reformists and conservatives, is also currently facing American demands to introduce an essential change in its policy regarding two main issues:

- Cessation of support for terror and terminating its utilization;
- Shelving its plans to acquire weapons for mass destruction and the means to launch them.

These American demands are backed up by the U.S. military presence on Iran's borders with Afghanistan and Iraq, and by the increasing American influence in the Muslim republics on Iran's northern border. The United States is also taking determined action vis-à-vis Syria—Iran's strategic ally—and demanding that it cease its aid to Palestinian terror organizations and to the Hizballah, and prevent the Hizballah's terror activity from South Lebanon. (A similar demand was also made on the Lebanese administration, along with the demand to deploy the Lebanese army along the border with Israel instead of the Hizballah's militia that is currently aligned there). A positive Syrian response to the American demands will impair and significantly reduce Iran's ability to aid the terror organizations supported by them today, primarily the Hizballah and the Palestinian terror organizations, such as the Palestinian Islamic Jihad, the Jibril Front, the Hamas, and more.

Following the American steps to implement the peace initiative (The Road Map) between Israel and the Palestinians, Iran has come up against escalating problems in the Palestinian arena as well. Since the beginning of the Al Aksa Intifada, Iran has been one of the strongest supporters of the armed struggle against Israel, and directly and indirectly has aided Palestinian entities that were involved in the conflict. Iran was one of the few countries that did nothing to conceal its intention to bring about Israel's destruction, and it acted to facilitate this concept by supporting the Palestinian armed struggle and constantly eroding Israel's social and economic strength. But when the United States succeeded in mobilizing most of the Arab world in support of the Road Map during the Aqaba and Sharm-a-Sheikh conferences, Iran remained isolated in its opposition to the growing consensus. At first, Iran acted to torpedo the Road Map and attempted to sabotage Abu-Mazen's efforts to form a government. Avi Dichter, head of the General Security Services (GSS), noted in this connection that "Iran is trying to fan the flames of terror in order to make Abu-Mazen's assumption of his role more difficult." He noted that "Iran is placing pressure on the various terror organizations to act against Abu-Mazen and not to consent to a ceasefire."[51] But, subsequently, Iran was forced to fall into line, if only temporarily. Reflection of Iran's distress in this connection can be seen in its consent to the "*Hudna*" (cease fire) which was achieved between the Palestinian factions, while even its closer protégés—the Palestinian Islamic Jihad, the Hamas, and the factions in the Fatah that enjoy its support—joined the agreement.

Perhaps for the first time, Iran is currently facing the need to introduce a strategic change in its approach to the issue of the utilization of terror, and the Iranian resolution will undoubtedly also be affected by the controversy that now exists in Iranian society and within the higher levels of government, between those who support the reformist approach and those who oppose it.

At this point in time it is impossible to state what Iran's policy will be changed regarding the issue of terror, but there is no doubt that Iran's ability to support the terror organizations acting under its patronage has been impaired due to the massive American presence in the Middle Eastern arena. An Iranian decision not to concede to the U.S. demands may place it in a political and perhaps even military confrontation with the United States, which is determined to take resolute action against global terror and the states that support it.

The ongoing "chaos" in Iraq is Iran's "insurance policy," for if there were peace and quiet in Iraq the Americans might decide to pay more attention to Iran. The coalition's failure to stabilize the situation in Iraq forces them to maintain a military presence and they suffer from a growing number of losses and a reduced legitimacy for their presence in Iraq.

Iran's terrorist record described above coupled with its operational and technological prowess mean that Iran could become a serious threat to any opponent—even the United States.

Iran could act:

- Against American allies
- Against American targets around the world
- Against targets in the United States.

Iran could act directly through its revolutionary guard and intelligence or indirectly through terrorist organizations. Iran has the ability to attack its targets by means of conventional and unconventional weapons.

One must emphasize that lately most of the attention in the United States and around the world is focused on Al Qaida and its terrorism, but one should take into account that an Iranian decision to initiate an intensive terror campaign against the United States would be a far greater challenge than one Al Qaida poses today (Iranian cooperation with Al Qaida is also not out of the question—especially joint ventures against American targets).

The United States must aspire to create a situation in which it is able to deter Iran from attacking American targets around the world and at home. If, however, deterrence proves ineffective America must go on the offensive or at least engage in operations designed to thwart terrorist attacks outside of its borders or to exact a price from Iran that would dissuade it from persisting in its terrorist camping.

Terror supporting countries, among them Iran, usually calculate potential gains and losses and take into account the international response to their activities. Each country sets the maximum price it is willing to pay for its continued involvement in terrorism. The "price range" differs from country to country as does the "breaking point." This means that countries combating terror have to exact a higher price from countries that support terror—a price so high that these countries will eventually decide that supporting terror is unprofitable.

The possibility that Iran may renew its attacks was suggested by a senior member of the Revolutionary Guard just a few months ago. In a May 2004 article, the London-based Arabic daily *al-Sharq al-Awsat* quoted senior Iranian officials regarding Iran's position vis-à-vis the West, Israel, the war in Iraq, and suicide attacks. These statements reflect, the current position of Iran's conservative elite.

The following is an excerpt from a speech by a senior member of the Revolutionary Guard to student members of the "Anassar Hizballah" organization at Al-Hussein University.

> The west sees us terrorists and describes our strategy as one of terror and oppression. If our youth ever agreed to Khatami's edicts and commentary, he [Khatami] would never fight the [Western] arrogance or protect the holy places, because Khatami speaks of lenience, reconciliation, tolerance and opposition to terror, while we encourage violence and warfare against the enemies of revolutionary Islam. I am proud of my activities which put fear into the Americans. Is it not true that the Jews and the Christians further their goals by means of oppression and violence? We have written strategy aimed at destroying Anglo-Saxon culture and uprooting the Americans and the English.
>
> Our missiles are ready to strike at their culture, and when the orders come from our leader (Ali Khameini) we will launch our missiles at their cities and facilities. Our motto during the Iraqi war was: "Karbela we are coming, Jerusalem we are coming," but because of Khatami's policies and his dialogue between civilizations we have been forced to freeze our plan to free Islamic cities. We are now ready, however, to proceed with the plan.

He added:

> The axis of blasphemy is an axis against Allah and the Muslims, and we must do all in our power to strike at this axis by means of our suicide attacks and our missiles. There are 29 sensitive sites in the United States and the West. We have examined these sites and we know how we'll attack them.

The key to effectively facing the Iranian challenge is adequate intelligence deployment which could provide at least some warning of imminent attacks. Since the Iranian terrorist organizations and Iranian-sponsored terrorist organizations (such as the Hizballah) are so effective and so compartmentalized, there is a dire need for more human agents ("Humint") to gather information that would help thwart attacks. Since the Iranian terrorists infrastructure is global the antiterrorist apparatus must be global as well. The terrorist attacking American targets at home and abroad make sure to leave no "Iranian fingerprints," and the United States must have the global reach and the necessary means to stop them.

Notes

1. This chapter is based on the following sources: *Hizballah*, A Special Collection of Information, the Center for Intelligence Heritage, The Information Center for Intelligence and Terror, March 2003, pp. 115-123; *Time Come*, "Hizballah is Moving Up the Threat Chart," Timothy J. Burger, Elaine Shannon,"December 10, 2001.
2. Edgar O'Ballance, *Islamic Fundamentalist Terrorism, 1979-95,* New York University Press, 1997, pp. 137-139.
3. The accepted assessment today is that Colonel Higgins was already executed in April 1988, about two months after his abduction, and that his "execution" in 1989 was faked.

4. Magnus Ranstorp, *Hizballah in Lebanon—The Politics of the Western Hostage Crisis*, St. Martin's Press, New York, 1997, pp. 108-109.
5. The content of the press conference held by Rafsanjani on October 24, 1989 was published in the following articles: Christopher Walker, *Times*, October 25, 1989; Harvey Morris, *Independent*, October 25, 1989.
6. Iran stipulated three conditions for its willingness to assist in the release of Western hostages, which are familiar from past dealings: (1) Freeing the Iranian funds frozen in the United States; (2) Renewal of diplomatic relations with the United States and Britain; (3) Condemnation of Iraq for using chemical weapons against Iran. These conditions were laid out by Iranian Foreign Minister Valyati.
7. Anat Kurtz, Maskit Burgin, *Inter-International Terrorism*, JCSS, Tel Aviv University, 1990, pp. 96-105.
8. *Washington Post*, December 16, 1989.
9. *Kihan*, June 9, 1990.
10. Office of the Secretary of State, Office of the Coordinator for Counter Terrorism, *Patterns of Global Terrorism*, U.S. Department of State Publications, 1992-1999.
11. "Jackie Chugi, The Iranian Intelligence Killed My Father—The Grandson of Ayatollah Khomeini Casts Unprecedented Accusations in the Iranian Press," *Ma'ariv*, November 28, 2000.
12. Ibid.
13. Ibid.
14. Ibid.
15. Zvi Barel, "In the terms of the Demonstrators even Khomeini is Considered Conservative," *Ha'aretz*, November 20, 2002.
16. Ibid.
17. Ibid.
18. Ibid.
19. Sharam Chubin, *Wither Iran? Reform, Domestic Politics and National Security*, The International Institute for Strategic Studies, Adelphin Paper 342, UK, 2002, p. 31.
20. Ibid., p. 32.
21. *IRNA News Agency,* February 12, 2001.
22. *IRNA News Agency,* June 4, 2001.
23. *Wall Street Journal*, November 5, 2001.
24. James Drummond, "Ministers Seek Diplomatic Balance," *Financial Times*, October 11, 2001.
25. This statement was included in a speech delivered by Khamenei in Isfahan on October 30, 2001, and was broadcasted on the BBC on November 1, 2001.
26. The "Forum of states bordering on Afghanistan," called the "6 + 2," aspired to bring an end to the war between the rival factions in Afghanistan. The countries bordering on Afghanistan (Tajekistan, Uzbekistan, Turkmenistan, Pakistan, Iran, and China) were members of this forum as well as Russia and the United States.
27. John Ward Anderson, "Teheran Uses Crisis to Reinforce Its International Influence," *International Herald Tribune*, October 8, 2001.
28. "Iran as a State that Supports and Activates Terror," a special collection of information, the Center for Intelligence Heritage, The Information Center for Intelligence and Terror, April 2003, pp. 61-62.
29. Ghassan Charbel, "Our Neighbor, The Great Satan," *Al-Hayat*, April 29, 2003.
30. Parisa Hafez, "Iran Tries to Avoid Row with US over Iraq," Reuters, Teheran, April 27, 2003.
31. Ibid.

32. These statements are presented as they were quoted by the Iranian News Agency (IRNA News) on April 11, 2003.
33. Donna Bryson, "Iran Opposition has Few Postwar Options," AP, Cairo, April 23, 2003.
34. This section is mainly based on: Zvi Barel, "An Islamic Revolution? Perhaps a Deal with the 'Great Devil' is Preferable," *Ha'aretz*, May 2. 2003; Donna Bryson, "Iran Opposition has Few Postwar Options."
35. *Islam Online*—News Section, April 11, 2003.
36. Ibid.
37. Ibid.
38. IRNA News Agency, April 11, 2003.
39. Daniel Sobelman, "The Shiite Leader al-Hakim Returns to Iraq after 23 Years of Exile," *Ha'aretz*, May 11, 2003.
40. Ibid.
41. Ibid.
42. Ibid.
43. Ibid.
44. Zvi Barel, "An Islamic Revolution? Perhaps a Deal with the 'Great Devil' is Preferable."
45. Ibid.
46. Ibid.
47. Ibid.
48. Ronen Bergman, "The Shiite State of the Americans," *Yediot Aharonot*, April 25, 2003.
49. This section is partially based on the following sources: *Yediot Aharonot*, May 4, 2003; *Ma'ariv*, May 4, 2003; *Ha'aretz*, May 4, 2003.
50. Daniel Sobelman, "Iranian President Visits Lebanon for the First Time since 1979," *Ha'aretz*, May 12, 2003.
51. *Yediot Aharonot*, April 28, 2003.

Index